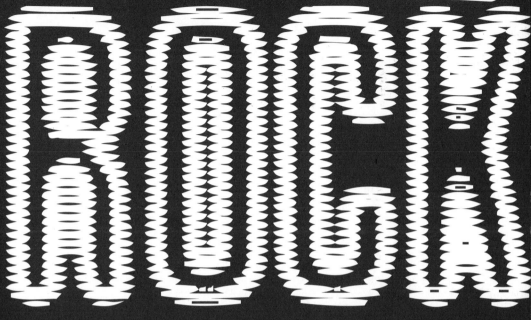

# ROCK

# EXTRATERRESTRIAL

# CTION

# MICHAEL C. LUCKMAN

**POCKET BOOKS**

NEW YORK     LONDON     TORONTO     SYDNEY

**POCKET BOOKS**

POCKET BOOKS, a division of Simon & Schuster, Inc.
1230 Avenue of the Americas, New York, NY 10020

Luckman, Michael C.
Alien rock: the rock'n'roll extraterrestrial connection / Michael C. Luckman.—
First VH-1 Books/Pocket Books trade paperback ed.
p. cm.
Includes bibliographical references (p. )
ISBN-13: 978-0-7434-6673-8
ISBN-10:      0-7434-6673-X
1. Rock musicians—Miscellanea. 2. Human-alien encounters. I. Title

ML3534.L83 2005
781.66—dc22
2005043017

This VH-1 Books/Pocket Books trade paperback edition July 2005

10   9   8   7   6   5   4   3   2   1

Designed by Charles Kreloff

Manufactured in the United States of America

For information regarding special discounts for bulk purchases, please contact
Simon & Schuster Special Sales at 1-800-456-6798 or
business@simonandschuster.com.

This book is dedicated to my mother, Dorothy Luckman, who isn't a believer in extraterrestrials, but does believe in rock 'n' roll; and Harold D. Salkin, America's oldest living UFO researcher, who is a believer, but doesn't believe in rock 'n' roll.

The author wishes to express his special thanks to his personal assistant, internationally known author and lecturer Antonio Huneeus, who has made a significant contribution to public knowledge about extraterrestrials and the paranormal.

The following individuals have also played a significant role in the development of this book: editor Mitchell Ivers and editorial assistant Joshua Martino at Simon & Schuster; literary agents Lisa Hagen and Sandra Martin of Paraview; Larry Geller; Daniel Transit of the Globe in Transit website; Maia Christiane of the Spirit Heart Sanctuary; Wanda June Hill; Reg Presley of the Troggs; Dave Davies of the Kinks; Angela Bowie; Uri Geller; Marc Davenport and Leah Haley of Greenleaf Publications; Sam Sherman of Independent International Pictures; Bill Cote of B.C. Video; attorney Robert Bletchman; Virginia Lohle of the Star File photo agency; Sandi Miller; astronomer Tom Van Flandern of Meta Research, Washington, D.C.; attorney Donald Cameron; Craig Silver; Corey Gotkin; Al Cohen aka Aloid of ACM Records; Maria Cuccia of Elijah Records; George Rackus; Dennis Richard Molloy; Sherwin Winick; Helene Iulo; Frank Scott; and James Karnbach.

The author appreciates the cooperation of Ringo Starr and Yoko Ono for granting him permission for the use of album cover artwork pertaining to the theme of this book.

Rock musicians who have had close encounters with UFOs and who are interested in telling their story and participating in a worldwide campaign to contact extraterrestrials are invited to contact the author at alienrockstars@aol.com.

# CONTENTS

# AUTHOR'S NOTE

Warning to readers: This is not your typical rock-music book. *Alien Rock: The Rock 'n' Roll Extraterrestrial Connection* provides evidence of a direct link between extraterrestrials and Elvis, the Beatles, the Rolling Stones, David Bowie, Jimi Hendrix, and Michael Jackson.

When I started doing research on this book some years ago, I was aware that quite a number of famous rock stars had been turned on to the UFO subject and had written songs about alien visitation during their careers, but I had never imagined that so many musical icons had had direct communication with intelligent beings from other worlds and that musicians such as Jerry Garcia, Dave Davies of the Kinks, Sammy Hagar of Van Halen, Rick Wakeman of Yes, Cat Stevens, and others had experienced alien abductions firsthand. Nor did I have the slightest clue that many rock and pop musicians credited an unseen cosmic superpower that I've titled Extraterrestrial Musical Forces (EMF) for helping them create some of their biggest hit songs and directing their onstage performances. Another remarkable discovery I made was that UFOs were inextricably drawn to some rock concerts and had been seen hovering above the crowds at the Woodstock, Altamont, and Isle of Wight festivals. The cosmic/ musical connection now seemed complete.

I once told a seasoned New York City pop-music critic about the rock 'n' roll/extraterrestrial link, including a close encounter with a spaceship and possibly aliens reported years ago by members of the progressive rock group the Moody Blues. The writer said that he wouldn't know what to do with the information. Now that the rock 'n' roll/extraterrestrial connection is being exposed, the extraterrestrial subject, like rock 'n' roll, is here to stay. The ball is now in the media's court.

*Alien Rock* crosses the cosmic threshold from UFO sightings in the here and now to apparent messages received from the other side. From Elvis's apparent ability to heal the sick and Jimi Hendrix's out-of-body experiences to Jerry Garcia's battle with "insectoid presences" aboard a flying saucer and Carlos Santana's cosmic companion, Metatron, guiding him through the recording of his Grammy Award–winning CD *Supernatural, Alien Rock* is a sweeping investigation into the last half century of rock 'n' roll and the paranormal that could permanently expand your view of human consciousness. You will also learn about mankind's possible origins from Planet X, located on the edge of our solar system beyond Pluto, and view dramatic photographs of a new human face on Mars and strange tunnels that crisscross the Red Planet.

Skeptics will, of course, be quick to try to knock down many of the encounters reported in this book on the grounds of alleged drug use by rock stars. To put it mildly, this is a paper tiger. Certainly many rock stars have taken drugs, but the majority of the cases cited in this book appear to have little or nothing to do with drugs and follow a now familiar pattern that coincides with the experiences of thousands of individuals from all walks of life throughout the world. John Lennon went to great lengths to explain that he wasn't using drugs when he sighted a flying saucer in New York City. Many of the cases cited in this book are backed up by sober eyewitnesses. We're dealing with an exciting new phenomenon that is the *real* high: a cosmic connection that is musically driven.

One of the rewards of writing *Alien Rock* was the realization that a multitude of other rock stars out there have had similar experiences with extraterrestrials and will hopefully now be moved to step forward to share them with the public at large.

Rock 'n' roll has always been at the forefront of important social movements. It is my sincere hope that rock stars can and will play a pivotal role in efforts to inform the public about UFOs presently visiting our planet and help pave the way for peaceful contact with members of advanced civilizations.

We're all living in unusually turbulent times in which global terrorism and the rapidly declining post-Tsunami environment compete for daily headlines. Rock 'n' roll remains one of the few forces on Earth that can appreciably raise the human spirit by broadcasting a powerful message of peace and love to all within hearing range. Space is rock 'n' roll's final frontier as mankind makes plans to eventually inhabit the stars.

Astronauts have already taken their beloved musical instruments along with them on NASA's space shuttle and the International Space Station. Both NASA and the European Space Agency have gone to considerable lengths to incorporate music into their present missions to Mars and other parts of our solar system.

All of this has set the stage for one of the world's largest outdoor entertainment events, the Signal to Space Concerts, which are planned to take place starting in the summer of 2006 in Berlin, New York, and Tokyo.

The crowning achievement of the Signal to Space Concerts would be the receipt of an unambiguous signal from space that would prove beyond the shadow of a doubt that we are not alone in the universe. The absence of an intelligent extraterrestrial signal so far has kept astronomers on edge and offered comfort to a chorus of skeptics.

There is new reason for optimism. A signal detected in February 2003 known as SHGb02+14a has sent shock waves throughout the Search for Extraterrestrial Intelligence (SETI) community. The signals, which add up to about a minute in length, have been picked up three times by the Arecibo radio telescope in Puerto Rico. They don't carry the specific signature of any known astronomical phenomenon. Equally intriguing is that some scientists have speculated that aliens would be likely to transmit a message at 1,420 megahertz, the same frequency used by SHGb02+14a.

According to the *Fortean Times*, astronomers are puzzled because SHGb02+14a seems to originate from a point between the constellations Pisces and Aries, where there is no obvious star or planetary system within a thousand light-years. No one ever said that solving these mysteries would be easy.

The latest cosmic curveball hurled in the direction of astronomers is an unexplained phenomenon likened to a car wash in space that mysteriously improved the performance of NASA's Mars Opportunity rover from five hundred watt-hours to nine hundred watt-hours per day. *New Scientist* magazine reported that something—or someone—regularly removed heavily built up dust from the rover's solar panels during the night.

Was some Martian cleaning person trying to lend assistance to America's space program? We'll probably never know the true answer. But the case of the "Martian car wash" illustrates how the rules that normally apply on Earth may no longer apply in space.

The best advice for humans is to be prepared for any and all eventualities. Conventional wisdom among eighty distinguished scientists and futurists who belong to the

Welcome ETI (Extraterrestrial Intelligence) to Earth Project is that aliens could be thousands or even hundreds of thousands of years in advance of us. This is a personal invitation to take the ultimate trip and become a full-fledged citizen of the cosmos.

May the force be with us all, humans and extraterrestrials.

Michael C. Luckman
January 1, 2005

# ELVIS: MUSICAL AMBASSADOR FROM THE STARS

The home where Elvis was born in Tupelo, Mississippi, was visited by a strange blue light when the King of Rock 'n' Roll entered this world, perhaps from another one.

**A**ppearing on the *David Letterman* show, Elton John said that when he first saw a photograph of Elvis Presley from *Heartbreak Hotel* on the cover of *Life* magazine, he thought Elvis resembled "a man from Mars."

Little did the Rocket Man know how close to the truth he was. You're about to blast off into the outer reaches of the paranormal for an unforgettable close encounter of the musical kind involving rock 'n' roll's biggest legend: Elvis Presley. Fasten your seat belts and prepare for a cosmic roller-coaster ride. We're clearly not in Kansas anymore. In the case of the undisputed King of Rock 'n' Roll, truth is stranger than fiction by light-years!

It turns out that there really were two Elvises—the one whom we all worshiped who started out as a skinny kid on the *Ed Sullivan Show*, swiveling his hips for all to see, and capped his career performing glitzy musical extravaganzas in Las Vegas, and the private Elvis, whose birth was anything but normal, who reportedly had direct contact with cosmic beings between the ages of five and ten and who continued to encounter UFOs throughout his life in the pressure-cooker world of show business—UFOs that visited him even at his gravesite.

Unknown to hundreds of millions of his fans around the world, the cosmic beings Elvis encountered as a child allowed him to peer deep into the future and invested him with supernatural powers, including the ability to move clouds in the sky, levitate objects in his living room, and heal the sick. They also told him of his origins from a blue planet far, far away in the Orion constellation.

Orion is one of the major constellations in the sky on the celestial equator, representing the hunter in Greek legend, and is visible in the south during the northern hemisphere's winter. Orion Nebula, a giant cloud of gas and dust in the Orion constellation, makes up the sword hanging from Orion's belt. Many of the stars in Orion are hot and relatively young and burn out in spectacular explosions known as supernova. They are born and die in periods of tens of millions of years. The star Rigel in the Orion constellation may be equal to the power of at least sixty thousand Suns.

News of Elvis's outer-space origins may sound impossible—the stuff that supermarket tabloids are made of—but you will soon discover a whole new side of Elvis Presley that will challenge what you thought you knew about the King of Rock 'n' Roll.

"I am not of this world," Elvis confided to Wanda June Hill, a fan who was Elvis's close friend for the last fifteen years of his life who met Presley through an actress friend of hers who appeared with Elvis in the 1962 Hollywood film *Girls! Girls! Girls!* With Elvis's permission, Wanda recorded numerous now-historic telephone conversations with the greatest rock-music legend of all time. Many of Elvis's statements, published here for the first time, shatter the myth that the man who left the building was merely an entertainer. "I am a man, a human being now, but what is 'me' is not from here," said Elvis. "I am from out there. . . . You think I'm making this up, but it's true—you'll know that one day."

Wanda's extraordinary claims are backed up by voiceprint analysis of the Elvis tapes by detective Arland Johnson, copies of old telephone bills proving that Wanda had indeed called Elvis's private, unlisted phone number at Graceland on numerous occasions, and handwriting analysis of Elvis's writing and signature on gifts he bestowed upon her. Johnson said in a sworn notarized affidavit, dated January 12, 1979, that he had run the tapes through "extensive electroanalysis" and compared the voiceprints to those taken from a spoken portion of a Las Vegas recording by Elvis. "It is my opinion determined by 6 voice print check points, that 5 out of 6 checked to be positively Elvis' voice. The 6th test was neutral and could be read as positive," said Johnson. "It is my conclusion based on the extensive comparison examinations performed on each separate conversation . . . that the male voice contained on all 15 cassettes is Elvis A. Presley."

On the tapes, Elvis told Wanda that he met two men when he was a child who revealed themselves as "light forms." "One of them touched me," Elvis said, "and I felt light inside me—floating sort of." Often Elvis heard voices when he was alone, sometimes when he was in the closet being punished. They played music for him, spoke about his home planet, and showed him a man under stage lights dressed all in white. "I didn't know what he was doing . . . ," said Elvis, "but then I later saw karate [Elvis loved practicing the martial arts], and I knew immediately then—it was me—they had shown me the future."

Wanda was one of the last people who spoke to Elvis before his death. Elvis told her that the "blue star planet" had several moons. Wanda quoted Elvis as saying that the people on Earth would soon learn about people on other planets outside our solar system who had mastered the techniques of longevity and who knew how to cure deadly diseases such as cancer. Once, in person, Elvis pointed out various stars to Wanda and named them one by one. When Wanda asked how he knew so much about the cosmos, Elvis grinned, pointed to the stars, and said he was "from up there." During his whirlwind romance with Deborah Walley, the costar of the movie, *Spinout,* Elvis said that he didn't want to waste time on "trivialities." Elvis announced, "I got the word. I want to give it to you. I'm not a man. I'm not a woman. I'm a soul, a spirit, a force. I have no interest in anything of this world. I want to live in another dimension entirely."

Today the King's records still sell millions of copies, and six hundred thousand people make the pilgrimage each year to Graceland, Elvis's estate in Memphis, Tennessee, from all over the world to see his tomb, located in the peaceful Meditation Garden, which is marked by an eternal flame and flowing fountains.

Many fans visiting Graceland leave behind personal messages to Elvis on the stone Wall of Love that is in certain respects not unlike Jerusalem's Wailing Wall and join the evening's candlelight vigil. "You can feel his presence here," observed Bea Williams, an onlooker in the crowd. "I don't really understand the phenomena myself, but you feel it." Tens of thousands of fans from all walks of life have built shrines in their own homes to their cultural idol. There are increasing signs that what started out as an Elvis cult is blossoming into a full-fledged religion with Elvis positioned to become a possible new Messiah.

"He [Elvis] is considered by many to be a religious figure, like Jesus," declared singer Dolly Parton. "I don't know how to explain it, but it's there, it's real, and people love it." Bob Dylan had a different take. He called Elvis "the deity supreme of rock 'n' roll religion as it exists today."

Unquestionably, Graceland is music's mecca—an American pop-culture symbol without equal anywhere on Earth. Singer Paul Simon reflected the sentiments of millions of Elvis fans when he declared, "We will all be received at Graceland."

In one memorable episode of television's *The X-Files,* a show that frequently delved into UFOs, space aliens, and the paranormal, FBI agent Fox Mulder informed his partner, Dana Scully, that he was about to embark on a spiritual journey to a special destination. That episode ended with Agent Mulder donning Elvis shades at Graceland. Perhaps Agent Mulder was there to investigate a minor incident that happened in 1990 during a photo shoot for *Rolling Stone* magazine. Elvis's "moon and stars" lamp from the

1950s, which sits atop a small refrigerator in the office at Graceland, jettisoned one of two satellites for no apparent reason while the lamp was being photographed. Or perhaps Agent Mulder was there for a far bigger reason—a scenario involving Elvis and men from outer space that even Hollywood couldn't manufacture.

# ROCK'S OWN STAR OF BETHLEHEM

Thousands of Elvis fans also make the pilgrimage to the Elvis Presley Center in Tupelo, Mississippi, to see the small two-room wooden shack where Elvis was born on January 8, 1935, at 3:30 A.M. on a snowy winter day in the midst of the Great Depression. Apparently this was an extraordinary birth marked by the appearance of a mysterious blue UFO that shone over the house from above at the exact moment that Elvis made his grand entrance into this world, perhaps from another.

Ironically few visitors to the Elvis Presley Center have ever heard of the inexplicable blue light that may have more to do with rock 'n' roll history than any other single event. The Presley home, which has been restored to its original Depression-era look and is now designated an official state landmark, is part of Elvis Presley Park, a complex comprising a museum, a memorial chapel adorned with stained-glass windows, and a gift shop. A life-size bronze statue of "Elvis at 13," carrying a guitar, stands on the grounds, which contain facilities for picnics and recreational events.

Elvis's father, Vernon Presley, referred to the story of the strange blue light—rock 'n' roll's own Star of Bethlehem—when he needed information about the exact time of Elvis's birth to give to a waiting astrologer. According to Larry Geller, Elvis's hair-stylist turned personal spiritual guru, who witnessed the conversation with Elvis while sitting in Graceland's Meditation Garden around 1975, Vernon said, "As I looked around, son, I noticed something strange. The whole area around the house was lit up with a blue light. It seemed to surround the house. And just at that moment, the wind stopped blowing. It was so still you could hear a pin drop."

The blue light startled Vernon, but he ran back into the house when he heard noise. Elvis's twin brother, Jesse Garon, was stillborn. There was also the unconfirmed report that bottles lining a shelf inside the Presley home were shaking. UFO literature is rich with examples of blue UFOs, but the cosmic kicker is that thousands of UFO abductees report encountering a strange blue light-beam as their odyssey unfolds, taking them to a room in a spacecraft where they commonly find themselves on an examining table being communicated to by extraterrestrial beings. Consequently, the appearance of a blue light that heralded Elvis's arrival on Earth is no small matter to UFO researchers and could provide an important clue to the fifty-years-plus rock 'n' roll/extraterrestrial connection.

Significantly, it was the dramatic sighting of a glowing flying saucer hovering above the backyard at Graceland for five minutes—witnessed by both Elvis and his father, Vernon—that initially triggered Vernon's memories of that unexpected blue light. The UFO observed at Graceland moved erratically in the sky at breakneck speeds, darting from one position to another. Elvis confided in Ed Parker, his personal bodyguard and karate instructor, who had seen a similar UFO in his native Hawaii in 1974, "My father was so moved by the sighting of that [space] craft that he shared with me an occurrence that happened at my birth. I had a still-born twin brother, and at the time of our birth my father said that there was a canopy of light over the house. Its aura lighted his way to the well outside the home in Tupelo. My father was amazed. He wondered in his mind what manner of occurrence this was. What was its significance? What did it mean? He had never spoken of it until that night we saw the unidentified flying object together.

"Ed, I still don't know what this [the blue light] means," said Elvis, "but I'm convinced that there must have been some significance to it. Was my brother, who was stillborn, such a special person that the light was for him? What does it mean? Could it have been for me?"

The mysterious blue light, which may indeed have come from an extraterrestrial source, left a indelible impact on Elvis. Nowhere was that better illustrated than in Elvis's approach to healing the sick. Whenever the King did healing prayers, he would invoke the words "First we must think of the blue light." He felt that the blue light held deep spiritual significance and empowered him to perform miracle healings.

Blue was Elvis's favorite color. He loved to wear blue shirts, blue jumpsuits, blue capes, and blue shoes and owned a flashy blue Cadillac. The song "Indescribably Blue" is believed to be Elvis's heartfelt tribute to the indescribably beautiful blue light that accompanied his remarkable birth. Many of Elvis's best-selling songs had such titles as "Blue Suede Shoes," "Blue Moon of Kentucky," and "Blue Christmas." And some of Elvis's biggest-grossing films also had the word *blue* in their title, including *G.I. Blues* and *Blue Hawaii.*

It seems eerily appropriate that Elvis's hair, which he dyed black, looked bluish in the Technicolor films of that period. In some people's minds all he would have needed to qualify for musical sainthood was a halo around his head. Poignantly, the last song Elvis sang while sitting at home at the piano just hours before his passing on August 15, 1977, was "Blue Eyes Cryin' in the Rain."

For his funeral, the King was dressed in a blue shirt and a white suit in an open gold casket. The blue star planet's favorite son had come home.

# ELVIS'S UFO ENCOUNTERS

"I've always felt there was a guiding hand directing the events in my life," Elvis confided to Larry Geller early in their relationship. "My overnight success didn't just happen." UFOs were obviously a part of the cosmic equation. Members of Elvis's innermost circle have come forth with riveting eyewitness accounts of Elvis's UFO encounters while living both in his mansion in Bel Air, California, and at Graceland and while traveling the countryside for major concert and film appearances and recording sessions. Most people don't get an opportunity to view a single UFO in their lifetime, but Elvis saw more than his share of flying saucers and was convinced that vastly superior intelligences were monitoring planet Earth "to prepare us for transition into the New Age." Was Elvis chosen by cosmic beings to be an important player in events that are still unfolding on Earth to this day?

Joe Esposito, Elvis's close friend and road manager, confirmed that UFOs were frequently on the King's mind while he was on the road. Describing a typical day, Esposito said, "Just before dawn we would check into a motel and grab some sleep, and we were back on the road by dusk. Every few hours we stopped by the side of the road to toss a football or let Elvis practice a karate kick on us or just sit under the stars, listening to him speculate about beings from another world. He genuinely believed in UFOs. Outer space was another piece of the puzzle of life Elvis was determined to solve."

Ed Parker said that Presley was "interested in all facets of life, death, resurrection, psychic healing, and other phenomena which, when put together, seemed to give many answers to the mysteries of the universe." Parker indicated that UFOs were always a prime concern: "Stories of contact with alien beings held a fascination for Elvis."

One of Elvis's earliest encounters with a UFO occurred sometime during the 1950s in the desert, an encounter with a rare cigar-shaped mother ship that almost cost Lamar Fike, Elvis's three-hundred-plus-pound bodyguard, his life and made Elvis think that he was about to be abducted by space aliens. Elvis spoke to Wanda June Hill about the incident that left him, like Elvis's famous lyrics, all shook up.

"We were away from the fire [in the desert] and we saw this light in the sky, movin' weird, you know, not like a plane or anything like it. And it was different-looking than a plane, it got brighter and it was comin' in closer. Hell, it was way up there, but we could see it on account of the Moon and the way it was lit up. It was cigar-shaped, oblong and rounded, and had some window portholes on one end and had lights along the bottom, but the damn thing had no wings, no means of bein' up there at all that we could see."

Elvis continued, "Well, we were watching it and the guys at camp started hollerin' 'cause they saw it too. And then we all ran to each other and got quiet when we heard the sound it made—it was like electricity, a buzzing and metallic sound, not like any engine we ever heard, and then it got kinda over us, still high, mind you, but up there over us. Our hair began to prickle, it stood up on my arms and on my head, and I got this weird feeling like I was about to float any minute. Like when you have two people put their hands over the top of your head and then lift you off the floor and you're real light, go up fast like an elevator, you ever do that?

"Well, I thought they were going to take me, man! But we all

Elvis Presley is flanked by his manager, Colonel Tom Parker, left, and Larry Geller, his spiritual advisor. Larry turned Elvis on to New Age philosophy, much to the displeasure of Colonel Parker, who eventually fired Larry and ordered all of Elvis's cherished metaphysical books burned.

felt it and then Lamar started groanin' and he fell on his face—man. Flat in the sand on his face! And we all got kinda got spooked 'cause he was like dead! He had no heartbeat and I started pounding his chest and Jerry [bodyguard Jerry Schiling] was giving him mouth-to-mouth, you know, and he came around fast—he was yellin' about flying saucers takin' him off . . . but the thing was gone when he came around."

Elvis said that he and his friends didn't see the cigar-shaped object disappear and stayed up all night looking for it to reappear. They even called the air command post at the local U.S. marine base, which said that they had a UFO report that turned out to be nothing. "You know how they are," said Elvis. "But, man, we saw it!" What Elvis and company saw was something that few people have ever seen, a giant mother ship that could have been as large as three football fields or bigger, which carries smaller scout ships.

It wasn't the first time that Elvis had sighted a UFO: "A bunch of us saw one, one night comin' out of the studio. It was right over us, right over L.A. big as life, man it was weird. It was round! Like a saucer—and that night there were blackouts around the area and across the country. You can't tell me that they aren't doin' that—checkin' out how our things work. I mean, they are comin' and, goddamn, I hope I'm here. Man, I want to see one! I want to see 'em up close! Hot damn! That would be a blast! I'm from out there, I told you that."

UFOs often commanded Elvis's attention. The King's bodyguard Sonny West worried once that a flying saucer had grabbed Elvis when he was briefly out of West's sight. A UFO had been spotted above Elvis's mansion in Bel Air, California, in 1966. "We were in the back of the place and suddenly Elvis says to me, 'Do you see that? It's a flying saucer!' I thought it was the light of a plane," West recalled, "and I just waited until I heard the sound of the motor. Well, I didn't hear any sound, the light kept coming, and it went through the trees and sort of over the roof of the houses."

Then the light disappeared, said West, "and it seemed to have dropped in the front of the house and we were in the back. Elvis tells me to go back into the house and get Jerry Schiling [a member of the King's inner circle]. I rush in, grab Jerry, and we go outside looking for the light. When we got outside, we couldn't find Elvis. We're hollering and yelling and we run into the front of the house and we still can't find him.

"Finally I hear him [Elvis] yell, 'I'm down here.' We run down about two or three houses and there he is in the driveway. I say to him, 'Jesus, I thought they got you!'" West said that he was only half-joking when he remarked that Elvis might have been space-napped "because I believed I had seen some kind of flying saucer or a phenomenon of some kind which I can't explain."

Elvis's wife, Priscilla Presley, revealed that she once spotted Elvis in the backyard of their Bel Air home staring up at "planets moving across the sky" for long periods in the darkness of the early-morning hours. "He was convinced, and nearly had us convinced, that there were energy waves so powerful they caused the stars to glide through the universe," said Priscilla. British psychic Craig Hamilton Parker claimed that following Elvis's death Priscilla heard noises coming from the stable. She reportedly saw Elvis's favorite horse upset by some sort of "shimmering form" hovering nearby.

While driving through New Mexico on Route 66 with Jerry Schiling and Larry Geller in the late 1960s, Elvis sighted a flying saucer crossing the night sky in a giant arc. The UFO grew bigger and brighter, then abruptly made a right-angle turn and shot off into the distance. Elvis proclaimed, "That was definitely not a shooting star or a meteor." Schiling and Geller agreed. "That was clearly something different," said Schiling. "We don't make anything that moves like that," said Geller. "That object maneuvered like a flying saucer." Elvis nodded and said, "It had to be!" Later Elvis told Geller, "It's ridiculous to think we're the only life with millions of planets in the universe."

Geller asked Elvis, "If they want to tell us something, why don't they land on the White House lawn or the Pentagon and contact our leaders instead of visiting an occasional individual out in the boondocks in the middle of the night?" "I've thought about that," said Elvis. "Maybe they don't want to cause panic, plus they want us to evolve spiritually by giving us a chance to make our own decisions. They'll work quietly behind the scenes, influencing us without appearing to." Geller asked, "And how will they do that?" Elvis answered, "By the power of their minds, which must be vastly superior to ours, or they couldn't be flying across the sky. They wouldn't let us blow ourselves up." According to formerly top secret documents, UFOs have visited U.S. air force bases and shown a "clear intent" in nuclear weapons storage areas.

Elvis took out his ever present Bible and read from the prophet Ezekiel, who described a UFO in ancient times. "They even had a landing pad," said Elvis excitedly. "What do you make of that? And they had lights, like the ship we saw in the sky over New Mexico!"

Elvis's UFO sightings, which he considered signs from God, deeply influenced him throughout his entire life. All three of his Grammys were for gospel albums, and today the King is permanently enshrined in the Gospel Association's Hall of Fame. Elvis's version of the nineteenth-century Swedish hymn "How Great Thou Art" is arguably to gospel fans what "Blue Suede Shoes" is to rock 'n' roll fans. A group of musicians and friends of Elvis's who gathered in RCA's Studio B in Nashville to hear him perform "How Great Thou Art" one night in May 1966 weren't prepared for what happened. "Something almost frightening happened when he finished that song," said a member of Elvis's Memphis Mafia. "It was like he was just drained. He turned white and almost fainted, as if something happened outside of the normal experience."

Elvis's infamous gyrations, which critics initially blasted from one end of the United States to the other, are now believed to have been inspired by the free-spirited First Assembly of God, a Holy Roller church he attended as a youngster with his mother and father. Churchgoers often spoke in tongues and jumped up and down in wild abandon during the services, which were initially held in an old-fashioned revival tent. Much later, Elvis incorporated gospel singers into his unforgettable, no-holds-barred Las Vegas shows. Elvis opened the Vegas shows with the thundering theme from *2001: A Space Odyssey,* a film he watched over and over in rapt fascination. The music he used to make his triumphant entrance, "Also Sprach Zarasthustra," secretly signaled Elvis's cosmic connection—a connection that began when he was a young child in Tupelo and in some sense still carries forward to this day.

On Elvis's first full-length gospel album, *His Hand in Mine,* released in 1960, the King revealed his search for unlocking the great mysteries of life in a song titled "Known Only to Him Are the Great Hidden Secrets." In his 1971 tune "Life," Elvis alluded to the origins of the universe and love becoming "an ageless soul." And while on that subject, that same year he performed a song called "I Was Born 10,000 Years Ago."

Elvis's wardrobe contained many stunningly designed, bejeweled caftans that were similar to the vestments worn by the spiritual masters he adored. His pricey jumpsuits worn during his over-the-top Las Vegas shows were loaded with ancient American Indian and Mayan symbols. One of Elvis's favorite symbols, the phoenix, was repeated in separate jumpsuits he owned in red, blue, and black versions. The phoenix symbolizes immortality, resurrection, and life after death. In Greek and Egyptian mythology, it is associated with the sun god. Betty Luca Andreasson, a famous UFO abductee from Massachusetts, reported that the aliens she met on a spacecraft wore a surprisingly similar phoenix symbol on the sleeve of their uniforms—a cosmic coincidence if ever there was one.

Ultimately Elvis felt that he had a special calling to spread his spiritual message of peace and love throughout the world as a sort of latter-day musical messiah, according to Jess Stearn, author with Larry Geller of *Elvis' Search for God.* Elvis was prepared to put his career on hold and go to the Middle East to help defuse tensions between Israel and its Arab neighbors—an offer that still resonates today. Elvis wanted to use music, the universal language, "to communicate with people who can't get across cultural and language barriers. Bringing Jew and Arab together, with someone from the land of hope, America, providing the musical theme that will bind us together."

# ELVIS'S SPIRITUAL JOURNEY

Elvis was a voracious reader and maintained a large personal library of over three hundred metaphysical books stored in several trunks so he could bring them with him wherever he went. He didn't just own the books, he read them from cover to cover. Elvis's handwritten notes can be seen in pencil in the margins of many of the books. On the official Graceland tour, visitors file past the King's desk, which contains a copy of Erich von Däniken's *Chariots of the Gods,* Kahlil Gilbran's *The Prophet,* Yogananda's *Autobiography of a Yogi,* and *The Impersonal Life,* which was channeled by one Joseph Bennett in the early twentieth century.

Von Däniken was the first major researcher to popularize the theory that is steadily gaining worldwide acceptance about ancient astronauts visiting Earth and interacting with human beings at the dawn of civilization. Von Däniken contends that the so-called mythical gods from all cultures were really flesh-and-blood, technologically advanced beings who traveled to our planet from the stars. He recently opened Mystery Park, a multimillion-dollar Disneyland of the gods in his native Switzerland. It isn't hard to figure out why Elvis considered *Chariots of the Gods* one of his favorite books. He constantly spoke of the space brothers as if they were members of his family (which they may have been).

Among other books in Elvis's library were *Strange World* by Frank Edwards, *The Secret Teachings of All Ages* by Manly P. Hall, *Doors of Perception* by Aldous Huxley, and *The Secret Doctrine* by Helena Blavatsky. Myrna Smith, one of Elvis's backup singers, noted that the King was fond of reciting passages to his flock from various books he studied.

Elvis's spiritual guru, Larry Geller, had much to do with turning Elvis on to metaphysical subjects from the New Age to numerology, psychic phenomena, pyramid power, and ancient mysticism. Geller, who was a twenty-four-year-old hairstylist, met Elvis on April 30, 1964. Elvis needed a trim for a movie he was working on. Not only did Elvis get that trim, but he soon discovered that Geller was just the person he was looking for, someone outside his circle of close friends and hangers-on who could provide important new insights into the very meaning of life.

Elvis was quickly hooked on Geller and bought him a white Cadillac in appreciation for his special work. The Memphis Mafia, a group of security and advance men who followed the King everywhere, were not impressed. They considered Larry a threat and nicknamed him Swami, a name that obviously displeased Geller no end. Elvis's manager, Colonel Tom Parker, grew increasingly suspicious of Larry and made sure that someone else was in the room whenever Geller cut Elvis's hair. Parker was concerned that Larry was steering Elvis away from the business of show business. Eventually the Colonel fired Geller and ordered all of the King's beloved metaphysical books burned. This made Elvis furious and was one of the reasons that in the end he wanted to fire the Colonel.

Under Geller's guidance Elvis had discovered that he possessed supernatural powers that enabled him to move clouds in the sky. He demonstrated this cloud-moving ability to his friends in the desert in New Mexico. They found it hard to believe what they had apparently just witnessed with their own eyes. Wanda June Hill said that when she asked Elvis for his views about levitation, he moved a heavy green glass ashtray from one side of a marble-topped cocktail table to the other without touching it. The ashtray is in Wanda's collection of presents Elvis gave her over the years. Elvis's supernatural powers didn't stop with moving clouds and ashtrays. To his amazement, the King discovered that he could heal the sick simply by the laying on of hands. Soon people who were afflicted with a variety of illnesses sought Elvis out, flocking to his performances and even waiting patiently outside Graceland, hoping he would take time out to see them. He did his best not to let them down.

Ted Dungan, a UFO believer who attended the International UFO Congress held in Laughlin, Nevada, in 2002, was blown away the time that he met Elvis at Memphis radio station WHBQ in the fall of 1956. "It was a promotional appearance," said Dungan, "and there were lots of pretty young girls who were all making a fuss about him. Elvis was real polite and he was signing autographs when he noticed this unfortunate girl in a wheelchair. She was deformed and it wasn't easy to look at her. Well, Elvis just dropped everything and walked over to her and knelt by her wheelchair. He put his arm around her and talked to her. He must have spent twenty minutes with her, and I swear, when Elvis got up, that girl was beautiful."

Joe Esposito, Elvis's friend and road manager during the 1960s and 1970s, recalled an incident in which one of Elvis's backup singers, a woman named Sylvia, who was a member of a group called The Sweet Inspirations, was diagnosed with cancer. According to Esposito, Elvis came to her dressing room, put his hands on her stomach, and began to pray. The next day, the hospital gave Sylvia a clean bill of health. There was no sign of cancer whatsoever. Elvis had performed what can only be called a miracle.

Larry Geller was riding with Elvis on a bus when the King saw a man fall into the gutter with a heart attack. "Elvis stopped the bus and I watched as he put his hand on the man's chest," said Larry. "The man said, 'It's you, it's you, and just got up.'"

Despite the never-ending jokes about "Elvis sightings" over the years on late-night television shows, Dr. Raymond A. Moody, a well-respected doctor and longtime researcher on near-death experiences, has documented case after case where Elvis Presley appeared to have visited people after his death, providing some measure of comfort and assistance to those in need.

Dr. Moody, who graduated from the Medical College of Georgia in 1976 and then served his residency at the University of Virginia Medical School, emphasized that these life-altering psychic experiences happened to psychologically normal people "with little or no interest in the paranormal. Not one of them ever questioned the reality of the experience. They questioned only why Elvis chose to communicate with them." Dr. Moody's subjects included young and old, truck drivers and psychologists, devoted Elvis fans and people who had little interest in the King of Rock 'n' Roll.

Among the *Twilight Zone* type of cases chronicled by Dr. Moody during his nine-year study is that of a father who found his runaway son using information supplied by Elvis in a dream, the parents of a dying girl who were comforted by her last words, "Here comes Elvis," and the young divorcée, terrified of being alone for the birth of her third child, who found comfort and joy in Elvis's presence in the delivery room. Rod Serling would feel right at home with these strange accounts involving Elvis that seemingly transcended time and space.

Hans Holzer, the famous ghost hunter and author, investigated several cases where people claimed to have seen Elvis's ghost or had some kind of spirit communication with him from the other side. Some of these claims came on the heels of the King's death in 1977. Holzer found most of the cases inconclusive, but one case drew his undivided attention.

Dorothy Sherry, a New Jersey housewife and mother in her thirties, claimed that beginning in January 1978 the spirit of Elvis appeared to her regularly and took her on a number of astral flights to show her that there was life on the other side. Although Holzer was initially skeptical, Dorothy gradually won him over with her sincerity and details of Elvis's life few would know, which turned out to be true.

Holzer said that Dorothy "just happened to be psychic and somehow fell into this bizarre situation very much against her will." The spirit of Elvis would appear to her at night and grab her hand. She would then follow him in an out-of-body experience or astral flight. Dorothy told Holzer, "I took Elvis's hand, and as I turned around, I looked back at myself sitting on the couch. Then we went through a sort of tube or tunnel, with bright lights on the other end." Sometimes Elvis took her to beautiful landscapes, and other times they visited Graceland or Elvis's dressing room at the Hilton Hotel in Las Vegas. From these visits Dorothy learned important details about particular pieces of furniture in a room or the names of people in Elvis's life that led Holzer to believe that she was the genuine article.

An important piece of evidence was that Dorothy's mother witnessed some of her daughter's astral trips. Whereas Dorothy would see Elvis as a real man, the mother could only make out "a shadow." In time Dorothy turned to automatic writing, a trance technique with a long history in the psychic realm, to communicate with Elvis. The messages were mostly spiritual. "Please make people aware of the other side, that we are not dead," Elvis pleaded to Dorothy. "Life goes on. This is only a bus stop; death is not the end."

Elvis told Dorothy that he was upset with the cult developing around his personality and the marketing of his image: "This is like a sideshow, a zoo. They have got to realize that I was a person and not some kind of god." Elvis said that he still played songs on the other side. There were concerts, but no records.

Eventually Holzer put Dorothy under a deep hypnotic trance, and one key séance, held on July 13, 1978, was witnessed by David Stanley, who was Elvis's bodyguard for six years, and Elvis's stepmother, Dee Presley. Both David and Dee came away from the session believing that the presence of Elvis had indeed been in the room. They were also impressed that some of the information Dorothy conveyed during the séance was strictly personal and never publicized in books or other media.

Of course the question remained as to why Elvis had chosen this New Jersey housewife as a channel. This, too, was answered in the many communications that Dorothy had with Elvis. Elvis told Dorothy that they had been married in a previous life, so he felt comfortable with her.

# ELVIS'S POSTHUMOUS ENCOUNTERS

But even Elvis's death didn't put a stop to his cosmic link with UFOs, which appeared to take a special interest in his burial site. Shockingly, during the spring of 1978 a total of thirteen flying saucers were reportedly seen over Elvis's grave at Graceland. "Several times orange-lit saucers have hovered as close as twenty feet over the silent tomb and shone laserlike lights onto the cold stones before zooming off into the clouds," said one security guard at Graceland's rear gate, adding, "Use my name and I will lose my job!" The guard said that he had seen spacecraft around Grace-

Elvis claimed he was from the Blue Star Planet and reportedly met cosmic beings of light when he was a young boy. The King of Rock 'n' Roll saw UFOs through-out his lifetime and believed that extraterrestrials were monitoring Earth. UFOs were seen near his gravesite at Graceland.

land several times. "They usually come between two and four in the morning when hardly anyone is around."

The guard said that the first time he saw a UFO at Graceland was on a rainy night in April. "I heard a strange noise near the grave . . . like an electrical popping, like a high-tension wire that's been blown down. I ran out there and saw a strange glow in the clouds, just above the tomb. Then a saucer-shaped object dipped out of the clouds and came down within a few yards of the grave. The whole area was lit up by a ray of light that came from the underside of the ship.

"Now, my job is to protect the tomb with my life if necessary, but I was so scared I couldn't reach for my gun. After a few seconds the light suddenly went off and the ship zoomed away." The guard attempted to call for help on his walkie-talkie, but the device was full of interference. "All of us who work here have seen UFOs," the guard confided, "but we are under strict orders not to talk. I have told you too much already."

The electrical popping sound made by the saucers hovering over Graceland yielded an important clue: Elvis's previous contact with a cigar-shaped mother ship in the desert was also marked by an unusual electrical buzzing noise.

Three teenagers from suburban Memphis who attend regular vigils at Graceland claimed to have seen UFOs at Elvis's beloved mansion one night. "I like to sneak out in my mama's car and drive there late at night," said sixteen-year-old Sandi Lee Smith. "The night I saw the UFO I was with my friends Debbie Barnes and Rhonda Flowers. We saw a flying saucer dart down from the sky. There was a strange humming in the air. It was raining. A beam lit up the tomb. The UFO started to go away, but it came back and hung around for ten seconds or so before disappearing. We drove to the [front] gate and told the security guard, but he said get the hell out of there and not tell anyone or they would call the police."

# BILL CLINTON: ELVIS'S SOUL MATE

Sounds like a case for the commander in chief of the United States. Former president Bill Clinton, who calls Elvis his "musical hero," plays a mean saxophone, and was dubbed "Elvis" by the media, privately shares the King's obsession with UFOs and extraterrestrials. The Clinton Presidential Library opened in 2005 in Little Rock, Arkansas. Library officials have forged a partnership with Graceland to encourage Elvis fans to drive 140 miles west to learn more about the Clinton White House and the man who regards himself as Elvis's soul mate. To drum up interest in the project, the Clinton Library took the unusual step of putting together a special exhibit of Elvis records and memorabilia, collected by Clinton, at the Cox Creative Center in Little Rock. What was left out was the air force report on the Roswell UFO incident, which Clinton had kept in the Oval Office.

While he was president, Clinton asked his golfing buddy Webster Hubbell—who for a brief time was appointed assistant attorney general in the Justice Department under Janet Reno—to find out the truth about UFOs. President Clinton also wanted to know who killed President John F. Kennedy and made it clear to Hubbell that he considered both issues equally important. Today John Podesta, former Clinton chief of staff, is leading a major investigation into the U.S. government's cover-up of UFOs for the Sci Fi Channel. A team of high-powered lawyers is assigned to the case.

Billionaire New York philanthropist Laurance Rockefeller launched an initiative aimed at persuading President Clinton to open the government's X-files and to provide presidential immunity to a group of former Pentagon officials who claimed to have direct knowledge of the 1947 UFO crash in Roswell, New Mexico, where bodies of space beings were allegedly recovered.

A special report distributed by Rockefeller to one thousand movers and shakers on the world scene, including Bill Clinton, former U.S. secretary of state Henry Kissinger, and members of Congress, concluded with the bombshell announcement that UFOs apparently under intelligent control were visiting Earth—a fact that Elvis Presley could have told Clinton a long time ago.

To Elvis, the Space Brothers, who for thousands of years have done acrobatics in our skies in highly advanced spacecraft, were the greatest entertainment phenomenon of all—an enduring mystery in the heavens that held out the prospect of a bright new future for the entire human race. Now that Elvis has long ago left Earth, UFOs maintain the dream that someday soon our civilizations may meet face-to-face. That's one rock 'n' roll party you (and Bill "Elvis" Clinton) won't want to miss!

# THE BEATLES AND THE ROLLING STONES

## INTERGALACTIC ROCK 'N' ROLL ROYALTY

A poster depicting the Fab Four as space aliens combines the public's fascination with the Beatles and extraterrestrial creatures. John Lennon believed that he might have been a UFO abductee.

**W**hen the Beatles invaded New York City on February 7, 1964, they might as well have been visitors from another planet. Not only their outrageous new sound but also their peculiar looks made them seem totally alien to most Middle Americans, who were completely blown away by the rock group's British mop-top haircuts, which were as far away from conventional crew cuts as you could get.

But these same conservative Americans would have been positively shell-shocked to learn that only ten years later a naked John Lennon would shout to an alien flying saucer hovering over his Manhattan apartment building, "Stop, take me with you!" and would apparently send signals to his fans from the other side following his assassination—a superhuman feat that even the great Houdini could never accomplish.

At the dawn of the Space Age during the early 1960s, musical groups commonly adopted names that had a familiar outer-space ring such as Bill Haley and the Comets, the Telstars, the Zodiacs, the Starlets, and so forth. Albums by these and a galaxy of other space groups from the period are highly prized today by savvy collectors for their cool retro cover artwork showing planets, rocket ships, and men in space suits. Consequently, before they were the Beatles, John Lennon and school chums Paul McCartney and George Harrison billed themselves as Johnny and the Moondogs, playing school dances, coffeehouses, and beer halls in and around Liverpool, England. Later they changed their name to the Silver Beatles and ultimately to the Beatles, the group we all came to love.

Asked how they arrived at the name Beatles, John replied it was given to them by a man in the sky who handed them "a flaming pie"—an interesting choice of words given Lennon's later penchant for flying saucers.

# JOHN LENNON'S CLOSE ENCOUNTERS

John's mind-blowing, up-close-and-personal UFO sighting occurred on August 23, 1974, at 9 P.M. The setting was the small penthouse of the Tower Apartments on East Fifty-second Street overlooking New York City's East River, a place John shared with his personal secretary and then-girlfriend, May Pang. Among the parade of celebrities who regularly stopped by were Mick Jagger, David Bowie, and Paul McCartney and his wife, Linda.

Writing in friend Andy Warhol's *Interview* magazine, Lennon recalled, "I was lying naked on the bed when I had this urge . . . so I went to the window, just dreaming in my usual poetic state of mind . . . as I turned my head, hovering over the next building, no more than a hundred feet away was this thing." The hair on the back of his neck stood up, a phenomenon long associated with UFO reports.

Lennon said that the object appeared to have "ordinary electric lightbulbs flashing on and off round the bottom, one not-blinking red light on top. What the Nixon is that? I says to myself . . . is it a helicopter? No. It makes no noise . . . ah, then, it must be a balloon . . . but no. Balloons don't look like that, nor do they fly so slow (about thirty miles per hour)."

According to May Pang, she had just stepped out of the shower when she heard John scream for her. He was standing naked on the terrace of the apartment, looking toward the sky, pointing. "My eye caught this large, circular object coming towards us," said May. "It was shaped like a flattened cone, and on top was a large, brilliant red light, not pulsating as on any of the aircraft we'd seen heading for Newark Airport. When it came a little closer, we could make out a row or circle of white lights that ran around the entire rim of the craft—these were also flashing on and off. There were so many of these lights that it was dazzling to the mind. It was, I estimate, about the size of a Learjet, and it was so close that if we had something to throw at it, we probably would have hit it."

The UFO, which had a dark metallic color, floated silently less than a hundred feet away from the couple. May jokingly said to John, "Suppose it's looking at us. Maybe they think that everyone who lives on the East Side wanders around naked on their terraces on Friday evenings. We look like Adam and Eve!" The object went past the United Nations Plaza building, which houses many U.N. delegates, slowly turned left, crossed over the East River, and eventually headed in the direction of Brooklyn, disappearing from view.

John shouted to the UFO, "Stop, take me with you!" then they both went inside. "I almost didn't call you [to go outside]," John confessed to May. "I was afraid you wouldn't believe me. I thought you would say, 'What is John on?' I didn't think anyone would believe me." The rest of that night John kept repeating, "I can't believe it . . . I can't believe it . . . I've seen a flying saucer!" John and May were in total shock.

Lennon went to great lengths to assure his friends that he

John Lennon sighted a flying saucer big enough to hold two passengers from a Manhattan rooftop. The former Beatle yelled to the UFO, "Stop, take me with you!" John opposed the UFO coverup and regularly read UFO publications, such as the *Flying Saucer Review*.

wasn't high on any substance when he spotted the flying saucer. Among the people he told about the sighting was his trusted friend and adviser Elliot Mintz, who believed the story. Unfortunately photographs John had taken of the saucer came back "like they had been through the radar at customs." John asked friend Bob Gruen, a well-known photographer of rock stars, to call the newspapers to see if anyone else had sighted the UFO. Sure enough, reports had been received by both the local police station and the news media. The New York *Daily News* received five telephone calls from people who saw the UFO. Two people gave UFO sighting reports to the New York City Police Department.

John speculated that the UFO was part of a fleet stationed in upstate New York, from which they could siphon off energy. "UFOs were probably responsible for the last blackout," he said. "It's possible that they drained too much juice from Con Ed all at once." John's observations were right on the money. A pilot sighted UFOs operating near a major power station on November 9, 1985. Some eight hundred thousand people were trapped in the blackout, some for hours, in subways or elevators. Strange blue lights were also seen at about the same time on New York's Lower East Side.

Lennon referred to his UFO sighting on the liner notes of his *Walls and Bridges* album. He wrote, "On the 23rd of August 1974 at 9 o'clock I saw a UFO—J.L." He further referred to UFOs on "Nobody Told Me," sadly one of the last songs he wrote: "There's a UFO over New York and I ain't too surprised."

John thought that the governments of the world were covering up the truth about UFOs. "If the masses started to accept UFOs, it would profoundly affect their attitude toward life, politics, everything. It would threaten the status quo," he said.

Spiritually, Lennon believed that "Christ, Buddha, Krishna, Muhammad, were all messengers of the Supreme Being. They were all saying basically the same thing, laying down the laws of the universe in language appropriate to their culture. The trick is to make all this subconscious knowledge conscious."

John naturally incorporated his cosmic views into his music. For example, in his solo effort "Instant Karma," the memorable chorus goes, "We'll all shine on like the moon and the stars and the sun." In "Across the Universe," which he recorded with both the Beatles and David Bowie and which was John's favorite song, Lennon referred to "limitless undying love which shines around me like a million suns, it calls me on and on and across the universe." In "Yer Blues," John stepped out of his mortal skin entirely, proclaiming, "My mother was of the sky, my father is of the earth but I am of the universe." And in "Out the Blue," a song on John's *Mind Games* LP that boasts a heavenly choir in the background, Lennon recalled that his soul mate, Yoko Ono, suddenly appeared to him one day "like a UFO" out of the blue.

John actually thought that he might have been abducted by space aliens as a child and certainly shared an affinity with tens, perhaps hundreds of thousands of people worldwide who believe they have been taken on board flying saucers in the middle of the night by gray humanoids. "It [UFO abductions] can be traced through hypnotic regression," John said. "That would explain why I've always seen things so differently." He wondered aloud if these aliens might be humans from the future who had mastered the art of time travel.

UFOs sparked John's interest ever since the late 1960s, when he started subscribing to the respected British UFO journal *Flying Saucer Review*. Elton John introduced

Lennon to psychic Uri Geller at a party in the mid-1970s. The two men immediately struck up a friendship. Geller's New York City apartment was about one block away from the Dakota building, where John and Yoko lived. Uri said that he secretly met John about once a week in a coffee shop at the nearby Sherry Netherland Hotel to discuss UFOs and similar subjects near and dear to their hearts.

John Green (also known as Charlie Swann), John and Yoko's personal tarot card reader from 1975 to October 1980, indicated that the Lennons were heavily tuned in to the spirit world. Green quoted John as saying, "The wife [Yoko] tells me I'm getting stronger and stronger psychiatric messages. She says the spirits are coming to me all the time now and they say I'm an initiate. Isn't that amazing? We won't need all of those psychics anymore because I will get all the messages."

John Lennon asked Green, in his first job interview, if he believed in UFOs, saying that he'd seen one: "I was on the roof . . . when I saw this thing, this ship. It wasn't much of a ship, maybe big enough to hold two people." Lennon told Green that he didn't report the UFO sighting, fearing newspaper headlines like "'Ex-Beatle Sees Saucer" and articles asking "What was he on?" Green considered Lennon's question about UFOs a "test." Green passed the test with flying colors, blurting out that everything we see is affected by "selective perception," created by our own beliefs and conditioning, and the conversation promptly moved on to other topics.

Around 1969 John and Yoko became briefly involved with a mysterious character from the San Francisco area named Dr. Don Hamrick, who claimed to have made direct contact with extraterrestrials in Norway and wanted the Beatles to promote communication between humans and space beings. According to biographer Albert Goldman, author of *The Lives of John Lennon*, the Lennons visited John's old friend Tony Cox, who lived with his new wife, Melinda Kendall, in a remote Norwegian farmhouse near the town of Alborg. Melinda was the daughter of a rich Texas family and one of Hamrick's devoted followers. During their three-week stay, John and Yoko were introduced to Hamrick, who sometimes used the alias Z. Charneau, and two hippie concert producers from Canada, John Brower and Ritchie Yorke, who were organizing a huge Toronto peace festival, which Hamrick envisioned being headlined by the Beatles. Hamrick also wanted to have Elvis Presley perform at the mega-event.

Brower said that when he later met Hamrick in a hotel room in Norway, the leader of the Frontiers of Science group claimed that John had already been taken up in a spaceship. "The next thing Hamrick does is to take us over to this table, and here's this scale model of a little Buck Rogers city," said Brower. "It's floating mysteriously about a foot above the table. He runs his hand under it and says, 'I have been given by the space people the antigravity secret. We're building a city above Brazil in the clouds. This is the model and it illustrates the power.'" Hamrick, a former seminarian, was on a mission to unite the physical and metaphysical aspects of science.

Brower noticed that a tremendous change had come over John the second time he visited him at the Coxes' farmhouse. He claimed that Lennon's primary focus had gone from world peace to space and cosmic consciousness. Furthermore Lennon insisted that the rock festival in Toronto had to be free. Hamrick's flamboyant chief disciple, Leonard Hollahan—a man with long red curls who dressed in purple velvet—unveiled plans at a key strategy session at the Jefferson Airplane's house in Haight-

Ashbury in January 1970 for John and Yoko to arrive at the festival in a "kosmic kraft"—a bubble-bodied helicopter that supposedly had no engine and operated entirely on psychic energy. The psychic helicopter proved to be the straw that broke the camel's back. Rock musicians, including Paul Kantner of the Airplane, weren't buying it. The whole project quickly dissolved.

In an article published in *Rolling Stone* magazine on April 16, 1970, John wrote, "Yoko and I still think we need it [a festival] not just to show that we can gather peacefully and groove to the music, but to change the balance of energy power on earth and, therefore, in the universe." John alluded to staying in a "far out farmhouse" in Norway with no telephone and referred to his friend "Dr. Don Hamrick or Zee to his Martian friends." As Lennon biographer Albert Goldman noted, "Lennon's interest in UFOs and space people didn't disappear. It just became a private interest rather than a public statement."

Just a few weeks before his assassination, John reportedly handed Uri Geller an object that he claimed he got "from an extraterrestrial entity." According to Uri, the object, which he cherishes, is an "odd-looking, not-quite-egg-shaped piece of metal," resembling brass, "very smooth and very heavy, about an inch or so wide. I was astounded. I said it sounded like an alien encounter and he seemed to agree and said that he couldn't think of another explanation himself."

John told Uri, "About six months ago I was asleep in my bed, with Yoko, at home, in the Dakota Building. And suddenly I wasn't asleep. Because there was this blazing light round the door. It was shining through the cracks and the keyhole, like someone was out there with searchlights, or the apartment was on fire . . . There were these four people out there."

Uri asked John if they were fans. "Well, they didn't want my f—in' autograph," said John. "They were like, little. Bug-like. Big bug eyes and little bug mouths . . . I've told this to two other people, right? One was Yoko and she believes me. She says she doesn't understand it, but she knows I wouldn't lie to her . . . I was straight that night. I wasn't dreaming and I wasn't tripping. There were these creatures, like people but not like people . . . They did something, But I don't know what it was. I tried to throw them out, but, when I took a step towards them, they kind of pushed me back. I mean, they didn't touch me. It was like they just willed me. Pushed me with willpower and telepathy."

When John woke up with "this (egg-shaped) thing in my hands. They gave it to me." John presented it to Uri, saying, "Keep it, it's too weird for me. If it's my ticket to another planet, I don't want to go there." Uri said that "when I hold the cold, metal egg in my fist, I have a strong sensation that John knew more about this object than he told me. Maybe it didn't come with an instruction manual, but I think John knew what it was for. And whatever that purpose was—communication? Healing? A first-class intergalactic ticket? —it scared him. I wish I could have warned him . . . that however scary aliens seem, it's the humans you have to fear."

Geller said that he still has the physical evidence from John's alleged alien encounter, but is reluctant to have it tested by a laboratory. "I want to keep the mysticism around it," Uri explained. (For further information go to www.urigeller.com.)

John's wife, Yoko Ono, who has brilliantly reinvented her career recently by invading the dance-club circuit and the rave-music scene, scoring a smash hit with her song "Walking on Thin Ice," was well aware that someone else was out there in space listening. On her 1985 *Starpeace* album, Yoko sang about "blue star people" who inhabit outer space, while the title track of the album contained a long-distance phone conversation with aliens. Yoko's description of aliens coming from a "blue star" is nothing short of astounding when you factor in that the two beings of light who communicated to Elvis Presley when he was a young boy growing up in Tupelo, Mississippi,

Yoko Ono holds a clear, round cosmic ball on the cover of her album *Starpeace,* which expresses her hope for peace not only on Earth, but throughout the universe.

told him that his home was a "blue star planet" located somewhere in the Orion constellation. How could Yoko have possibly known about the existence of the blue star? It seems that she may have tuned in to the same cosmic wavelength as Elvis, who was John's musical idol.

Yoko also was inextricably drawn to Egyptology and collected museum-quality Egyptian artifacts that held valuable clues to the cosmos. Michael Jackson and David Bowie shared the same fascination with Egyptian art. "I make sure to get all the Egyptian things, not for their value but for their magic power," Yoko said. "Each piece has a certain magic power." The Sphinx and Great Pyramid at Giza, which Yoko featured on one of her album covers for the Plastic Ono Band, have their counterparts on Mars, where giant three- and five-sided pyramids and humanlike faces photographed on the Red Planet by NASA remind researchers of the powerful rulers of the Nile in ancient Egypt. One of the three humanlike faces discovered on Mars to date—the face found in the Syrtis Major region—is thought by many to be an Egyptian princess. The figure can be seen wearing a crown and is absolutely remarkable in detail, resembling an exact portrait of a woman. A separate carving found elsewhere on the Red Planet shows the outline of an Egyptian princess, again complete with a crown.

Informed scientists agree that all of these structures were artificially constructed by ancient Martian intelligences. Moreover, the outer sarcophagus in King Tut's burial chamber is covered with depictions of small humanoid figures that bear an uncanny resemblance to stereotypical space aliens, raising the question whether the Egyptians were in contact with extraterrestrials and vice versa. The answer undoubtedly is yes. An even more intriguing question is "Are Martians out there today?" No one knows for certain, but the mysterious disappearances of a great many space probes sent up by both the United States and Russia indicate that extraterrestrials may be operating near Mars. Some researchers think that aliens may be hiding inside Phobos, one of Mars's two moons, which is marked by deep craters and could be hollow—the perfect place for ETs to take cover and not be seen by prying humans.

Sean Lennon sang vocals on Yoko's *Starpeace* album and performed a tune titled "Spaceship" on his debut album, *Into the Sun*. Sean, who shares the same date of birth as his father, appeared in Michael Jackson's "Moonwalker" film in 1988.

# THE OTHER BEATLES AND UFOS

John wasn't the only Beatle to have a warm spot in his heart for UFOs. The Paul McCartney and Wings album *Venus and Mars* spoke of "waiting in the cathedral for Starship 91ZNA," presumably a mother ship. Paul's *Red Rose Speedway* album contains this tantalizing snippet: "All at

Ringo Starr waves hello to earthlings standing on the ramp of a flying saucer—the image based on the hit 1950s sci-fi movie *The Day the Earth Stood Still*. Ringo is flanked by Gort, an alien robot who came to Earth to help deliver a message of peace. The cover artwork is from Ringo's album *Goodnight Vienna*.

once we see things in the skies and we both realize it together." In 1975, Paul's brother, who goes by the name Mike McGear, released an album titled *McGear,* which includes the song "The Man Who Found God on the Moon." Produced by Paul and cowritten by McCartney and McGear, the song features sound clips of Apollo 11 astronaut Buzz Aldrin's broadcast live from the moon. (Despite earlier denials, Aldrin admitted on the twenty-fifth anniversary of the Moon landing that he and his fellow Apollo astronauts actually encountered a UFO on their way to the lunar surface.) Earlier, Paul coproduced "I'm the Urban Spaceman," the first top-five hit in England for the Bonzo Dog Band. In 1990 Paul compared being a former Beatle to being an ex-astronaut. "If you've been an astronaut and been to the Moon, what do you do with the rest of your life?" he asked.

Characteristically, Beatles drummer and all-around gadfly Ringo Starr managed to steal the UFO show by popping up on the cover of his 1974 album, *Goodnight Vienna,* dressed in a silver jumpsuit as Gort, the beloved hero of the classic 1950s flying-saucer movie *The Day the Earth Stood Still,* who came with a message of peace (and a warning) for all mankind. The last song on Ringo's *Goodnight Vienna* album, "Easy for Me," which was written by Ringo and Harry Nilsson, has the line "Love so bright could only blind us; how could reason hope to find us, hiding in the Milky Way, without a star to shine the way?"

Not long after Ringo's *Goodnight Vienna* was released, a previously unknown group called Klaatu released a title song, "Calling Occupants," which set about to make contact with space aliens by proclaiming World Contact Day. The song became notorious because of the rampant rumor that it was done by the Beatles under a pseudonym. After much investigation, the band members were identified as Canadian session players. But even to this day "Calling Occupants" remains the strongest musical overture summoning space brothers to Earth. In 1977, Klaatu released their second album, *Hope*, recorded with the London Symphony Orchestra, and several additional albums were released. But the group broke up following a Canadian tour in 1981, never to return to the stage.

Ringo, who presently tours major venues with his All Star Band, is convinced that intelligent life exists on Mars, but believes that it may not be visible to us because it is in another dimension. "We really don't know much about time," Ringo pointed out. As for UFOs visiting Earth, Ringo said, "All those people [who witness UFOs] can't be wrong, and I just wonder why the government's trying to squash that all the while."

Ringo's certainty that intelligent life is on Mars and has existed on Mars is supported by the mysterious disappearance of many probes sent from Earth to photograph the Red Planet and by the existence of the three giant humanlike faces in the Cydonia, Syrtis Major, and Terra Sirenum regions of Mars. In fact, so many Mars probes (mostly sent up by the Russians) vanished that the inside joke at the Jet Propulsion Laboratory in Pasadena, California, was that a "great galactic ghoul" was gobbling up the probes. Ringo's comment that aliens may not always be visible to us is also right on the mark. They seem to be able to materialize or dematerialize at will, which explains why it has been particularly difficult to capture certain key UFO events on film or videotape. To answer Ringo's question about the UFO cover-up, one of the chief reasons the government is uptight about admitting that UFOs are here is that it means that we might all have to answer to a higher authority. The other main reason for the cover-up is panic of the type created by Orson Welles's infamous *War of the Worlds* radio broadcast, which convinced millions of Americans that marauding Martians were on the loose. Rock fans know better.

George Harrison, the Fab Four's in-house mystic, introduced

the rest of the Beatles to Eastern mysticism and transcendental meditation via the Maharishi Mahesh Yogi, who operated a holy retreat in Rishikesh, in the Himalayan foothills of northern India. Although eventually the Beatles split from the Maharishi (John calling him a fraud), George continued to embrace Krishna consciousness, and his music came to be heavily influenced by Ravi Shankar, the well-known Indian sitar player.

Presently the Maharishi, who hadn't been heard from in some time, is seeking to assemble forty thousand yogis in India trained in meditation and yogic "flying" to create a spiritual force field to stop global terrorism.

Sid Bernstein, the man who produced the Beatles' historic Carnegie Hall and Shea Stadium concerts in the 1960s, disclosed that in the 1970s George transformed his dressing room backstage at Madison Square Garden into a private temple during his *Dark Horse* tour. "There he was sitting on the floor, meditating, doing his *ommm* chanting," Bernstein recalled fondly. Dan Ingram, a prominent radio deejay now with WCBS FM in New York City, said that George had told him that "he had reached the fourth level of consciousness—and that was how to learn to really feel the joy of playing music." Harrison's Concert for Bangladesh will forever be remembered for serving as the blueprint for countless charity events featuring performances by large aggregations of rock stars.

The "quiet Beatle" staunchly believed in extraterrestrial life. "The planetary spheres, with their countless forms of life, are naught but figures in a cosmic motion picture," observed George. The Hindu religion he embraced speaks about spacecraft known as *vimanas,* used by the gods. *Vimana* is a Sanskrit word that literally means "aerial car." According to Indian scholars, these UFOs were constructed of iron, copper, and other metals for travel to the solar and stellar regions.

George often spoke for hours with his sister, Louise,

"about life, God, and the universe." But he had absolutely no fear of death, based on the Krishna belief that "souls go to other planets." When George finally did succumb to cancer at age fifty-eight, his body was covered by a silk blanket and was sprinkled with rose petals. The air was filled with the essence of sandalwood. George's ashes were scattered on the river Ganges, forty miles from the Taj Mahal. Many months later, Louise attended the Bay Area UFO Expo at California's San Mateo Marriott Hotel, where a thousand people vigorously discussed flying saucers, alien abductions, and the UFO cover-up. Louise said that she had no specific UFO experience, but "I'm here for a spiritual path" and "my mind is open." She currently operates an environmental organization.

Just days before the end, Paul and Ringo visited George in the hospital. Friends described the meeting as "joyful, tearful, and magical." Ringo was quoted in 1980 as refusing to go to funerals "because I don't believe in them. I totally believe your soul has gone by the time you get into the limo . . . I'm sure . . . I can't wait to go half the time."

# MESSAGES FROM JOHN

When the Beatles were young, they made a well-publicized pact that whoever died first would try to send some sort of message to the surviving members of the group. "When John died, I thought, 'maybe we'll get a message,' because he knew the deal," said Paul in 1997. "I haven't had a message from John," he said sadly. "I don't know if you can get messages back after death. Maybe you live but there's no postal service."

But John may have sent a message to the Beatles and their fans on the twentieth anniversary of his assassination. It happened inside Gotta Have It! Collectibles on East Fifty-seventh Street in New York City, where a black upright piano once owned by art dealer Sam Green and used by John and Yoko to compose their *Double Fantasy* album one summer in Green's Fire Island home was on display in tribute to the slain Beatle. A single candle shone in the window.

Co-owner Robert Schagrin was all alone in the shop at about 3 P.M. when luckily a woman tourist came in. "Did you hear that?" the woman asked. Schagrin answered, "Yes!" Both he and the woman, who was a lawyer from down South, were astonished when a single low note was struck on the piano keyboard, although the lid on the keyboard was still down. Experts were certain that this could not occur by itself, without pressure being applied to the keys.

Yoko, who also had a memorial candle burning in the window of her Dakota apartment that day, was notified of the possible paranormal event. Earlier her spokesman, Elliot Mintz, asked questions about what exactly had happened and was open-minded about the incident. Yoko said nothing in public and still hasn't to this day. However, assuming that really was John striking the piano keyboard, he'd managed to out-Houdini Harry Houdini, the internationally known magician and escape artist who'd vowed to send a signal from the other side but failed hopelessly in that ultimate quest to cross over. Perhaps John had figured out a way to break through the cosmic barrier separating this world from the next and in so doing brought us all one step closer to life in the great beyond.

Cynthia Lennon, John's first wife, said, "John told Julian [their son] that if there is life after death, he would prove it by sending a feather as a sign." When Julian found a dead jackdaw wrapped in old newspapers dated 1956 behind

John Lennon's half sister, Julia Baird, chats with Connecticut psychic Helene Iulo at a Beatles convention. If you look carefully, John's head can be seen crouched between Julia's and Helene's heads. The faces of two alien grays are hidden on the right side of Julia's hair, but difficult to see without special equipment.

the fireplace of her home in Cumbria, England, he was "really shaken," said Cynthia. "It's as if John is trying to get in touch with us." Believing that John might be trying to send Julian some sort of signal, Cynthia went to court to retrieve the feathered Indian headdress John had given Julian that had somehow fallen into outside hands and was being offered for sale. She won the court case on Julian's birthday. "I gave it [the headdress] to him before his first major concert at the Royal Albert Hall, because he was so nervous. It seemed to work—the show was a great success." Julian has released an album called *Space.*

Uri Geller's belief that John may have had some kind of a premonition of his impending death is supported by statements made by Lennon sometime before he was assassinated in front of the Dakota on December 8, 1980. Recalling the breakup of the Beatles, John said, "We were not bored and certainly didn't run out of songs. I was paranoid about someone trying to bump us off." When John heard that a former Beatles road manager had been shot and killed by the Los Angeles police, he said, "I'm next, I know it." Nonetheless, John insisted, "I'm not afraid of death because I don't believe in it. It's just getting out of one car and into another."

"We all physically leave this planet," said Yoko. "For me, I believe that this is only the first act, if you will. That this life is a very small part of eternity, that we're preparing for the next, not reincarnation, but the spirit, the soul. Eternal life. Like John said, prayer and meditation are a great way to be still and feel the energy of life and the spirit. Every morning I get up and pray and meditate to start my day, and when I don't, I find that I'm not as peaceful that day.

"When you take a few minutes to direct yourself to your own concerns, realize that life is a series of levels and that the difficult times are often our best teachers, you will find great joy in life. Live well today. You may not be here tomorrow."

Extraordinary proof that John may still be with us, albeit on a much higher plane, exists in the form of several intriguing and highly controversial "spirit photographs" produced by Connecticut psychic Helene Iulo and published here for the first time exclusively for readers of this book. The most controversial photograph, which was taken at a Beatles convention in February 1989 in Trumbull, Connecticut, shows what appears to some to be John's head between his half sister, Julia Baird, and Helene. Helene asked well-known Beatles author Geoffrey Giuliano to snap a

A friend of psychic Helene Iulo's poses at the entrance to the Dakota apartments in Manhattan where former Beatle John Lennon was murdered. A ball of light with a star and a tail like a comet streaks across the picture. The object is believed to be John's spirit.

picture of Julia and herself, never imagining that John's image would mysteriously appear. What is even more astonishing about this photograph is that the tiny heads of two small gray aliens can be seen by closely examining the left side of the original print. It is important to note that Helene wasn't even aware of the existence of one of the alien images until this author pointed it out to her.

New York City UFO artist and sculptor George Rackus was the first person to notice the hidden aliens in the picture. Assuming that the photograph is genuine, this would be the only time that an alien—much less two—has ever successfully been photographed. No small accomplishment, but the billion-dollar question is what are the aliens doing in the same picture with John? Helene believes that aliens intertwine with spirit on a nonphysical plane and that John may have wanted to commu-

A brighly lit, oval-shaped UFO, left, turned up on a photograph taken of the Moon and Mars in the sky directly above the Dakota apartments where Yoko Ono lives. The UFO was not visible to the photographer, but materialized on the film that came back from the lab.

nicate that extraterrestrials are real. Adding fuel to the controversy is some type of writing—possibly Japanese—in white across Julia's face on the photograph. Helene has offered to undergo a lie detector test to prove that none of her photographs or negatives have been tampered with.

A second photograph, taken by Helene of a male friend standing in front of the Dakota apartment building during the day in 1997, not far from the very spot where John Lennon was gunned down, shows a clearly defined small ball of light with a cometlike-trail blazing across the picture along with an ominous-looking black form, an unexplained white shape in the foreground, and smokelike effects. None of these images were visible to Helene or her friend with the naked eye.

A third photograph (not shown here) has underground, East Village street singer David Peel, who was closely associated with John and Yoko during their so-called radical period in the 1970s, standing in front of a memorial tree that Yoko planted in Strawberry Fields, surrounded by glowing spirit orbs that seem to be dancing in midair. Once again the orbs were not visible until the film was processed. The orb phenomenon is the latest wrinkle in UFO research. The rise of orb sightings in both the United States and England has led to debate over what causes the orbs to form. Some investigators maintain that the orbs are simply caused by fine mist forming on the camera's lens due to humidity or the presence of dust particles. The Peel photograph, however, was taken on a day when the Sun was shining brightly. Any lens anomalies would invariably turn up on other frames on the roll, which didn't happen in this instance.

A fourth photograph captures images of the Moon and Mars when the Red Planet was at its closest to Earth in fifty thousand years—and a brightly lit companion UFO. At Peel's urging, Helene snapped the picture at night on John's birthday while standing on the edge of Strawberry Fields directly across the street from the Dakota building, where Yoko lives. The pattern was the same. The Moon and Mars were seen by Helene, David, and other observers from the ground. When the finished film came back, it showed a large, oval-shaped UFO radiating light in the sky adjacent to the two heavenly bodies. Was John trying to send his fans another signal that he is still with us? Had he joined the space brotherhood?

With the exception of the first photograph, which was taken with a standard 35mm camera, the three other photographs were made by Helene with a simple throwaway camera, enormously reducing the chances of negative tampering. Images of John and the strange orbs have shown up in other photographs taken by Helene. Some of the pictures have been taken at friends' homes as well as at Beatles conventions. The purported image of John's head in a black window in a distant trailer is noticeable in the background of another photograph Helene took of Sean Lennon backstage at a concert he did with his mother, Yoko, in Central Park in New York City around 1999.

Helene once promoted the Beatles look-alike, soundalike group Abbey Road. She said that she started to get messages from Lennon in the form of automatic writing shortly after he was assassinated. Both Helene's mother and grandmother had psychic powers and maintained contact with the spirit world. Helene claimed that she was able to make physical contact with John in front of a friend in 1995 at her previous home in Milford, Connecticut. "We were sitting there meditating," said Helene. "I lit a candle and I said, 'Let's try to talk to John and see what happens.' Suddenly the candle flame flew up and he was standing in my doorway. He had his hands in his pockets. He didn't say anything. He had jeans on and a bright shirt. Five to seven seconds later he vanished."

What happened next defied all logic. "We both saw this big spiral rotating at incredible speed. The spiral was one foot long and half a foot wide. It was different colors, purple and red and had bright silver edges. It started spinning across the room. The spiral got smaller until it turned into a white ball of light. We said, 'John, we know you're here.' Then it went pop, like a sparkler went off. We were both so caught up in our emotions that we had tears in our eyes. I said, 'God, he was here!'"

Helene said that she had seen John's spirit before, at a wake for her boyfriend John Conte at a funeral home in Bridgeport, Connecticut, on Halloween 1997. Conte had played the role of John Lennon for the East Coast tour of Beatlemania. "John [Lennon] was at his funeral, standing there in a suit and long beard and was seven foot tall," said Helene. "I know in real life he wasn't seven feet tall. During the service someone tapped me on the shoulder and I saw him standing there looking at me with a kind of slight smile on his face. Quite a few people saw him. I asked him if he was a friend of John's. He nodded his head. I turned around for a second. When I turned back, he was gone."

Helene said that John contacted her prior to the United States declaring war on Iraq. He wanted to voice his steadfast objection to the coming invasion. Helene quoted Lennon as saying, "We're being lied to in this country [the United States] and in England. We're destroying ourselves."

A paranormal research group called Parajax located in Jacksonville, Florida, is currently circulating two photographs of Yoko Ono giving a conceptual art performance onstage with spirit orbs clearly present in each shot. In one photograph an orb can be seen floating in the background, but in the other a circular ball of light seems to be practically touching, almost kissing, the back of Yoko's head. Taken on their own, these orbs might be dismissed by some as photographic anomalies, perhaps reflections from the stage lights, but it seems far too much of a coincidence that nearly identical orbs would repeatedly appear in Helene Iulo's photographs and at an avant-garde performance by Yoko documented by a different photographer. And then the icing on the paranormal cake—the extraordinary photograph of a UFO in the sky above the Dakota on a night when Mars and the Moon had to share the astronomical spotlight with a bright, oval-shaped visitor from space. It was enough to send chills up and down the spine of any die-hard Beatles fan.

Joey Harrow, a New York musician who lives near the Dakota building, absolutely swore that he spotted John's ghost in 1983 standing in the main doorway "surrounded by an eerie light." Harrow was accompanied by Amanda Mannes, a writer, who claimed to have witnessed the exact same phenomenon. "I wanted to go up and look at him, but something in the way he looked at me said no," she said. High-profile New York psychic Shawn Robbins also claimed that she was confronted with John's spirit in the Dakota. Yoko Ono reportedly saw John sitting at his white piano. He turned to her and said, "Don't be afraid. I am still with you."

Actress Robin Givens went further out on a limb, claiming that Lennon's "ghost" inhabited her new $1.9 million home overlooking Hollywood and Beverly Hills, although she offered no actual proof of her story. "John stayed in this house when the Beatles were on the West Coast," said Givens, who bought the property soon after her divorce settlement with heavyweight champion Mike Tyson. The star of television's *Head of the Class* sitcom recalled, "I was wakened by the sound of a man singing—and wondered what was going on. I got up and looked around and suddenly realized it was John Lennon's voice, so I went back to bed." Givens said that she didn't feel the need to send for an exorcist to rid the home of the ghost because she doesn't mind sharing her space with such a friendly and talented spirit.

A permanent shrine in space that orbits the Sun every 3.6 years pays tribute to John's life and his enduring music. Minor planet 4147, officially named Lennon, will keep his message of peace and brotherhood burning bright for an eternity. In fact, all four of the Beatles are represented by planets in space. Minor planets 4148, 4149, and 4150 are officially named McCartney, Harrison, and Starr, in honor of Paul, George, and Ringo, the musicians who permanently transformed all of our lives.

But what could possibly top that? Scientists at the Harvard-Smithsonian Center for Astrophysics announced their stunning discovery of the biggest known diamond in the universe, which they tagged Lucy in tribute to the beloved Beatles song "Lucy in the Sky with Diamonds." The 10-billion-trillion-trillion-carat gem, found by American astrophysicists on Valentine's Day, is positioned fifty light-years away from Earth in the constellation Centaurus and is technically known as BPM 37093. (By comparison, the largest diamond on Earth is the 530-carat Star of Africa, which is part of the collection of British crown jewels.) The cosmic jewel is a chunk of crystallized carbon twenty-five hundred miles across and weighs 5 million trillion pounds. "You would need a jeweler's loupe the size of the Sun to grade this diamond," quipped astronomer Travis Metcalfe, who led the team of researchers who discovered the giant gem.

Coupled with the announcement by scientists was the amazing revelation that Lucy—the mother of all diamonds—constantly plays a song that sounds like the ringing of a gigantic gong. By measuring the pulsations of the ringing, scientists were able to study the interior of the star, much as geologists use seismograph measurements of earthquakes to study the interior of Earth. "The hunt for the crystal core of this white dwarf has been like the search for the Lost Dutchman's Mine," commented scientist Michael Montgomery of the University of Cambridge.

Mick Jagger spotted a rare cigar-shaped mother ship during a UFO skywatch in England and had to contend with a sensitive UFO alarm that frequently went off when he left his estate. A UFO put in an unexpected appearance at the ill-fated Altamont Concert in California right in the middle of Mick's onstage performance with the Rolling Stones.

Earth's Sun will eventually become a white dwarf when it dies, but that will take another 5 billion years.

# MICK JAGGER'S FLYING SAUCERS

Despite their symbolic conquests in the sky, however, the Beatles still faced competition from their old rivals, the Rolling Stones, who gathered no moss in the cosmic field of dreams. After all, who could explain why a UFO detector that Mick Jagger had installed in one of his estates in England kept going off every time he left the premises? UFO detectors, which are marketed throughout the world, operate on the principle that flying saucers create electromagnetic fields. The warning alarm is triggered whenever an electromagnetic impulse is detected, indicating that a UFO is in the neighborhood. Were flying saucers following Mick?

Jagger, who recently purchased real estate on the Moon from a company called The Lunar Embassy, hit the jackpot when he and other New Age believers, including his close friend singer Marianne Faithfull, encountered a rare luminous, cigar-shaped mother ship while camping at Glastonbury Tor in England in 1968. Mother ships are said to be giant spacecraft bigger than a football field, sometimes as big as three football fields, which carry smaller scout ships—not the type of thing you see every day.

Mick was also fortunate enough to see nightly displays of UFO lights, according to John Michell, who led the hippie expedition. Jagger's interest in UFOs apparently stemmed from what was described by Michell as a natural curiosity and a keen analytical mind. "Mick is the Great Observer," said Michell. "He is in-

GIGAR-SHAPED SPACE SHIP (#2 OF 4)
10:30 A.M. 3-5-1951
PHOTOGRAPHED AND COPYRIGHTED
BY PROF. G. ADAMSKI.
©

Cigar-shaped spaceship photographed in California is similiar to the mother ship sighted by Mick Jagger and Marianne Faithfull in England.

terested in everything that goes on around him. He takes nothing for granted. He's thinking all the time and he wants to know what everyone else is thinking." Michell said, "The New Age grail questers . . . were searching for UFOs, ley lines, and other totems of the Age of Aquarius."

Mick and Marianne hung out in the 1960s with Desmond Leslie, the nephew of Sir Winston Churchill and coauthor with George Adamski of a sensational book called *Flying Saucers Have Landed.* Leslie was a composer of electronic music in the field's pioneering stages. Several of his musical scores were used in BBC productions, and he was featured on a musique concrète album titled *Music of the Future.* The term *musique concrète* was coined in 1948

Another cylindrical mother ship, this one photographed in Rhode Island, is estimated to be hundreds of feet long and big enough to carry several smaller scout ships.

by Pierre Schaefer, a French radio broadcaster who created the first electronic-music studio. Schaefer pushed the boundaries of established musical composition by employing a multitude of microphones, record players, and the then recently invented tape recorder.

Leslie and Adamski's book, *Flying Saucers Have Landed*, was translated into scores of languages and became an international best seller, earning Leslie the title "The Royal Saucerer." Leslie met Adamski—the world's most famous UFO contactee—in the early 1950s. Adamski claimed to have met a space being by the name of Orthon in California's Mojave Desert in November 1952. A group of socially prominent individuals later signed affidavits that they had witnessed Adamski's face-to-face encounter with the space alien, although most responsible UFO researchers now dismiss Adamski's fantastic claims. That notwithstanding, Leslie, having investigated UFOs himself, insisted that there was a factual basis for flying-saucer sightings.

Leslie commented that after studying reports of over two thousand UFO sightings, several hundred historical reports, and scores of ancient Sanskrit books, he concluded the majority of flying saucers were interplanetary and originated "both within and without Earth's solar system." At his castle, Desmond spent much time with Mick and Marianne. Castle Leslie in Glaslough, Ireland, where Leslie was born and lived for a good part of his life, is believed to be haunted and is known by paranormal researchers for its levitating bed. A bit of an eccentric, Desmond established a nightclub at the castle. Leslie coauthored a book, *The Space Race*, with noted astronomer and friend Patrick Moore. At one time Leslie belonged to a spiritual-healing group that tried to establish mental contact through meditation with members scattered around the globe.

Around this same period Mick was determined to produce a cosmic album that would upstage the Beatles' crowning musical achievement, *Sgt. Pepper's Lonely Hearts Club Band*. At great expense, Jagger hired Michael Cooper, the same photographer who created the *Sergeant Pepper* fantasy album cover, to come up with a cosmic fantasy suitable for the cover of the Rolling Stones' *Their Satanic Majesties Request* album released in 1967. The finished product was a 3-D holographic portrait of Mick wearing a wizard's hat and robe surrounded by his bandmates, who were dressed up in their Elizabethan finery. Planets could be seen in the background sky. The album was nearly renamed *Cosmic Christmas* to take advantage of the holiday shopping season.

Primrose Hill, a celebrated UFO site located in North London, was where photographer Gered Makowitz shot the cover for the Rolling Stones LP *Between the Buttons*.

Penelope Tree, the year's most talked-about model and daughter of a wealthy investment broker, moved into David Bailey's home near Primrose Hill in 1969 and promptly installed a UFO detector on the roof of their home. Bailey, a famous photographer, was a good friend of Mick Jagger's who had served as best man at his wedding to actress Catherine Deneuve in 1965. Reports about flying saucers popping up at Primrose Hill proved to be an enduring folk legend. Billy Bragg's 1996 single explored a dream the singer had involving "a treeful of angels over Primrose Hill."

According to psychic Craig Hamilton-Parker, at one time Mick "was frightened off [from] buying a Gothic mansion by a bell-ringing eighteenth-century ghost." Anna-Maria Sliwinski, the housekeeper of the Domnington Grove House in Newbury, said, "I've heard the ghost firsthand. I heard strange chimes on a windless night. The bells were ringing in the tower, but there was nobody else in the house."

Mick Jagger's home apparently wasn't the only rock 'n' roll residence in England visited by UFOs and other strange phenomena. Keith Richards reported seeing several daylight discs near his estate in Sussex, England, at 6 A.M. one day in 1968. "I've seen a few [UFOs]," Keith commented, "but nothing that any of the ministries would believe. I believe they exist—plenty of people have seen them. They are tied up with a lot of things, like the dawn of man, for example. It's not just a matter of people spotting a flying saucer. I'm not an expert," Keith admitted. "I'm still trying to understand what's going on." Toward that goal, Keith read books like *Chariots of the Gods* by Erich von Däniken. The Swiss author and researcher, who also was a big favorite of Elvis Presley's, presents stunning evidence that Earth was visited thousands of years ago by ancient astronauts who directly charted the development of the human race.

On March 7, 1968, Keith and his girlfriend, Anita Pallenberg, discussed an idea for an offbeat film about sky people and flying saucers with Anthony Fontz at the Carlton Towers in London. The film was to star Mick and his girlfriend, Marianne, Keith and Anita, and Rolling Stones golden boy Brian Jones. However, the project never made it to the big screen.

While the Rolling Stones were putting the finishing touches on the *Let It Bleed* album in a Los Angeles recording studio, Keith went off in search of UFOs in the desert outside Joshua Tree in 1969. Gram Parsons, the original Space Cowboy, and Anita Pallenberg joined him in the overnight excursion. Gram packed a picnic basket and high-powered binoculars. "We went there to watch the UFOs," said Keith rather matter-of-factly. The trio took turns sitting in a barber chair someone with an obvious wry sense of humor had placed on top of the mountain, and they gazed up at the sky, watching the sunset and sunrise. Searching for UFOs "was part of the period," recalled Anita. "We were just looking for something." But alas no space visitors joined the all-night cosmic vigil on the mountaintop. On another excursion Keith and Mick visited Stonehenge, the famous prehistoric circular stone monument and astronomical observatory, which some students of ancient history believe may have been built with the help of extraterrestrials.

Today Keith calls himself a spiritual person, but not religious. "Spirit is all around us," opined Keith. "That's why I did the *Wingless Angel* album, very spiritual music. But mine is a very rebellious spirituality. I wouldn't care to put a name on it." As for his feelings about death and the possibility of an afterlife, Keith said, "I never got a postcard from anyone who left. Maybe they don't sell postcards up there."

Marianne Faithfull said that at the height of the 1960s Brian Jones and other friends in the Rolling Stones circle were "convinced that there was a mystic link between druidic monuments [such as Stonehenge] and flying saucers. Extraterrestrials were going to read these signs from their spaceships and get the message." Asked by friends if he would climb aboard a flying saucer if one descended in front of him, Brian said that he was primed and ready to go. "Our friends are questioning the wisdom of an almost blind acceptance of religion compared with the total disregard for reports relating to things like unidentified flying objects," said Brian. He decried the Vietnam War, the laws against abortion, and the persecution of gays, saying, "I believe we are moving towards a new age in ideas and events."

Jones, who performed the eerie extraterrestrial music on the mellotron on the Stones' classic *2,000 Light Years from Home*, was fond of séances to communicate with the dead and was known to drive many miles from his home around midnight to search for UFOs. Brian was so focused on the space theme that he purchased two planetary paintings to decorate the walls of his home just one year before he was found tragically drowned in a swimming pool. Brian commissioned David Hardy, the award-winning British science fiction illustrator, to create two large acrylic paintings, thirty-six by twenty inches. One was titled *Uranus from Titania* and the other *Jupiter from Io*. The first depicts a sea of liquid methane in which the planet is reflected; the depiction of the surface of Io was highly influenced by the buttes of Monument Valley, which look volcanic.

Veteran Stones guitarist Bill Wyman, a multitalented personality who has taken photographs, opened a restaurant, produced other musicians, and even dabbled in archaeology since leaving the world's greatest rock 'n' roll band, theorized that "maybe ten percent" of all unidentified flying objects are genuine, which judging by the number of UFO reports in every country on Earth, would add up to quite a huge number, perhaps thousands or even tens of thousands over the years.

"The media tend to really kill it [the UFO subject] because it's the only way of stopping everyone getting shit scared," declared Bill. "There actually are beings who might be cleverer than us and might use us as cattle fodder, so they ridicule it and fob it off." He urged people to "look at the factual evidence. I'm very logical, very black-and-white, and when I'm presented with proven facts I have to think about it."

Wyman's reference to "cattle fodder" stands as a bleak reminder of a possible dark side of the UFO scene, with reports of hundreds of cattle being found horribly mutilated for unknown reasons. In some of these "cattle mutilation" cases, strange lights have been seen by eyewitnesses in the areas of the bloodletting. Some researchers think that cults or military experiments might explain the strange events, and no one has ever produced clear proof that extraterrestrials are actually responsible for the carnage. On the other hand, a visit to your friendly neighborhood butcher shop might demonstrate how humans feel about cows, and when you get right down to it, it's not a pretty picture.

Guitarist Mick Taylor, who performed admirably with the Stones on their *Sticky Fingers* and *Let It Bleed* albums before pursuing a solo career, spotted several UFOs over Warminster, England, on a dark Sunday morning in January 1970. Taylor was among seven people in a skywatch party surveying an area of dense crop fields that had been the scene of repeated UFO activity over the previous fifteen years. Taylor and several American friends trudged through two feet of snow to get a better look. Arthur Shuttleworth, editor of the daily *Warminster Journal,* was an eyewitness.

"The UFO was so bright that we could actually distinguish the sheep on the nearby hillside huddling together for warmth," said Shuttleworth. Two additional UFOs could be seen off in the distance. According to Shuttleworth, Taylor mulled over what was happening and wondered if his eyes were playing tricks on him. "But he eventually had to conclude that UFOs were quite real, as all seven in the sky-watch party had seen the identical thing."

Just recently Mick Jagger endorsed the sending of rock 'n' roll music to outer space aboard the European Space Agency's Huygens probe, which landed on Saturn's moon, Titan, on January 14, 2005. "Music has always been at the center of cultures all over the world and it will continue to play an important part in thousands of years' time," predicted Mick. "Music has a role [to play] in the same way as technology and science in reflecting the age we live in and generally exploring new areas beyond accepted boundaries and beyond Earth," said the rock legend.

The probe carried four rock songs, "Lalala," "Bald James Deans," "Hot Time," and "No Love" composed by French musicians Julien Civange and Louis Haéri. "The music on board the spacecraft offers a very human touch to the project and at the same time provides an important educational aspect to the mission," said Mick.

When UFOs finally land openly here on Earth, look for Earth's Intergalactic Rock 'n' Roll Royalty—the surviving members of the Beatles and the Stones—to join musical forces and help roll out the red carpet for these space emissaries, together with leaders of the world's governments. The Beatles and the Stones can then hopefully master the secrets of music performed throughout the galaxy and in other galaxies existing on the very edges of our imagination, opening a brave new world of sound for the waiting masses.

# 2

# EMF

## EXTRATERRESTRIAL MUSICAL FORCES

ohn Lennon, Paul McCartney, Keith Richards, Michael Jackson, Jim Morrison, Jerry Garcia, Robert Plant and Jimmy Page of Led Zeppelin, Robert Fripp, Robert Palmer, John McLaughlin, Ginger Baker, Rick Wakeman, and many other rock and pop superstars have all reported feeling some kind of an unseen mysterious power—let's call it the Extraterrestrial Musical Force (EMF)—that enabled them to write their songs and/or perform onstage. Far-fetched as it may sound, the Beatles and their contemporaries appear all along to have been cosmic sounding boards, which raises the larger question: Exactly who or what was transmitting the music and lyrics to the Beatles and others for all these years? Were intelligent beings involved, and if so, what did they look like, where did they live, and what was their purpose anyway? To quote *Alice's Adventures in Wonderland,* it just gets curiouser and curiouser.

"They [the Beatles] were like mediums," Yoko Ono explained while in Berkeley, California, in 1982. "They weren't conscious of all they were saying, but it was coming through them." John Lennon put it this way: "When the real music comes to me—the music of the spheres, the music that surpasseth understanding—that has nothing to do with me 'cause I'm only the channel. The only joy for me is for it to be given to me and to transcribe it. Like a medium. Those moments are what I live for." John said, "It is amazing that the tune to 'In My Life' just came to me in a dream. That's why I don't profess to know anything. I think music is very mystical." The exact same thing happened to Paul McCartney. "The music to 'Yesterday' came in a dream," said Paul. "You have to believe in magic. I can't read or write music." George Harrison said that Beatles had "cosmic energy" until the day that they broke up.

In the fall of 1980, several weeks before his assassination, Lennon dropped a musical bombshell. He disclosed to John Green (aka Charlie Swan), his trusted tarot card reader, that he depended on a secret female muse—whom he refused to name—for much of his songwriting success. And he complained to Green that "me muse" had sometimes left him high and dry. "All of these years, it's like I've been deaf," Lennon told his seer. "The music was always there, but I couldn't hear it, and now I can't help but hear it . . . and sing it and write it. I've finally got her [the female muse] back. It's such a pleasure. I really thought that I had lost her forever this time."

When pressed by Green for further details about the identity of his secret muse, Lennon said, "Never you mind. This is a very private relationship and I have no intention of being even the least bit unfaithful. If I tell people her name, they might go calling her up, and if someone more desirable than me comes along, I will lose her again. And I never want to go through that again." Lennon wasn't joking.

Lennon made the unexpected disclosure of "me muse" in a telephone conversation he had with Green from Bermuda, where he had rediscovered reggae music and had entered a particularly creative period. "There are these street musicians everywhere, the place is full of music, and it kind of inspired me," said Lennon enthusiastically.

Bob Dylan said that his trademark protest song, "Blowin' in the Wind," just came to him "right out of that wellspring of creativity." Dylan confessed that he didn't know how he wrote this and other early songs. "Those early songs were magically written," said Bob.

"In the end you have to look at the song and not know where it came from," commented Bruce Springsteen.

Some students of the often magical and mysterious songwriting process attribute the source of the music directly to a higher God-like cosmic power. On the other hand, certain religious groups like the Way of Life Organization are convinced that the source of most, if not all, rock music—especially heavy metal—is the devil (Christian rock may be the only exception). In a larger context, is a battle being waged for the heart and soul of rock 'n' roll?

"We receive our songs by inspiration, like at a séance," said the Rolling Stones' Keith Richards. The songs he writes sometimes materialize out of thin air. "People say they write songs, but in a way you're more the medium," said Keith. "I feel that all the songs in the world are floating around; it's just a matter of [being] like an antenna, of whatever you pick up. So many uncanny things have happened to us. A whole new song appears from nowhere in five minutes, the whole structure, and you haven't worked at all."

Michael Jackson said, "I wake up from dreams and go, 'Wow, put this down on paper.' The whole thing is strange. You hear the words, everything is right there in front of your face. I feel that somewhere, someplace it's been done and I'm just a courier bringing it into the world." The Gloved One said, "When I hit the stage, it's all of a sudden a 'magic' from somewhere that comes and the spirit just hits you, and you just lose control of yourself."

Led Zeppelin's Robert Plant and Jimmy Page don't have a clue who wrote their megahit song "Stairway to Heaven." They insist it certainly wasn't them. "Pagey had written the chords and played them for me," said Plant. "I was holding the paper and pencil, and for some reason I was in a very bad mood. Then all of a sudden my hand was writing out words. I just sat there and looked at the words, and then I almost leapt out of my seat."

Robert Fripp said that "amazing things would happen" when he played guitar with King Crimson. "I mean, telepathy, qualities of energy, things that I had never experienced before with music. You can't tell whether the music is playing the musician or the musician is playing the music."

Robert Palmer called "Sweet Lies" "a lovely record," but confessed it wrote itself. "It came out of the blue. I was merely channeling it," said Palmer. "These chord changes—I have no idea where that came from." The same held true for another Palmer song, "She Makes My Day." "I didn't give much thought to it at all. It was like automatic writing. It's nice to be in the right place at the right time, catch it unaware, and then people go, 'What's that?' And I go, 'I dunno, good isn't it?'"

John McLaughlin, who led the Mahavishnu Orchestra, remembered, "One night we were playing and suddenly the spirit entered into me, and I was playing but it was no longer me playing."

Ginger Baker, drummer for the popular 1960s band Cream, said, "It happens to us quite often—it feels as though I'm not playing my instrument, something else is playing it, and that same thing is playing all three of our instruments." Baker confessed, "It's frightening sometimes. Maybe we all play the same phrase out of nowhere. It happens very often with us."

Stevie Nicks of Fleetwood Mac said that she has felt the magic of music moving on its own momentum. "It's amazing, 'cause sometimes when we're onstage, I feel like somebody's just moving the pieces. . . . I'm just going, 'God, we don't have any control over this.'"

Rick Wakeman of Yes said, "There's this really weird thing that happens when I know exactly what he [bandmate Steve Howe] is going to do [onstage] at any time, and he knows exactly what I'm going to do at any given time. There's a weird type of telepathy that goes on that's really strange." Rick said that he has had the same sort of experience while performing with Jon Anderson. Rick called the phenomenon the X-factor and said, "When you try to look at it or analyze what it is, it'll all collapse. You just have to be thankful that it's there."

Vocalist Marc Storace of the heavy metal group Krokus, compared playing rock music to "a mysterious energy that comes from the metaphysical plane in my body." Fellow heavy metal musician Bill Ward of Black Sabbath said, "I've always considered that there was some way where we were able to channel energy and that energy was able to be from another source; if you like, like a higher power or something that was actually doing the work. I've often thought of us just being actually just the Earth beings that played the music, because it was uncanny." Angus Young, lead guitarist of AC/DC, said that something—he doesn't know what—appears to take control of the band during concerts. "I'm on automatic pilot," said Young. "By the time we're halfway through the first number, someone else is steering me. I'm just along for the ride."

Punk Godmother Patti Smith said that she taps into an unknown creative vehicle whenever she composes songs: "I don't want to seem conceited or anything . . . but I do have an ability that is [in] some ways like a channeling kind of ability. . . . So I surrender and let these things come into me. . . . Sometimes I feel that I don't know where certain things come from, sometimes I believe they come from angels, from God, from an ancestor. . . . I have experienced enough things to know that even if they are part of my subconscious, they are a real thing, and I think that they are often helpful."

Grammy Award–winning singer and songwriter Rodney Crowell of such hits as Bob Seger's "Shame on the Moon" and the Oak Ridge Boys' "Leaving Louisiana in the Broad Daylight" compared songwriting to "doing card tricks on the radio." Crowell said that he didn't write the songs on his new album, *Fate's Right Hand*. He said, "These songs picked me. These songs exist somewhere else, fully written. My job is to bring them into the time and space we're in. I'm careful to let the song tell me what to do. My intention is to be the receiver for the inspiration. It'll come to visit, and then [the songs] come pouring out of me."

Jim Morrison, leader of the Doors, had a name for the spirits that provided his musical inspiration. He called them The Lords and even authored a book of poetry about them. The Doors' name sprang from Aldous Huxley's book *The Doors of Perception.* Huxley wrote, "When the doors of perception are cleansed, we will see things as they really are—infinite." Morrison's signature song, "Break on Through," described his group's mystical mission: "There are things that are known, and things that are unknown, and in between are the Doors."

Morrison claimed that when he was onstage the spirits of dead Indians took over him. Ray Manzarek, the Doors' keyboardist, said, "Every once in a while from the microphone, I would hear some strange guttural Indian utterances. I'd say, 'What on Earth, where did that come from?' And sure enough, it came out of Jim Morrison's mouth and you could see his eyes roll back ever so slightly in his head and he was gone, man. He was gone and somebody else had come out.

"Jim was an *electric* shaman and we were the shaman's band," said Manzarek, who now performs with the Doors of the 21st Century, complete with a look-alike stand-in for the Lizard King. "When the Siberian shaman gets ready to go into a trance, all of the villagers get together . . . and play whatever instruments that they have to send him off into a trance. . . . Sometimes Jim wouldn't feel like getting into the [shamanistic] state, but the band would keep on pounding and pounding, and little by little it would take him over. God, I could send an electric shock through him with the organ. John could do it with his drumbeat." Manzarek added that Perry Farrell and Eddie Vedder

Jim Morrison, leader of the Doors, credited unseen extraterrestrial musical forces he nicknamed The Lords for helping him write and perform his music. Morrison claimed that when he was onstage, the spirits of dead Indians took over him.

of Pearl Jam "definitely have a shamanistic side to them that comes out when they sing onstage." Shamans are spiritual healers who can invoke the divine and have the power to transform anyone within their reach.

Jerry Garcia of the Grateful Dead called performing onstage "a kind of channeling." Jerry said, "We're opening the door, but we're not responsible for what comes through. So in that sense, I can't take credit for it. We're like a utility, like a conduit for life energy, psychic energy—whatever it is." Joseph Campbell, the renowned mythologist, attended several Dead concerts and thought that they resembled a modern shamanistic ritual. Campbell told Garcia, "This is the antidote to the atom bomb."

Joni Mitchell, who wrote the theme song "Woodstock," credited her creative powers to a cosmic being—in her case a "male muse" named Art. Joni feels married to Art, whom she claims has lent her his key to the "Shrine of Creativity." She has reportedly often roamed naked with him on her forty-eight-acre estate. You can't just make up this stuff.

Elisabeth Kübler-Ross, a Swiss-born psychiatrist who was generally regarded as the world's foremost expert on death and dying, admitted that she was once serenaded by a guitar-playing "spirit guide" named Willy. A believer in extraterrestrials, Kübler-Ross claimed that she has experienced several encounters with spirit guides who imparted great wisdom to her. She said that she has no idea if the spirit guides were aliens.

The late Cyril Scott, an eminent composer and student of theosophy, claimed that spirit "takes a special interest in the evolution of Western music," adding, "The great initiates [in the spirit world] have vast and imposing plans for the musical future to use music as an occult medium to develop altered states of consciousness, psychic abilities, and contact with the music world. Music in the future is to be used to bring people into yet closer touch with the Devos [spirits]."

Could an ancient muse or at least a reasonable modern facsimile have orchestrated many of the past and present top-ten rock 'n' roll hits? Somebody or something seems to have been assisting many rock stars for years in composing some of their best-known songs, yet they have never received royalty payments. The muse phenomenon dates back five thousand years to ancient Greece, when poets and prophets—rock stars for their time—were understood to be the direct mouthpieces of superior beings.

Outstanding Greek philosophers and artists attributed their special talents to nine different invisible beings in the sky. Calliope was the muse of epic poetry; Clio, the muse of history; Euterpe, the muse of lyric poetry; Melpomene, the muse of tragedy; Terpsichore, the muse of choral song and dance; Erato, the muse of love poetry; Polyhymnia, the muse of sacred poetry; Urania, the muse of astronomy; and Thalia, the muse of comedy. Besides the muses, three goddesses called Graces presided over dining, the arts, and "all social enjoyments."

Poetry in ancient Greece was not meant to be read but heard, creating a new art form that was the forerunner of today's live pop music concerts. Poets often accompanied themselves on a string instrument called the lyre, invented by the god Mercury. According to legend, one day Mercury found a tortoise, removed the shell, made holes in the opposite edges of it, drew cords of linen through the holes, and behold, the lyre was born. Nine cords were used in honor of all nine Muses. Mercury gave the lyre to Apollo. From then on Apollo was considered a key source of inspiration for the arts and also of prophecy, which was linked to poetry from the beginning. Legend has it that Apollo's son, Orpheus, the first poet-musician in mythology, produced such moving sounds that "nothing could withstand the charms of his music." He turned people on the way Mick Jagger still does today.

The merging of music and lyrics went on for many centuries after the collapse of the classical world, eventually laying the groundwork for modern songs ranging from jazz and rhythm-and-blues to folk, rock 'n' roll, and pop. During the Middle Ages troubadours carried on in the same tradition. The troubadours came out of southern France around the twelfth-century, spreading their ideal of pure love and romance to other parts of Europe despite being suppressed during the Great Inquisition. Many parallels can be found between the medieval troubadours and modern rock 'n' roll troubadours of the 1960s, such as Donovan and Cat Stevens, who replaced the lyre with the guitar as their instrument of choice. Both the original troubadours and their latter-day counterparts rebelled against authority and were seekers of higher consciousness and spirituality.

Medieval troubadours were in some ways the hippies of their day, preaching tolerance and seeking truth. And they unabashedly loved to have a good time. Wandering minstrels would travel from castle to castle, bringing new songs, gossip, and the latest news. A variety of performers from acrobats to dwarfs and jesters joined in the freewheeling celebrations. Troubadours laid the groundwork for future musicians to communicate their ideals to mass audiences and encourage new ways of thinking.

# 3

# DAVID BOWIE
# AND
# JIMI HENDRIX

## MEN WHO FELL TO EARTH

David Bowie, in his full makeup regalia as Martian Ziggy Stardust, played the role of ultimate extraterrestrial performer. In real life Bowie spent considerable time searching for the aliens he sang about. He wasn't disappointed.

avid Bowie's creation of Ziggy Stardust, his beloved alter ego, instantly blasted pop culture to a galaxy far, far away. Flaunting glowing red hair, wild makeup, and body paint beneath outrageous costumes, accompanied by surreal lighting and special effects and a backup band called The Spiders from Mars, Bowie was like no previous showbiz personality who ever lived. Offstage, David was consumed with making contact with aliens and passionately searched the skies for extraterrestrials. He found what he was looking for—spacecraft from another world.

*The Rise and Fall of Ziggy Stardust and the Spiders from Mars*, one of the most important concept albums of all time, was released in June 1972. The story was about a Martian who comes to Earth in human form and finds a desolate planet that only had five years remaining. Ziggy's essential message was to let the children lead the way to the future. To reach out to them, he was forced to become a rock 'n' roll star, and eventually it cost him his life. "Ziggy was my Martian messiah who twanged a guitar," recalled Bowie. "I fell for Ziggy, too. It was quite easy to become obsessed night and day with the character. I became Ziggy Stardust." The Spiders from Mars band consisted of guitarist and vocalist Mick Ronson, bass player Trevor Bolder, and drummer Mick Woodmansey.

"In one instant, in a spiritual breaking of the clouds, Ziggy was born," observed one Ziggy historian. "He hung on to the stars and gestured with infinite grace and precision. He breathed the cool winds and caressed divinity as if it were his lover. And then he wove his web of poetry and beckoned from the skies to the children. And the children heard. . . . In their thousands they came and listened. And in his word they found life and hope. Manifested in Ziggy's words they perceived the truth . . . they demanded more and more, until they tapped the very source of this fragile creature and sucked out his energy . . . until finally the truth had become like shattered fragments of glass, and his soul had been ravaged. And there was nothing left to mark his passing except tiny grains of Stardust, which were swept up by the wind and sprinkled into the colored hair of children all across the planet Earth . . ."

Bowie based his Ziggy Stardust character on Vince Taylor, an unbelievably eccentric rock star with a heavy messiah complex and a love for Elvis Presley, whom Bowie encountered at the Gioconda café on Tottenham Court Road in London in 1966. Taylor's best-known work was his 1959 single, "Brand New Cadillac," which was covered by the Clash on their London Calling album in 1977. The Clash's Joe Strummer said, "Vince was the beginning of British rock 'n' roll. Before him there was nothing. He was a miracle."

The Ziggy Stardust album opened with a song called "Five Years," which set the stage for extraterrestrial intervention. The second song, "Soul Love," offered the hope of peace, love, and redemption. Then came the momentous arrival of Ziggy in "Moonage Daydream," in which he announced, "I'm the space invader, I'll be a rock 'n' roll bitch for you." Bisexuality had arrived on the scene.

Talking about "Starman," the centerpiece song on the Ziggy album, Bowie said, " 'Starman' can be taken at the immediate level of 'There's a starman in the sky saying, "Boogie, children!" ' but the theme of it is that the idea of things in the sky is really quite human and real and we should be a bit happier about the prospect of meeting [these] people." The song included the lines "There's a starman waiting in the sky, / He'd like to come and meet us, / But he thinks he'd blow our minds."

On side two of *The Rise and Fall of Ziggy Stardust,* Ziggy met his disciples in "Lady Stardust," playing before a crowd of worshipers. In "Star" he revealed his plan for intergalactic superstardom. But by the time of the title song, "Ziggy Stardust," the sheen had started to come off the space messiah's vision. The narrator talked about fights within the band and Ziggy's loss of momentum. In "Suffragette City," Ziggy was in full decline and he lamented, "My work is down the drain." Many years later, Bowie envisioned mounting *The Ziggy Stardust Show* on Broadway with five new songs added. It was a clever idea, but it never got off the ground.

David had launched his first hit song, "Space Oddity," about an alienated astronaut named Major Tom, on July 11, 1969, just nine days before America's first moon landing. The BBC played "Space Oddity" as its theme song for its coverage of the Apollo 11 Moon landing, unaware that the song culminated with its hero Major Tom's implicit refusal to return to Earth. Bowie watched the television tube intently as Neil Armstrong set foot on the lunar surface. The song's title was a parody of Stanley Kubrick's epic film *2001: A Space Odyssey,* released the year before. Yet another extraterrestrial song, "Life on Mars," from Bowie's album *Hunky Dory,* rocketed to number three on the charts in 1973.

Looking back, David said, "I really do support that theory [of extraterrestrial life] wholeheartedly. But for my writing, I used it merely as imagery, as symbolic generally of some kind of spiritual search. And it was the idea of whatever that godhead or the higher being or whatever that could be. It manifested itself in my songs as saucers or aliens or otherness, so really it was used as a subtext more than anything else. It wasn't used as hardware."

But behind the scenes, contacting aliens proved to be David's real-life obsession in the 1970s. "My mother saw her first flying saucer," said David, standing nearly naked backstage during the opening of the D. A. Pennebaker film, *Ziggy Stardust and the Spiders from Mars*, depicting Ziggy's retirement concert at the Hammersmith Odeon in July 1973. Bowie would routinely interrupt interviews with the media to go to the window to see if any saucers were waiting outside. David owned a thousand books on the subject and had a telescope set up to peer through the open moonroof of his limousine so he could search for aliens during his concert tour in the United States.

In 1974, David and his then wife, Angela, were transfixed in their Detroit hotel room by an afternoon television news flash that a UFO had crashed in the area with several aliens aboard. The spaceship was reported to be about six feet wide and thirty feet long. "The three creatures were killed on impact when the spaceship plummeted to Earth," recalled David in *Mirabella* magazine, "but they were taken to a hospital to be examined anyway. These people looked like human beings but were much smaller, and when they were examined, it was discovered that their vital organs were like human beings' too! The catch is that their brains were found to be much further advanced! Wow!"

An update on the UFO crash was promised on the six o'clock news. At 6 P.M. the news crew confirmed the landing, but were vague about its location. David and Angela waited until the eleven o'clock news, when it was announced that the prime-time news crew had perpetrated a hoax and had summarily been fired. "No UFOs had landed; no aliens were in custody, dead or alive; the United States air force had not intercepted any craft whatsoever in the skies above Michigan," said Angela. The case seemed closed, but there was really no way to be certain.

Angela said, "David believed very strongly that aliens were active above our planet. . . . That's why we were so alert in the limo on the way to Minneapolis [the next stop on Bowie's American tour], watching intently for signs of further UFO activity in the bright night sky." David had his eye pressed to a telescope that had just been purchased for him in Detroit by his personal assistant, Corrine Schwab. He looked out the open moonroof of the limousine, hoping to see aliens, but none appeared. "I suspect he [David] wouldn't have been surprised at all if the aliens had come right down to the limo and tractor-beamed him up for an exchange of ideas," said Angela. Bowie talked about the six o'clock broadcast on the UFO crash during his show at Detroit's Cobo Arena. "I asked the audience at the concert that night if they had heard about the spaceship landing," said David, "and just about all of them had, so I wasn't hearing things! I'd really like to know more about it, though!"

Angela said recently, "I would like to visit alien planets." She traced her interest in UFOs to St. George's School in Switzerland, which she attended with girls from fifty-seven countries and twenty-eight religions. "The girls from South America and their magazines and newspapers were full of UFO sightings, and I wondered why none of these events were reported in the media in the rest of the world," Angela said. "Who knows how many countries have the remnants of destroyed landing craft sitting in hangars; the evidence of various visitations?"

"I've always felt like a vehicle for something else," said David, who was born David Robert Jones on January 8, 1947—the same year that a UFO crash-landed in Roswell, New Mexico, carrying four alien creatures. David's mother, Margaret Burns, said that the midwife told her, "This child has been on this Earth before." Margaret added, "I thought that was a rather odd thing to say, but the midwife seemed quite adamant."

Michael Hutchence of INXS said in a 1997 interview that he met with Bowie in the 1970s. "I thought that he was not of this earth!" remarked Hutchence. "But, then, why should rock stars be treated that way? At the moment people are all into aliens again, but not rock stars. Aliens have replaced rock stars." The iris in Bowie's left eye was damaged in a childhood fight, adding to his alien persona.

"If you listen to Bowie's song 'Loving the Alien,' you will realize that he is in reality the son of a starman and an Earth mother," insists Nina Hagen, Germany's Queen of Punk, who believes that on many occasions throughout history extraterrestrials have landed and mated with Earth women, a scenario that is well supported by much current research into the origins of humankind. The promotional video of "Loving the Alien" has a curious moment in which Bowie faces the camera and for no apparent reason his nose starts bleeding. Whitley Strieber's book *Communion*, published two years later, describes UFO abductees having nosebleeds from nasal probes inserted by alien visitors. Bowie starred along with Catherine Deneuve and Susan Sarandon in the horror-film adaptation of Strieber's book *The Hunger*.

David's passion for UFOs began in childhood. He spent his hippie years spotting UFOs from the rooftop of his south London home. In 1969 he edited a UFO magazine in England and took part in regular UFO skywatches. He sighted UFOs six or seven times a night for about a year from a small observatory. "We had regular cruises that came over," said David. "We knew the 6:15 was coming in and would meet up with another one. And they would be stationary for about half an hour, and then after verifying what they'd been doing that day, they'd shoot off." Bowie said that what is important is what people do with UFO information. "We never used to tell anybody [about the UFO sightings]. It was beautifully dissipated when it got to the media."

During the filming of Nicolas Roeg's 1976 film, *The Man Who Fell to Earth*, shot over six weeks on location in

New Mexico—a hot zone for UFO activity—David, who plays space alien Thomas Jerome Newton, claimed that he had several UFO sightings. "You could look up into the sky and see strange things every day," recalled Paul Mayersberg, the film's writer. Bowie reportedly spent his spare time between film takes locked in a trailer poring through his library of mystical books and listening to his song "Young Americans" played backward on a special turntable, which made the recording sound like a Tibetan chant. Bowie had wanted to visit monasteries in Tibet. "The Tibetan monks, lamas, bury themselves inside mountains for weeks and only eat every three days," said David. "They're ridiculous—and it's said they live for centuries."

The Man Who Fell to Earth told the story of an extraterrestrial who came here in search of water for his barren planet. Bowie's alien joined forces with a lawyer played by Buck Henry to patent nine advanced technological processes he hoped would allow him to amass a fortune big enough to finance the construction of his own spaceship to return home after obtaining water to save his planet. But despite his successes, the powers-that-be felt threatened by the potential disruption of their monopolies that Bowie's character and company, World Enterprises, represented. He was eventually betrayed in a suspense-filled plot enhanced by breathtaking special effects. As his plan faltered, the alien tycoon all-too-humanly embraced sex and booze as solace for his sense of failure. At the film's dramatic climax, the depressed and depraved Bowie character ripped aside his human skin and revealed the alien within.

Roeg said that in making The Man Who Fell to Earth he was trying to establish "a link between the alien from another planet and the alien within our own culture." Bowie commented that the film "works on spiritual and primal levels of an incredibly complex, Howard Hughes–type alien." No one could have been better cast for the film than Bowie. Asked in the film, "Are you the first visitor?" Bowie's alien responds, "No, there have always been visitors."

Bowie's producer, Tony Visconti, said that Bowie was hanging out in a nearby room when Visconti sighted a UFO while standing on an outdoor balcony belonging to Bowie's friend, the singer and songwriter Leslie Duncan. "We both visited Leslie at her top-floor flat in West Hampstead [England] one day," said Tony. "Leslie and her boyfriend talked about UFOs for hours. It was their specialty, and the purpose of our visit was for David to introduce me to them. After dark I went out on their balcony with the boyfriend, who eventually said, 'They are up there all the time.' Then he suddenly pointed up and we could see a faint moving object, about the size of a medium-bright star, moving rapidly across the night sky. 'There's one,' he said. I said it couldn't be; it was only a satellite. He said it wasn't and we should just keep watching it. Quickly, very unlike a satellite, it disappeared. David was inside the flat when this happened, but we ran to tell him and Leslie about it."

Visconti further recalled that Dennis Davis, who played percussion on Bowie's 1977 album, Low, claimed that he had taken a shortcut through a highly classified air force hangar and, from the catwalk he was standing on, saw a crashed UFO. Davis said that he stared at the strange spacecraft for what seemed an eternity, until a guard ordered him to leave because he wasn't authorized to be there. Davis said that he was warned to never mention what he'd seen to anyone. Visconti said that he didn't know if Davis's story was true. Davis played drums for Bowie on all his albums from Station to Station through Scary Monsters.

According to Spiders from Mars guitarist Mick Ronson, "David became convinced he was being stalked by men from Mars," around 1969 or 1970. Through the years David became increasingly concerned that aliens might be trying to control his thoughts. But appearing on the British television show *Russell Harty Plus* in 1973, Bowie appeared cool, calm, and collected. "I stopped flying a year and a half ago," he said. "I had too many bad flights. I'm waiting for flying saucers." The following year, appearing on Dick Cavett's *Wide World of Entertainment* in the United States, Bowie demonstrated how a flying saucer can take off vertically as opposed to the liftoff of a conventional airplane. Bowie's song "Memory of a Free Festival" painted a seldom-equaled portrait of UFO contact. David wrote, "The sun machine is coming down and we're gonna have a party."

A well-known French ufologist, Thierry Pinvidic, reported that he accidentally met David's manager on a train heading from White Plains to New York City in 1979 and was promptly invited to a party at Bowie's mansion in Westchester County. Pinvidic met Bowie and was apparently welcomed with open arms by the rock superstar and his friends.

David's 1996 album, *Earthling*, contained the catchy track "Looking for Satellites." He described the song as stream of consciousness: "I used words randomly: *shampoo, TV, boyzone.* What I said first stayed in." Bowie said, "It's as near to a spiritual song as I've ever written: it's measuring the distance between the crucifixion and flying saucers."

Bowie belatedly paid homage on his 2002 *Heathen* CD to Norman Carl Odam, also known as the Legendary Stardust Cowboy, by covering Odam's 1968 song "I Took a Trip on a Gemini Spaceship" and arranging for him and his band to be flown from San Jose, California, to perform at the Meltdown Arts Festival in London. David said that he borrowed the name *Stardust* for his album, *The Rise and Fall of Ziggy Stardust and the Spiders from Mars.* The lyrics for "I Took a Trip on a Gemini Spaceship" include references to "Two or three flying saucers, parked under the stars." Now that he has had his fifteen minutes of fame, Odam dreams one day of visiting Mars.

Bowie's entire *The Rise and Fall of Ziggy Stardust and the Spi-*

ders *from Mars* album was beamed into space in January 2003. He has created an archive of *Ziggy*-related documents that along with a CD will be sent on the launch of humanity's first starship in 2005. Team Encounter, a commercial spaceflight company based in Houston, Texas, is sponsoring the solar sail, which is the size of a football field. The ship will be propelled by solar waves into deep space, passing Pluto after seventeen years. Major Tom will soon be coming to a planet near you.

# JIMI HENDRIX: EXTRATERRESTRIAL GUITAR WIZARD

Carlos Santana once witnessed Jimi Hendrix onstage playing his electric guitar without touching the strings. Talk about a hard act to follow! The multimillionaire, Grammy Award–winning Latino musician credits Metatron—a bearded cosmic being whom he has seen—for guiding his platinum album *Supernatural.* But could Jimi Hendrix, who didn't know how to read or write music, have also possibly been in touch with some similar type of supernatural cosmic being that drove his far-out performances?

The Allen Twins, Taharqa Aleem and Tunde-ra Aleem, who once shared an apartment with Jimi and were background singers on Hendrix's *Cry of Love, War Heroes,* and *Rainbow Bridge* albums, claimed, "Jimi was able to make visible musical entities from the ethereal world of sound, and on numerous occasions he actually performed that for us. . . . Jimi would take us into a room and he would perform an act that would summon up entities that we were able to see. Of course this was mind-boggling to us."

The Allen Twins first came into contact with Jimi when he was touring with Little Richard and the Isley Brothers in 1965, and organized a famous street concert for Jimi in Harlem in 1969 to benefit the charity Biafra Calls. The twins opened up their own recording studio in the late 1980s. Attempts to get the twins (also known then as the Ghetto Fighters) to describe exactly what these so-called beings looked like hit a brick wall, but there is little doubt that Jimi played like an extraterrestrial guitar wizard plugged into an ultimate source of musical power, combining fuzz, feedback, and controlled distortions in ways never done before by any other artist on this planet.

Hendrix truly accomplished the impossible. He took music kicking and screaming into another dimension. And just to make it more interesting, he accomplished it as a left-hander using a right-handed Fender Statocaster turned upside down. This is roughly the equivalent of playing a piano backward. "All of the strings and notes are reversed, and instead of bending a string, you have to pull it," noted ex–Rolling Stones guitarist Mick Taylor.

Hendrix's manager, Alan Douglas, said flat out that Jimi "believed that he was possessed by some spirit, and I got to believe it myself and that was what we had to deal with."

"Jimi was not of this Earth," claimed longtime friend Curtis Knight, who hired Hendrix to join his group, The Squires, appearing at nightspots in Greenwich Village in rock 'n' roll's formative days. One of the songs The Squires recorded once Hendrix was on board was "The UFO." "What I'm telling you is exactly what Jimi told me a long time ago," said Knight. "Jimi was a spiritual messenger. He was sent here from another place so that through his music and his guitar he could put his message across to the world."

Jimi once told a reporter from the *New York Times* that he was really from Mars. Commenting on life beyond Earth, Jimi told someone else, "There are other people in the solar system, you know, and they have the same feelings too, not necessarily bad feelings, but see, it upsets their way of living for instance—and they are a whole lot heavier than we are. And it's no war games, because they all keep the same place. But like the solar system is going through a change soon and it's going to affect the Earth in about thirty years."

"There's one thing about Jimi nobody ever wants to discuss, the metaphysical Jimi Hendrix," said his friend and longtime Band of Gypsies bass player Billy Cox. "Jimi's spirituality, his whole psyche, was that of someone from another planet. . . . There are those who come before the public eye and are commercialized into the consciousness of the masses. We are told they are popular, and we echo, 'They are popular.' Then there are a few who are so intuitively turned into the universe that they are beyond sight. This is immortality and Jimi Hendrix is immortal."

Jimi was High Priest of the Electric Church, finding a way of transforming music into a New Age religion: "It's just a belief that I have you know; and it's . . . we do use electric guitars; everything, you know, is electrified nowadays. So therefore the belief comes into, you know, through electricity to the people, whatever. That's why we play so loud, because it doesn't actually hit through the eardrums. . . . We're planning for our sound to go inside the soul of a person actually, you know; and see if they can awaken some kind of thing in their minds, you know, 'cause there are so many sleeping people."

Jimi assured legions of his young fans, "There'll be music in the hereafter, too. Everyone shouldn't get hung up when it's time for you to die, because all you're doing is just getting rid of that old body." He explained to his girlfriend Monika Dannemann that he "didn't believe that we are born simply to die. He felt strongly that everything has a reason and a purpose, and that there would be no sense in life if there is nothing beyond death." In his song "Voodoo Child (Slight Return)," Jimi scored this ironic one-liner: "If I don't meet you no more in this world, I'll meet you on the next one, so don't be late."

"The everyday mud world we're living in today compared to the spiritual world is like a parasite compared to the ocean, and the ocean is the biggest living thing you know about," said Jimi. "The music flows from the air; that's why I can connect with a spirit, and when they come down off this natural high, they see clearer, feel different things—don't think of pain and hurting the next person." Jimi went on, "Before I can remember anything, I can remember music and stars and planets. I could go to sleep and write fifteen symphonies. I had very strange feelings that I was here [on Earth] for something and I was going to get a chance to be heard."

Elvis Presley had precisely the same feeling, and so did John Lennon and David Bowie. They were here for some larger purpose, although they didn't know exactly what that purpose was in the cosmic scheme of life.

# JIMI'S MYSTIC EXPERIENCES

Mary Willix, who was a close friend to "Jimmy" when he was just a twelve-year-old attending public school in Seattle, Washington (she was two years younger), fondly remembered, "We talked about mysterious, mystical outer space, inner-space things—pyramid power, reincarnation, mental telepathy, precognitive dreams, and exotic places." In an "open letter" to Hendrix published in her book, *Jimi Hendrix: Voices from Home*, Mary said, "At school I learned quickly that I couldn't talk to most people about psychic phenomena, outer space, or spiritual things without being labeled as different. But I liked to keep testing the waters, looking for an opening. When I tested you, I felt as if I'd won the lottery. We had conversations that would knock most people over . . . I loved our mini 'what-if' brainstorming sessions. What if great people like Mozart lived before? What would you do if you were alone on a dark road and a UFO landed?"

While he was growing up in Seattle, Hendrix loved to paint cosmic pictures at school. "The teacher used to say, 'Paint three scenes,' and I'd do abstract stuff like a Martian sunset," said Jimi. "No bull. I wanted to be an actor or a painter. I particularly liked to paint scenes on other planets, summer afternoons on Venus, and stuff like that. The idea of space travel excited me more than anything else."

Jimi frequently experienced astral travel in adulthood. "Have you ever laid in bed, and you were in this complete state and you couldn't move?" he asked. "And you get . . . feel like you're going deeper and deeper into something. Not sleep, but something else." Jimi told Monika Dannemann that "while a person is living on Earth, his or her spirit could actually leave the body for a period of time," often at night. "The more evolved and spiritually active a person is, the more easily will his spirit be able to travel to Spiritland and meet the spirits of the dead," said Monika. "These are real astral journeys, and Jimi told me that they can be beautiful beyond description." Jimi said that many of his songs were triggered by astral travels and recollections of dreams he'd had. In a piece he dedicated to Monika in 1970, "Beam Me Up Jupiter," Jimi wrote, "In all your strength and splendor, / Do you hear my knocking? / I come running home to you Jupiter."

Hendrix had made an extremely exciting discovery. William Buhlman, one of America's leading experts on out-of-body experiences, has surveyed over sixteen thousand participants from thirty-two countries about their OOB (out-of-body) experiences. For more than a decade, the Michigan-based hypnotherapist and author has offered workshops that teach people how to project their consciousness outside the limits of their physical bodies and to explore dimensions and worlds beyond everyday life. Buhlman claims to have journeyed outside his body to parallel universes described in the new physics theories of Stephen Hawking, Paul Davies, and Fred Alan Wolf.

"All of us are interdimensional beings currently focusing our attention on energy-matter," said Buhlman. "Out-of-body and near-death experiences, dreams, altered states of consciousness, even death itself, are evidence of our interdimensional nature." Buhlman predicted, "Eventually all of us will evolve to the point where we are able to consciously experience and explore the entire universe. This will occur when our species grows to recognize that we and the universe are the same—multidimensional."

Evidence of out-of-body experiences dates back to Egypt between three thousand and five thousand years ago. Egyptian priests were aware of the existence of the astral body, which they called the ka. References to OOB experiences can be found in the writings of ancient Greek philosophers and in the Bible. Astral travelers are always keenly aware of a silver cord that connects their physical and extraphysical bodies. If the silver cord breaks, the astral traveler can never return to his or her body and will be pronounced dead.

Psychic Chris Burrows, who runs an animal sanctuary in North Yorkshire, England, claims that he has met space aliens during his astral travels for more than forty-five years. An ordained Zen Buddhist monk and onetime drummer for a band in London,

Burrows said that he'd traveled to the astral plane while living in all parts of the world and had come into direct contact with "little beings" identical to those reported by UFO abductees. "The conclusion I have come to," said Burrows, "is that although there may be certain beings from outer space, we should certainly be looking to inner space for some answers."

Hendrix went even beyond that. "Jimi seemed to have the ability to switch from one time dimension to the next," declared Monika. "He often spoke of ancient worlds and civilizations as if he had contact with them." The legendary lost continent of Atlantis inspired Jimi's song "Valleys of Neptune—Arising." Monika said that Jimi described Atlantis as "a magical place, full of force and energy, almost a living entity."

Hendrix was part American Indian and believed he had been a full-blooded American Indian in a past life. Jimi's beloved grandmother, Nora, belonged to the Cherokee tribe, and her grandmother was a Cherokee princess. The Cherokees, like other Native American tribes, believed that they had descended to Earth from the stars. Jimi's song "Red House" was inspired by *The Book of the Hopi* written in the 1960s by Frank Waters. A mysterious town in ancient Mexico, the Red Town of South, supposedly housed a four-level pyramid used for religious ceremonies, in which strange creatures called kachina trained men in the occult. After long training, adepts could access the fourth level and know all there was to know about the planets, the stars, and life by speaking to the Creator, hence the song's line "the key doesn't lock the door." If indeed Jimi did unlock the door and had outside cosmic contact during his meteoric three-and-a-half-year career as a rock avatar, he was far from alone.

# HENDRIX'S "ANGELS OF HEAVEN"

Carlos Santana, today's *Supernatural* troubadour, who has championed Hendrix as a cultural icon, said that his cosmic guide Metatron instructed him how to make important changes in his musical career that would catapult him ever higher into the musical stratosphere. "We want to hook you back to the radio airwave frequency," Metatron told Santana. "We want you to reach junior high schools, high schools, and universities. Once you reach them—because we are going to connect you with the best artists of the day—we want you to present them a new menu. Let them know that they are themselves, multidimensional spirits with enormous possibilities and opportunities. We want you to present them with a new form of existence that transcends religion, politics, or the modus operandi of education today."

Santana claimed that other artists who participated with him on his album *Supernatural* were brought to him supernaturally to be a part of Metatron's project. Among his guest soloists were Lauryn Hill, Wyclef Jean, Eagle-Eye Cherry, Rob Thomas, Dave Matthews, and Eric Clapton. He claimed that they heard his music or were communicated with in dreams about the forthcoming album. According to Carlos, cosmic spirits communicated to him as though he were "like a fax machine." The enormous success of *Supernatural* was "not a matter of coincidence or a lucky break," he said, "but something much bigger: a kind of holy synchronicity. I have sought to spread a kind of spiritual virus, and now I've received a great opportunity.

"We can all achieve things for the enrichment of mankind, if we have a mind to," said Carlos. "I want to use music as a means of healing, because there is so much suffering out there. To my mind, real success is sharing the cake and feeding as many people as possible. Only the truly ignorant eat it all themselves, and choke on it."

Santana said that he is tuned in to the same spiritual radio station that Jimi Hendrix channeled, and that is where his musical power comes from. "There's an invisible radio that Jimi Hendrix and [John] Coltrane tuned in to," Carlos explained, "and when you go there, you start channeling other music." For years Santana has dreamed about making an album that is mainly electric guitar like Jimi Hendrix and Sun Ra "with a little bit of lyrics and very little vocals to tell stories of interplanetary or galactical or celestial time rather than just Earth time."

Several of Jimi Hendrix's best-known songs were about space aliens and their impact on the human race. On his very first album, *Are You Experienced?*, Jimi envisioned an alien-invasion scenario right out of the movie *Independence Day* or *The War of the Worlds.* The song "Third Stone from the Sun" asked, "May I land my kinky machine?" (i.e., a flying saucer). On his second album, *Axis: Bold as Love,* Jimi presented an imaginary, tongue-in-cheek interview between a news announcer and a man from outer space (voiced by Jimi) in a segment called "EXP." The announcer (Jimi) introduces a *"very peculiar-looking gentleman"* (named) Paul Caruso to give his opinion on "this nonsense about UFO's and space people?" Caruso cautions, "You just can't believe everything you see," and then blasts off, leaving the announcer awestruck. The announcer exclaims, "I, I don't believe it!"

The peculiar-looking spaceman is quickly swallowed up in a spiral of dazzling guitar chords that lead to a song, "Up from the Skies," sung from the perspective of an alien who once lived on Earth in prehistoric times and has now returned to see how mankind is faring.

"Jimi and I once talked about the idea of astral travel," confirmed the real Paul Caruso, "and we came up with

Carlos Santana, the Grammy Award–winning Latin superstar, claimed that he couldn't have gotten where he is today without the help of Metatron, a bearded cosmic being who helped him produce his platinum album *Supernatural*.

the idea of space brothers; beings from two different worlds who would, as a means of 'cultural exchange,' reincarnate in each other's worlds from time to time, the native acting as host for the visiting time-space traveler. Most likely this exchange provided the background for the EXP skit on the *Axis* album. I was in the Tin Angel restaurant in Greenwich Village when a friend told me that I was on a Jimi Hendrix album. I had not recorded with Jimi so I ran over to the record store next door to investigate this unexpected phenomenon. It was like having your name skywritten for you by surprise. Needless to say, I was deeply and permanently touched by this unusual person, Jimi Hendrix."

In his song, "Hey Baby (The New Rising Sun)," Jimi merged his visions of woman-as-savior and alien-as-savior into a single, space-tripping message. In "Castles (Are) Made of Sand" on the *Axis: Bold as Love* album, Jimi portrayed a spiritually healing kind of UFO intervention. Even when Jimi sang about nothing more than a idyllic dream of a flower maiden in "One Rainy Wish," also from *Axis*, the whole scene was suddenly thrust to another world with multiple satellites: ". . . the sun kissed the mountains blue, and eleven moons played across rainbows above me and you."

He alluded to the great outer space beyond in the song "Midnight Lightning" from *Voodoo Soup*: "Gotta keep on movin', gotta keep on movin', to understand both sides of the sky." In "Purple Haze" Jimi excused himself so he could "kiss the sky," and in "Astro Man" on his *Cry of Love* album, Hendrix completely adopted the guise of an outer-space superhero, as "a hand came out from heaven and pinned a badge on his chest." Check out this cool line: "Astro man, flying across the sky."

Jimi's legendary real-life encounter with a UFO during the filming of his *Rainbow Bridge* concert film in 1970 in the Haleakala Crater on the island of Maui proved

Hendrix's intense desire to make contact with extraterrestrials. West Coast surf guitarist Merrell Fankhauser, who has spent considerable time living and performing on Maui, said, "The entire crew were making their trek through the crater at ten thousand feet with donkeys loaded down with cameras and other equipment when all of a sudden out of a clear blue sky a silver disc appeared hovering over a cinder cone. Jimi and some of the cast saw it first, and Jimi walked out on the cinder field of an eight-hundred-year-old lava flow with open arms saying, 'Welcome, space brothers!'" Dozens of phone calls came into the local radio station about the sighting.

Later Jimi told fellow musician Curtis Knight that "the craft had come down to put its spiritual stamp of approval on the show. He also said that he'd been emotionally and physically recharged by the experience." Knight said, "As the saucer streaked across the sky, Jimi announced to the audience over the microphone, 'There go my friends!'" Jimi played a total of three forty-five-minute sets. After each set he retired to a sacred Hopi Indian tent. Witnesses swore that they heard musical tones emanating from rocks and stones following the concert.

According to Fankhauser, "Everyone was amazed [by the UFO] except for a film producer who was riding on a donkey and had been drinking whiskey. He looked into the blinding sun and said he couldn't see anything and that they [the crew] were all crazy. The producer became so upset when people kept pointing to the glowing orb that he fell off the donkey, injured his back, and had to be airlifted to the crater by helicopter.

"There was also a very tall tale about one of the hippie girls in the movie wandering off the trail and going down into a lava tube where she encountered two gray aliens with great big dark eyes who were collecting plants and rocks," said Fankhauser. "The spaced-out girl said that the aliens sprayed her with something, and when she awoke, she couldn't talk. She claimed that it took her several weeks to regain her voice." A more plausible explanation is that the girl was stoned immaculate and imagined the entire episode.

Fankhauser, a longtime student of Hawaiian folklore, said that legends abound on all of the islands about strange lights seen in the night sky flying into the mountains. While performing on the same Hawaiian crater with his legendary band, Mu, Fankhauser spotted highly advanced UFOs that "were very real and made no sound. I've flown various kinds of aircraft and sailplanes and have a knowledge of aerodynamics. These objects did things no aircraft or helicopter can do." He said he met a tourist retired from the U.S. navy who saw them, too, and "he was thoroughly baffled." UFO activity seems to have centered around the Haleakala Crater on Maui starting in the 1800s, picking up again in the 1960s, and reaching a peak in the mid-1970s, said Fankhauser.

Filmed two months before Hendrix's death, the *Rainbow Bridge* concert film features a smashing seventeen-minute performance by Jimi accompanied by bassist Billy Cox from the Band of Gypsies and drummer Mitch Mitchell from the Jimi Hendrix Experience. At the outset of the movie, a voice states in no uncertain terms that the film was produced by individuals who are in direct contact with the space brothers. The film's central character, Pat Hartley, a black actress, travels from Los Angeles to the Rainbow Bridge Center for Occult Studies in Maui to check on the center's progress. Jimi, seated in the lotus position, holds forth in the film for several minutes about astral projection and the philosophy of the space brothers. Although quirky, the film heralded the arrival of the coming New Age. Unfortunately the UFO seen by Hendrix and his colleagues during the concert arrived much too early to be captured on film. But everyone who was there at the time agreed that they saw something in the sky they had never seen in their entire lives.

Curtis Knight claimed that an encounter Jimi and

other members of his band had with an exotic cone-shaped UFO and a tall alien near Woodstock, New York, on a cold winter's night in 1965 probably saved their lives. "It was four o'clock in the morning and we were trying to make it back to Manhattan—a drive of more than one hundred miles—through the worst blizzard I can recall," Curtis told veteran UFO researcher Timothy Green Beckley. The musicians' car got caught in a snowdrift and the temperature inside the car started to plunge, despite the heater being turned on full blast.

According to Curtis, a glowing cone-shaped object suddenly lit up the road in front of them and landed in the snow about one hundred feet away. The musicians were overcome with fright. Before they could do anything, the side of the alien spacecraft opened and out stepped a very tall being who floated toward the trapped occupants of the car. Curtis noticed that the snow was melting in the wake of the creature. Curtis said that in a matter of seconds the being came over to the right-hand side of the van where Jimi was seated and looked right through the window. "Jimi seemed to be communicating telepathically with it," said Curtis. The interior of the vehicle began to heat up. The snow drift completely vanished. Just then the creature disappeared and the strange UFO lifted off like a rocket from a launching pad.

"Jimi never did talk much about what happened," said Curtis. "He sort of let me know that the cool thing was not to bring up the subject. It was to be our little secret." Members of the group behaved as if they had been placed under hypnosis and had no conscious memory of the incident, said Curtis.

"Jimi was convinced that in the near future Galacticians from outer space, from another galaxy of great positive power, would come to our planet to help mankind in its struggle against evil," said his girlfriend Monika. "While explaining this, he drew two points representing this higher power coming closer and closer towards our galaxy, the Milky Way, finally reaching Earth. . . . He told me that the arrival of the extraterrestrials would bring about a great change on our planet, and that love, peace, and brotherhood among the peoples of the Earth would start to blossom again, just as they did in the ancient civilization of Atlantis." In his last poem, "The Story of Life," Jimi fittingly referred to the approaching UFOs:

> Angels of heaven, flying saucers to some,
> Made Easter Sunday, the name of the rising sun.

# JIMI'S LEGACY

Tragically Jimi succumbed to a drug overdose on September 18, 1970, at the age of twenty-eight. Hendrix's first single, "Hey Joe," reached number seven in the charts in 1967. He went on to appear at the Woodstock Festival, where he shocked and delighted hippies with his strident version of "The Star-Spangled Banner." His final appearance at the Isle of Wight Festival in England was watched by 250,000 people.

"Jimi and I often sat down together and talked about how there are other beings in different galaxies," commented his father, Al Hendrix. "He believed it and I do." Jimi's dad had a giant flying-saucer sculpture commissioned for his son's final resting place at Greenwood Cemetery in Seattle, Washington, saying, "The flying saucer is a fitting tribute because it was something that always fascinated Jimi. He loved to think about what else was out there." Before the saucer was commissioned, Jimi's grave had been marked by a simple guitar-embossed headstone. A second sculpture, a life-size bronze statue of Jimi, was commissioned for the gravesite by the late guitarist's sister, Janie. Later Jimi's body was moved to an elaborate floodlit aboveground mausoleum flanked by purple fountains in memory of Hendrix's hit song "Purple Haze."

Billionaire Paul Allen, the fourth-richest man in the world, is keeping Jimi's spirit alive at the Experience Music Project, a $240 million high-tech architectural marvel located adjacent to Seattle's illustrious landmark, the Space Needle. The Space Needle's design is actually based on a flying saucer. Allen, who ironically pumped tens of millions of dollars into the Search for Extraterrestrial Intelligence (SETI)—a project to contact space aliens that would have gotten Hendrix's juices flowing—hired award-winning architect Frank Gehry to design the entire building in the shape of a smashed guitar—one of Hendrix's best-known trademarks. Among the headliners who have performed concerts tied in with the Experience Music Project Museum are Matchbox 20, Alanis Morissette, Beck, the Eurythmics, Metallica, Dr. Dre, Eminem, Red Hot Chili Peppers, and Kid Rock.

Allen, a cofounder of Microsoft, plays guitar in a rock band called the Grown Men. The band sounds somewhat like Tom Petty and the Heartbreakers. Allen has also financed Space-ShipOne, the first private aerospace company to send a rocketship to the edge of space. The Experience Music Project, an alternative to Cleveland's Rock 'n' Roll Hall of Fame, is complete with eighty thousand musical artifacts, an eighty-five-foot-tall Sky Church that Jimi would have felt right at home in, and the Artists Journey, "part movie, part concert, and part theme-park ride." The Sky Church can be rented for the ultimate in hipness: rock 'n' roll weddings and parties. Hendrix memorabilia is everywhere you turn, most of it from Allen's personal collection, but Jimi isn't the only artist on display. Tributes to Nirvana, Pearl Jam,

Bob Dylan, Eric Clapton, Janis Joplin, the Beatles, and the Rolling Stones fill the 140,000-square-foot museum that traces America's rich and diverse musical heritage.

The Sound Lab located upstairs invites museumgoers to perform a virtual concert even if they can't play a single note. The Experience Music Project's own Electric Bus provides an outreach service to the community, bringing Hendrix's music directly to county fairs and to arts and music festivals. The museum's classrooms offer expert hands-on musical instruction. A two-hundred-seat theater is available for performances and lectures.

Soon to occupy part of the premises is a state-of-the-art Science Fiction Experience museum separately bankrolled by Allen to the tune of $20 million. Flying saucers and aliens from the 1950s era of classic films and television shows will take their place alongside props from Hollywood's latest multimillion-dollar sci-fi epics. Captain Kirk's original command chair from the *Star Trek* TV series will again bask in the spotlight. A Jimi Hendrix museum will be sharing space with flying saucers and extraterrestrials from out-of-this-world movies like *The Day the Earth Stood Still* and *Earth vs. the Flying Saucers*. Is somebody up there trying to tell us something?

Mysteriously, seven years after Hendrix's untimely passing, television broadcasts were suddenly interrupted throughout southern England by a so-called extraterrestrial intelligence named ASTARA on November 26, 1977, the eve of Jimi's birthday. An "off-the-planet" voice was heard warning that citizens must act immediately to avoid a nuclear holocaust. Many people took the message seriously, believing that a higher technology would need to have been used to interrupt the broadcast signals of major TV stations throughout Hampshire County and as far north as Berkshire and Oxfordshire.

The message from the UFOs read in part:

Jimi Hendrix, worshipped by millions as an electric-guitar god, was infatuated with extraterrestrials and told a *New York Times* reporter that he came from Mars. Upon sighting a UFO before filming *Rainbow Bridge,* Jimi shouted a welcome to the space brothers.

The New Age can be a time of great evolution for your race, but only if your rulers are made aware of the evil forces that can overshadow their judgment. Be still now, and listen, for your chance may not come again for many years.

Your scientists, governments, and generals have not heeded our warnings. They have continued to experiment with the evil forces of what you call nuclear energy. Atomic bombs can destroy the Earth and the beings of your sister worlds in a moment. The wastes from atomic power systems will poison your planet for many thousands of years to come. We who have followed the path of "evolution" for far longer than you have long since realized this—that atomic energy is always directed against Life. It has *no* peaceful application. Its use and research into its use must be ceased at once—or you will all risk destruction. All weapons of evil must be re-moved.

The time of conflict is now passed, and the races of which you are part may proceed to the highest planes of evolution—if you show yourselves worthy to do this. You have but a short time to learn to live together in peace and goodwill!

Jimi himself would have been proud to sign his name to this message. Finally, Jimi's mind-bending musical legacy is best summed up by the guitar genius's own telling state-ment: "What I don't like is this business of trying to classify people. Leave us alone. Critics really give me a pain in the neck. It's like shooting a flying saucer as it tries to land without giving the occupants a chance to identify them-selves. You don't need labels, man. Jus' dig what's happen-ing." Jimi was like that flying saucer lighting up the musical sky.

# 4

# MICHAEL JACKSON

## SINGING AND DANCING
## ON THE MOON

**L**eave it to the self-styled King of Pop to top P. T. Barnum. Bored by the physical limitations of performing on planet Earth, a gravity-defying Michael Jackson decided that he wanted to take it to the next stage and perform his trademark moonwalk on the Moon. And nothing was going to stop the beleaguered singer and dancer from launching his extraterrestrial show-business gambit on the lunar surface—not even a relatively minor technicality of how he was going to get there from here.

Managing briefly to eclipse pop singer Lance Bass of 'N Sync—who amid great fanfare had announced his intention to blast off to the International Space Station aboard the Russian Soyuz rocketship at a cost of $25 million—Michael consulted his closest friend and supporter, Uri Geller, the internationally renowned psychic spoon-bender who lives in England, about the best way to go about accomplishing his unprecedented musical mission to space.

Uri recalled that Michael asked him, "How can I get to the Moon?" Geller consulted his friend Apollo 14 astronaut Edgar Mitchell, who immediately suggested that the King of Pop settle for a rocketship ride to the International Space Station since NASA was no longer planning any manned missions to the Moon. Of course all of that has now changed dramatically with President George W. Bush's well-publicized announcement that the United States would return to the Moon and use it as a launching pad to Mars. NASA's Project Prometheus expects to put a man on Mars perhaps as early as 2030, using nuclear-powered propulsion. Manned missions to the Moon will come much earlier.

Moon exploration is officially back on the front burner. Europe, China, Japan, and India are all planning to launch unmanned Moon probes costing hundreds of millions of dollars, and manned ones are likely to follow in the near future. Scientists are searching for ice water believed to be hidden in dark polar craters that could hold the key to future space exploration of Mars and neighboring planets. And just recently TransOrbital, a California-based company, launched a flying craft that orbited the Moon for ninety days with a payload consisting of an eclectic mix of business cards, cremated remains, artwork, and other artifacts from good old Earth, charging customers $2,500 per gram for their new space-age FedEx. TransOrbital plans to cash in on the continuing lunar craze by using photographic images it has collected of the Moon in video games, movies, and educational products. Moon dust, incidentally, is second only to fragments of Martian meteorites in cost and is extremely hard to obtain. (For more on music inspired by the Moon, see chapter 8.)

Geller is convinced that one day the Gloved One will reach his lunar destination and sing and dance his way into the history books. "We are training Michael now to have that certain mind power to be able to complete such a task," said Uri. "We do visualizations, affirmations, contemplations. I told him he would have to do it all the way. He said, 'Yes, yes, let's do it.' . . . He is a very powerful person and athletic. His heartbeat at rest is like a runner's—forty-two beats per minute."

# MOONWALK

Michael had always been consumed with the moonwalk, which he picked up from kids on the street and referred to as "illusion dancing, where you create an illusion with the body." He is presently at work on a new step he calls skywalker. Who knows? Maybe the Marswalk will be Michael's next dance project.

After speaking with Uri, this writer released the story about Michael's moonwalk mission to the news media in the United States. That night it was topic A on the late-night television talk shows hosted by Jay Leno, David Letterman, and Conan O'Brien. Comedian Robin Williams quipped that the Gloved One "wants to do the Earthwalk on the Moon."

Meanwhile, news leaked out that Steve Tyler of Aerosmith also was "in serious talks to travel into space." Tyler—who once told extraterrestrial researcher Ellen Crystal that he was interested in visiting the town of Pine Bush, New York, to investigate unusually heavy UFO traffic—was eager to write a song while aboard the International Space Station and broadcast it live down to Earth. (Russian cosmonaut Yuri Romanenko composed the first songs from space, some twenty in all, during the 1980s, to relieve the boredom of the long orbital voyage.) The Russians, who were alarmed that Lance Bass might not be able to come up with the millions of dollars needed to make the journey to space (ultimately they were correct), remarked that they had thought about sending their own hot boy band, Na Na, into the stratosphere. Lost in all of this feeding frenzy was that during the days of the Soviet Union, John Denver was the first pop star to request a ride on a space shuttle, offering the Soviets a cool $10 million, which they refused to accept.

Buzz Aldrin, the second human to walk on the Moon, voiced his wholehearted approval of the Bass mission. "I've been extremely supportive of popular entertainers going to space," said Aldrin, who believed that Lance's trip might spur public support for more scientific exploration. Other entertainers with their eye on the sky quickly hopped aboard the space tourism bandwagon.

Actor Tom Cruise weighed in that he would go in a second if offered the chance to take a flight on NASA's space shuttle. "I'd be the first actor in space! I'd love to do it," said *Top Gun*'s Cruise. "It has always been a dream of mine since I was a little kid. I've always been fascinated with space." Cruise is starring in Steven Spielberg's $100 million movie remake of *The War of the Worlds*, depicting a full-blown alien invasion of Earth, and was shot on location in New Jersey. Cruise previously narrated the highly ambitious Imax film *Space Station 3D*, which gives viewers a spectacular astronaut's-eye view of the construction and daily operation of the International Space Station, orbiting Earth at 17,500 miles per hour. Twenty-five astronauts and cosmonauts from sixteen countries worked on the film over two and a half years.

Tom Hanks, who played a NASA astronaut in the film *Apollo 13*, about a near catastrophic disaster in space, was just as anxious as Cruise to be the first actor to reach the International Space Station. And following a news bulletin that supermodel Cindy Crawford would love to have a seat on board a rocketship to the space station, the Russian commander quipped that he would prefer to have Cindy to Lance as a crewmate.

But had they actually blasted off into space, superstars Michael Jackson, Lance Bass, Steven Tyler, Tom Cruise, Tom Hanks, and/or Cindy Crawford could have been in for the surprise of their lifetime—an experience with alien beings from another world. UFOs apparently operating under intelligent control had been observed and photographed repeatedly by astronauts and cosmonauts aboard both the International Space Station and the U.S. space shuttle. Official NASA videotapes showed unidentified pulsing lights outside the space station at night. These same type of strange pulsing lights and spacecraft, which often traveled at incredible speeds and made maneuvers that defied conventional physics, were photographed by space shuttle astronauts, offering the best tangible evidence to date that we are not alone in the universe.

Like Elvis, his onetime late father-in-law, Michael Jackson firmly believed that extraterrestrials were real. His short-lived but highly publicized marriage to singer Lisa Marie Presley was the inextricable cosmic bond between the King of Pop and the King of Rock 'n' Roll. If anyone doubted Michael's obsession with life in other worlds, they didn't have to look any further than his heavily hyped comeback concert in 2001 at Madison Square Garden, where he rose from the middle of the stage wearing an astronaut helmet and suit. Off came Michael's headgear, and he joined five of his brothers in a rousing medley of the Jacksons' greatest hits, including "ABC," "I Want You Back," and "I'll Be There." For a 1997 performance at the Johannesburg Athletics Stadium in South Africa, a rocket burst through the floor at the front of the stage in billows of smoke. Out of the portal came a spaceman dressed in silver foil. The figure removed his helmet to the sound of a thousand screams. Michael had made a perfect landing.

Elizabeth Taylor has stated on more than one occasion, "Michael Jackson is an extraterrestrial!" And Mr. Eccentricity himself revealed in November 2001 that he felt that he was from another planet, based in part on the difficulty of making the transition from child star to adult star. Michael identified the planet as "Capricious Anomaly in the Sea of Space" and said it was located "just beyond our solar system."

Earthling or extraterrestrial, one thing is for sure: Michael never failed to generate out-of-this-world controversy that regularly put him on the front pages. There was the time he supposedly wanted to buy the bones of the Elephant Man (the report proved entirely false); the fantastic claims about his sleeping in a hyperbaric chamber so he could live to the ripe old age of 150 (a publicity story planted by Michael's then manager, Frank Dileo); the surgical masks and other wild getups he regularly wore to hide his nose, which had undergone plastic surgery; his pet chimp, Bubbles, pet llamas, and an assortment of other animals running around a menagerie in Michael's sprawling 2,700-acre Neverland Ranch in Santa Barbara, California; not to mention the "baby-dangling" incident in Germany, for which Michael later apologized, his blistering attack on former Sony records honcho Tommy Mottola, and the sex scandal that threatens to wreck his monumental career as a singer who has sold well over 300 million records and owns the Beatles catalog of songs.

# MICHAEL AND IMMORTALITY

Unreported until now is that Michael has an unusual fear of death and has gone to extreme lengths to achieve immortality. New York celebrity fashion designer and health guru Andre Van Pier said that he learned through an associate at a longevity research organization based in Panama that Michael obtained GH3, the "fountain of youth" drug, by mail order. GH3, whose active ingredient is procaine, has long been popular in Europe to reverse aging, but users of the drug in the United States have been forced to acquire it through underground channels. John F. Kennedy and Winston Churchill head a long list of politicians and celebrities who have sworn that GH3 works health miracles. The controversial substance reportedly strengthens the heart, improves muscle tone, removes wrinkles, aids in hair growth, and most crucially, lengthens the human life span.

Many believe that millions of years ago extraterrestrials mastered the science of longevity. The Anunnaki, who some think genetically engineered the human race by joining their DNA with the DNA of prehumans, were said to be fond of ingesting a magical gold powder that permitted them to live long and prosper both on this planet and on their home planet, Planet X, located far out in our solar system. They lived to be thousands of years old. According to scholar Zecharia Sitchin, humans mined the gold here on Earth, which would eventually be pounded into fine particles to protect the atmosphere of Planet X.

Van Pier, the director of the Anti-Aging Rejuvenation Center on Fifth Avenue in Manhattan, said that researchers at the longevity group in Panama informed him that Michael had spent millions of dollars for scientists specializing in DNA to genetically engineer perfect offspring for him in the future and that he had secretly deposited his sperm in three different sperm banks in various parts of the world. This information came amid a flurry of reports that Michael had fathered quintuplets—a blessed event that the embattled performer flatly denied. It is not known whether the Fertile One has explored the possibility of having himself cloned to make himself truly immortal. La Toya Jackson told Van Pier that her psychic readings suggested that Michael—a longtime believer in reincarnation—might have been a woman in a past lifetime.

La Toya said that Michael frequently uses a floatation tank at his Neverland Ranch to escape from all the pressures that constantly plague him. Floatation tanks, which are usually egg-shaped, permit a person to float on salt water in the dark—a sensation that has been compared to a return to the womb. Some floaters plug themselves into

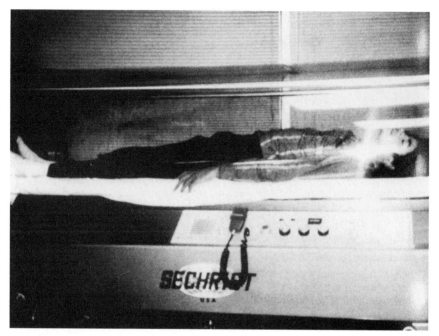

Michael Jackson lies in a hyperbaric oxygen chamber, hoping to increase his life span to 150. Although the photograph in the chamber was a publicity stunt, the King of Pop has an unusual fear of death and has gone to extreme lengths pursuing immortality.

relaxing music and can spend hours in the tank recharging their physical, emotional, and spiritual batteries.

After all that has been written about him, pro and con, Michael, the Man Behind the Mask, is really a deeply spiritual person who is in tune with the universe. "The songwriting process is difficult to explain because it's very spiritual," Michael explained in an online chat with fans while promoting his album *Invincible*. "You're in the hands of God and it's as if it's already written already. . . . It's like the songs have been written already in their entirety before you were even born and just fall into your lap. I feel guilty having to put my name on the songs sometimes because I write them, compose them, score them, and it's all really the work of God."

 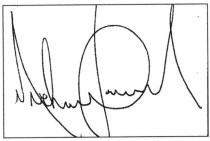

Michael Jackson's autograph on the author's extraterrestrial business card. Michael said that he believed in aliens and accepted a small silver alien keychain as a cosmic token of friendship.

Then Michael added, "All the planets in the universe make music—it's called Music of the Spheres—and all the planets make a different note and are making harmony as we speak."

Jackson composed many of his hit songs while sitting in a special place—a "magic tree" at the Neverland Ranch, the retreat he named after the magical kingdom featured in the beloved children's story *Peter Pan*. Michael was shown sitting in the tree and climbing on its branches in Martin Bashir's controversial television documentary about the singer's private life at Neverland. He had a great big smile on his face.

"Deep inside I feel that this world we live in is really one big symphonic orchestra," Michael told one interviewer. "I believe that in its primordial form of all creation is sound and that it's not just random sound . . . the same music that governs the rhythm of the seasons, the pulse of our heartbeats, the migration of birds, the ebb and flow of tides, the cycles of growth, evolution and dissolution. It's music, it's rhythm. And my goal in life is to give the world what I was lucky to receive: the ecstasy of divine union through my music and my dance. It's like my purpose, it's what I'm here for."

In 1980 a young Michael Jackson discussed an incredible UFO sighting that left him totally awestruck. He was sitting in the cockpit of an overnight flight over the north pole when, in his own words, he saw "illusions in the air that man has never seen. It was total dark and you saw these big icebergs that were glowing in the night. And then I looked far out into the sky and saw purple, green, and blue crystals sparkling and turning in the air. I said, 'What is that?' And the pilot said that he didn't know, they'd only seen that once before. I said, 'My God, I'll never forget this!'"

# CLOSE ENCOUNTERS WITH MICHAEL

"I do believe in aliens," Michael confirmed to me during a surprise encounter at the Abracadabra Superstore, a magic and costume emporium that has become a New York City tourist attraction. Michael called the meeting "a billion-to-one chance!" When I thought about it, I felt that I had made a cosmic connection myself. Michael was completely covered by a bright reddish orange outfit and dark glasses that made him look like the Invisible Man. He had on silver shoes and danced the moonwalk in front of the store's fun-house mirror. Michael signed the back of my New York Center for UFO Research business card that shows a photograph taken in France of a glowing red UFO emitting four light beams. He accepted a small silver alien keychain from me as a gesture of friendship. I told him that I had important evidence about UFOs that I would be happy to share with him. He asked novelty king Paul Blum, the store's owner, for the price of a life-size alien statue that was on sale in the shop, but winced when Blum offered him the chance to see his videos bigger than life on a giant video projection screen.

Michael Jackson recently announced that he's from another planet, which should come as no surprise to close friends like Elizabeth Taylor, who said "Michael is an extraterrestrial." The dethroned King of Pop once observed an awesome UFO from the cockpit of an airplane.

Michael purchased some magic tricks and the latest *Star Wars* mask and indicated he would return, but unfortunately a paparazzo was waiting for him when he left the store. Michael and the photographer promptly got into a shouting match on the street outside, and pictures of Michael landed in a tabloid newspaper. Months later when he did return, Michael was wearing a purple ski mask and was flanked by two young Russian-speaking bodyguards. "That's either Michael Jackson or we're being robbed," said Blum. Michael scooped up some new magic tricks involving mentalism and then beat it.

Michael originally unveiled plans to build an elaborate high-tech UFO landing strip in the middle of the Nevada desert to welcome extraterrestrials to Earth and to film the landing for a television special capturing the most important event in human history—contact between human beings and UFO occupants. According to Mike Walker, a nationally syndicated columnist and radio personality, Michael told of a dream where he saw a space alien—a dream that gave him the idea to build a state-of-the-art landing facility.

Michael's fascination with extraterrestrials was clearly influenced by two of Steven Spielberg's most popular films, *Close Encounters of the Third Kind* and *E.T. The Extra-Terrestrial.* Spielberg said that in both films he tried to illustrate his father's philosophy that technologically advanced life-forms would never travel light-years to Earth to spread hate and evil, but would instead be determined to satisfy their curiosity about us. "They would want to share their knowledge with other planetary systems and other species," declared Spielberg. The filmmaker said that the sneak preview of *E.T. The Extra-Terrestrial* at a theater in Texas was "almost a religious experience."

While he lay in bed in Brotman Medical Center in Culver City, California, the day his hair caught fire during the filming of a Pepsi commercial, Michael chose *Close Encounters of the Third*

*Kind* over ten different videos offered to him. The movie is based on actual UFO encounters, and the high-tech alien landing pad shown in the film is similar to the alien landing pad Michael wanted to construct in Nevada. The late Dr. J. Allen Hynek, the film's technical consultant, served on Project Bluebook, the U.S. air force's official investigation into UFO reports, and coined the term *close encounters* to indicate different types of contact with extraterrestrials.

Dr. Hynek, who was a highly respected astronomer at Northwestern University in Evanston, Illinois, quit Project Bluebook after he concluded that the air force was whitewashing UFO reports. Dr. Hynek founded the Center for UFO Studies (CUFOS) and can briefly be seen during the unforgettable climatic scene of *Close Encounters,* where the universal language of music is used to communicate with space aliens. He is sporting a gray beard and smoking a pipe. The small humanoid creatures playfully surround him.

Michael walked away with a Grammy for his narration on *The E.T. Storybook* record album. The moment that Michael first saw E.T. on the set of the movie, he wrapped his arms around the creature and wouldn't let go. "He was so real that I was talking to him," said Michael. "I kissed him before I left. The next day I missed him." Michael claims to have watched the movie *E.T.* over five hundred times, recently accompanied by his children. When Michael first saw the film, he "melted through the whole thing. The second time I cried like crazy."

Michael's unconditional love for E.T. is underscored by a $200,000 oil painting the King of Pop had commissioned depicting himself among those he regards as his peers: Albert Einstein, George Washington, Abraham Lincoln, the *Mona Lisa,* and E.T.—all wearing sunglasses and Michael's trademark white glove. The unusual painting lies hidden in Michael's Treasure Room, a secret bunker at the Neverland Ranch where he keeps his most prized possessions, including reportedly one million dollars' worth of precious jewels.

"If E.T. didn't come to Elliott [the film's child star], he would have come to Michael's house," commented Spielberg. "Michael is one of the last living innocents. . . . I've never seen anybody like Michael. He's an emotional star child."

Being a "star child" might explain why Michael spent $6 million to produce "Scream" in 1995, the most expensive rock video in history, which was directed by Mark Romanek, filmed in black and white, and took nine shooting days to complete. Michael and his sister Janet Jackson zoom across the galaxy in a high-tech flying saucer that tumbles endlessly through the vastness of space. In a zero-gravity environment that is both a home and a performance space, Michael dances on the walls and ceiling à la *2001: A Space Odyssey.* All together there are seven different rooms aboard Michael's futuristic spaceship: GRAvity, HABITation, GALLery, MEDia, MEDITation, OBSERVation, and reCREATion.

"Scream" had its world premiere on June 14, 1995, on *ABC Prime Time* with Barbara Walters during an interview with Michael and his then new bride, Lisa Marie Presley—a testament to the cosmic connection linking the King of Pop and the King of Rock 'n' Roll. "Scream" won Best Dance Video, Best Choreography, and Best Art Direction at the MTV Video Music Awards. It was also named winner of the Pop/Rock Video Award at the Billboard Music Video Awards and Best Music Video at the Grammy Awards. The gravity-defying special effects employed in the "Scream" video have since been used effectively in scores of music videos from Madonna and the Foo Fighters to Sheryl Crow and Jamiroquai.

# CAPTAIN EO

Believe it or not, two other Michael Jackson videos suggest that the King of Pop could possibly be a UFO abductee or at least a candidate for alien abduction. On "Thriller"—one of the most successful songs of all time—Michael sings of an "alien" creature looking for him around midnight. The song caused such a stir within the Jehovah's Witnesses, of which he is a member, that Michael was forced to issue a statement that he didn't endorse the occult. And Michael's video for "Black and White" opens with a close-up of the front page of a tabloid newspaper headlined "I Was Abducted" with a photograph of a flying saucer. Fans are left to make their own conclusions.

Michael's well-publicized cameo appearance in *Men in Black II*, the hit Hollywood sci-fi film about space aliens being chased by government agents, wasn't without controversy either. Released by Sony Pictures in the summer of 2002, *Men in Black II* proved to be a tough challenge for director Barry Sonnenfeld, but not for the reasons you might expect. Will Smith, the movie's costar, "thought it would be really cool" to have Michael in the movie, Sonnenfeld recalled. But Michael insisted that he have a much bigger role and had his mind made up that he should wear the equally cool Men in Black suit and appear on movie posters. Finally Michael was told he could wear the suit, but alas he never made it onto the posters.

Smith said that Michael was dead set on appearing in the picture and started campaigning for a role in the *Men in Black* sequel right after the first movie came out in 1997. During the 1950s and 1960s, real-life MIBs, who were believed to be working for the government or sometimes for the aliens themselves, kept a close watch over UFO eyewitnesses, particularly when some types of evidence such as photographs or soil samples were involved. The movie scriptwriters got their idea from the MIB comic book, which was in turn inspired by these stories.

The King of Pop did get to play the title role in "Captain EO," a seventeen-minute, 3-D space adventure shown at Disneyland's Kodak Magic Theatre in Anaheim, California, and Disney World's Epcot Center in Orlando, Florida, from 1986 to 1997. Produced by George Lucas of *Star Wars* and *Indiana Jones* fame and directed by Francis Ford Coppola at a cost of $20 million, "Captain EO" was originally titled "The Intergalactic Music Man" and took over one year to complete. The elaborate production required special theaters to be built for the sound and light show that had smoke emitted from the movie screen and a floor that tilted with the action. The fundamental idea was to take the whole audience along for a ride in a spaceship. Tourists lined up for hours to experience the ride again and again and again.

"Captain EO" pitted Michael and his offbeat crew against a wicked Supreme Leader played by Angelica Huston, who is magically transformed by the power of music and Michael's legendary dance steps into a beautiful queen. The songs Michael performed in "Captain EO" were "We Are Here to Change the World" and "Another Part of Me." The short feature film was also shown at Disney theme parks in Japan and France.

"Working on 'Captain EO' reinforced all the positive feelings I've had about working in film and made me realize more than ever that movies are where my future path probably lies," said Michael. "I love the movies and have since I was real little. For two hours you can be transported to another place. Films can take you anywhere." Michael would inevitably have done back-over flips if he'd known that the exact same site of Disneyland's Kodak Magic Eye Theatre that housed "Captain EO" once housed a wildly innovative children's ride called The Flying Saucers, which opened in 1961 and lasted for five years. Each kid was strapped into an individual flying saucer bumper car, which traveled on a cushion of air. For all of its wonders, Michael's Neverland Ranch never boasted a ride quite like that.

# MICHAEL AND URI GELLER

Michael's friendship with internationally acclaimed psychic Uri Geller, who was one of the Gloved One's staunchest defender against a chorus of critics, started with a phone call Michael made several years ago to Mohammed Al Fayed, the father of Dodi Fayed, who died in the tragic car crash in Paris that also claimed the life of Princess Diana and the driver. As fate would have it, Geller was sitting alongside Fayed, the owner of Harrods, the upscale department store in London, when Michael called to say hello. The King of Pop had been an admirer of Geller's spoon-bending and telepathic abilities ever since he was a schoolkid. The two men spoke, Uri flew to New York to meet Michael, and the rest as they say is "HIStory." The King of Pop served as best man at a ceremony in England where Uri renewed his wedding vows.

Uri claims that he was struck by a light beam from a UFO when he was only four years old, and he credits that cosmic event with giving him supernatural psychic powers. Geller said that when he was twenty-five years old, he was riding in the desert in Israel with three military personnel and an American scientist named Andrija Puharich when he spotted a giant spacecraft ablaze with lights moving silently a thousand feet in the air. Geller estimated that the object was twice the size of a Boeing 747, gray in color with a dull metallic hull, and not giving off a shadow. Uri's black-and-white drawing featuring a flying saucer and a monolith from the film *2001: A Space Odyssey* appears prominently in the booklet accompanying Michael's *Invincible* CD.

Despite all of his stardom and wealth, his $28 million mansion surrounded by twelve lighted tennis courts, a football field, several swimming pools, and an eighteen-hole golf course, plus a private eighty-seat movie theater, a petting zoo, a wax museum, and a candy store, Michael admits that when he is alone at night at the Neverland Ranch, he samples one ride after another in his personal $100 million amusement park, reaching for the stars all by himself. The aging pop star watches the sky continually to see what is waiting out there for him in the great beyond.

Today, despite his many detractors and his explosive trial, Michael is the farthest-out performer on the face of the planet—the man to watch when E.T. and friends finally decide to make open contact with the human race. Don't be surprised if there is also an Elvis sighting on that auspicious occasion.

# 5

# OTHER COSMIC PERSONALITIES

ELTON JOHN, MADONNA, STING,
BOB DYLAN, MOBY, TINA TURNER,
DAVE GROHL, DAN AYKROYD,
REG PRESLEY, MARC BOLAN,
SUN RA, GEORGE CLINTON,
MERLE HAGGARD, WILLIE NELSON,
DEBORAH HARRY, LANCE BASS,
PATTI LABELLE, JUDY COLLINS,
LAURIE ANDERSON, AND
JAMIROQUAI

The high-profile stars featured in this chapter all share a bold cosmic vision. Some of these performers have had close encounters with flying saucers. Some have clearly experienced supernatural events. Others have expanded their consciousness by embracing kabbalah, yoga, or other forms of mysticism. By entering new mind-expanding realms, these personalities are changing our culture.

# SIR ELTON JOHN: EARTH'S ROCKET MAN

Sir Elton John's name will forever be synonymous with the title of the beloved hit song "Rocket Man," his answer to David Bowie's "Space Oddity." Released in April 1972, "Rocket Man" skyrocketed to the top of the charts in both Britain and the United States, capitalizing on all of the publicity surrounding Apollo 16's successful three-man mission to the Moon, where at least one UFO was photographed by American astronauts. The song is so popular that Elton tries to play it at nearly every major performance in practically every country that he visits. Now that he is a regular headliner at Caesars Palace in Las Vegas, "Rocket Man" is destined to be one of Captain Fantastic's most requested tunes.

Elton's partner, Bernie Taupin, said that the inspiration

Earth's Rocket Man, Elton John, dazzles a concert crowd. Elton's tour-de-force musical performances have catapulted his name in lights on the cosmic marquee alongside piano great Liberace. Elton and his partner, Bernie Taupin, wrote "I've Seen the Saucers."

for "Rocket Man" came to him while he was driving under a starlit sky near his home in Lincolnshire, England. Bernie said, "The words just came into my head: 'She's packed her bags last night, preflight. Zero hour is nine a.m.' I remember jumping out of the car and running into my parents' house shouting, 'Please don't anyone talk to me until I've written this down.'" Appropriately, actor William Shatner, who played Captain Kirk on television's original *Star Trek* series, performed "Rocket Man" in the fall of 1997 during the National Science Fiction Awards, where it was named best song.

Few people realize that Shatner, who has himself released a number of CDs, had a lifesaving encounter with a flying saucer while riding a motorcycle in the hot California desert in the late

1960s. He became separated from his motorcycling friends and literally didn't know which way to turn. He was frantic. All of a sudden a golden disc appeared over his shoulder and telepathically communicated to him. He could only move his motorcycle in one direction. That proved to be the correct escape route. Had the saucer not intervened, the *Star Trek* movement as we know it may never have been born.

Shortly after "Rocket Man" was released, Elton demonstrated his commitment to space exploration by visiting the Johnson Space Center in Houston, Texas. Elton and members of his band spent four hours touring the facilities at NASA, trying out a flight simulator and lunching with Apollo 15 pilot Al Worden. Years later Worden became a poet and a proponent of the ancient astronaut theory.

Like so many astronauts before him, Worden underwent some kind of psychic transformation during his long and lonely Apollo voyage—the same type of voyage Elton sang about in "Rocket Man" on his *Honky Château* album. Interviewed by PBS in 1989 for a television documentary on the twentieth anniversary of the U.S. Moon landing, Worden said, "I think we may be a combination of creatures that were living here on Earth sometime in the past and having a visitation, if you will, by creatures from somewhere else in the universe, and those two species getting together and having progeny."

Always the consummate showman, Elton John gives tour-de-force musical performances—usually dressed in flamboyant costumes and spaced-out eyeglasses—that have not only won him fame and fortune on this plane, but also catapulted his name in lights on to the cosmic marquee alongside piano impresario Liberace. "When he [Elton] touches the keys of a piano, they respond as if to a supernatural command," observed paranormalist Uri Geller.

Elton and his partner Bernie wrote and recorded "I've Seen the Saucers," about mystery-shrouded UFOs that appear in the evening sky. The lyrics exclaim, "I've seen them, I've been there with them, / Maybe if I promise not to say a word, / They can get me back before the morning light."

Another Elton song, "Dan Dare (Pilot of the Future)," speaks of "the champions of destiny."

Elton and his partners formed Rocket Records in May 1973 with a stable of British and American singing stars including Neil Sedaka. Sedaka, a songwriter best known for such chart-busting hits as "Breaking Up Is Hard to Do," "Happy Birthday, Sweet Sixteen," and "Calendar Girl," sighted a UFO outside his home in the Catskills in upstate New York in the late 1980s. First he thought the object was merely a shooting star, but then it moved rapidly and subsequently slowed down, suggesting it wasn't a shooting star at all, but appeared to be operating under intelligent control. "Some people are still prone to laugh," observed Sedaka, "though the number of skeptics are getting to be fewer and fewer in number."

Despite Elton's close friendship with Princess Diana, whom he later immortalized in the haunting hit song "Candle in the Wind," it is unlikely that Earth's Rocket Man knew of her father-in-law Prince Philip's keen interest in UFOs, dating back to the 1950s. Philip reportedly had a map in his office at Buckingham Palace pinpointing the latest UFO sightings around the world. Precious little has ever been said about the prince's lifelong preoccupation with UFOs, which seems to escape the notice of the usually intrepid British news correspondents.

Davey Johnstone, Elton's longtime musical director, teamed up with fellow guitarist John Jorgenson for an instrumental album titled *Crop Circles*. Johnstone composed Elton's hit song "I Guess That's Why They Call It the Blues," and has worked with Alice Cooper. Jorgenson was a founding member of The Hellecasters. Crop circles have constantly been in the news in England. Although many of them are believed to be hoaxes, enough crop circles are left to suggest some kind of cosmic intervention. Scientific analysis of bent barley and wheat stalks indicate that they have undergone a radical change at the molecular level.

Moreover, Steve Canada, an American crop circle researcher from the West Coast, has found that the majority of legitimate crop circles have designs that correspond identically to symbols used by the Anunnaki from Planet X, who may be preparing us for their imminent return. The discovery of a planetoid dubbed Sedna that is three-quarters the size of Pluto and moves in a peculiar orbit has some astronomers convinced that another planet at least the size of Earth may be out there. If these astronomers are correct, it could be the tenth planet that passes in the vicinity of Earth every thirty-six hundred years.

# MADONNA: KABBALAH AND COSMIC SYSTEMS

Madonna lives, breathes, and drinks kabbalah, the ancient Jewish mystical doctrine that she calls "the punk rock of spiritual philosophy." Madonna has adopted the biblical name Esther, which she uses in spiritual services. *Esther* translates as "star." Among other things, kabbalah teaches devotees how to establish contact with spiritual beings. One of kabbalah's cornerstones is the Bible's book of the prophet Ezekiel and his vision of a chariot with spinning wheels in the sky that landed by the Jordan River and communicated with him. Ezekiel is considered one of the key texts for the ancient astronaut theory that has won millions of adherents world-

Madonna, who has adopted the Biblical name Esther, is a tireless supporter for the worldwide Kabbalah spiritual movement. She has donated millions of dollars to the Kabbalah centers in Los Angeles, New York, and London. She believes in reincarnation.

wide. Kabbalah scholarship is said to date back to the thirteenth-century and to have been studied by Sir Isaac Newton.

The Ethereal Girl consulted Rabbi Yehuda Berg's Kabbalah Learning Centre in Los Angeles when she needed to know just how many tracks to put on her 1999 album, *Ray of Light,* which is loaded with references to kabbalah, yoga, and other divine forces. An optic-fiber flying-saucer lamp bearing the *Ray of Light* logo that was distributed for promotional purposes is today worth thousands of dollars because few of them were ever manufactured.

In her song "Impressive Instant," released in 2000, Madonna sings, "Cosmic systems intertwine, / Astral bodies drip like wine, / All of nature ebbs and flows, / Comets shoot across the sky, / Can't explain the reasons why, / This is how creation goes."

Kabbalah forced Madonna to reevaluate her private and public life. She confessed, "Despite all the success and fame, I still felt like something was missing. . . . Suddenly I was concerned about the bigger picture. Why am I me? Why am I here? Why did my soul choose this body?" And the biggest question of all: "What is the point of all this?" Kabbalah provided her with many of the answers.

Consequently Madonna, or more appropriately Esther, donated a whopping $22 million to open a kabbalah school in New York City, donated $8 million to the Kabbalah Centre in London, and persuaded her husband, British film director Guy Ritchie, to write a movie based upon the kabbalah concept. Madonna even went to the length of flashing Hebrew letters on video screens during her last concert tour. Some of the letters translate to "Let go of your ego," a recurring kabbalah theme.

Flying in the face of critics who charge that the kabbalah group she belongs to is little more than a money-driven cult, Madonna proudly flaunts a T-shirt stamped "Cult Member," regularly consumes specially blessed "kabbalah water," which is said to have healing properties (including supposedly the ability to cure cancer), and is the poster girl for the burgeoning kabbalah movement; her group has opened twenty-three branches worldwide. She recently toured holy sites in Israel accompanied by hundreds of fellow kabbalah students. Madonna and husband Guy spent more than an hour inside a stone mausoleum placing candles on the tomb of revered Jewish mystic Rabbi Yehuda Ashlag in Jerusalem's Givat Shaul cemetery. They prayed and chanted over food and wine and circled the raised stone grave. A planned pilgrimage to the Western Wall had to be canceled because of swarms of unruly paparazzi.

Madonna introduced pop singer Britney Spears to kabbalah and has helped make the Kabbalah Centre's red-thread bracelet a red-hot fashion accessory worn by Britney, Mick Jagger, and many other celebrities. The bracelets are designed to fall off when they have absorbed as much evil as they can take. Britney revealed, "Mine falls off every day," and thinks, "We're just here as vessels to bring some light into the world." Among the big-name stars who have recently climbed aboard kabbalah's spiritual bandwagon are Ashton Kutcher and Demi Moore, Elizabeth Taylor, Paris Hilton, Naomi Campbell, Donna Karan, Marla Maples, Leonard Nimoy, Barbra Streisand, Courtney Love, Sandra Bernhard, Jeff Goldblum, Rosie O'Donnell, and Roseanne Barr. Ashton and Demi have even gone so far as to wear the movement's white uniforms, which are meant to attract positive energy.

Embracing reincarnation, Madonna said that she has spoken to many people about past lives and recently began to understand what it is all about. She confided that for years she sought the advice of fortune-tellers, who predicted that she was going to play Eva Perón in the movies. When the predictions finally came true, Madonna was convinced that her starring role in *Evita* was destiny knocking at her door. "I have a strange affinity for Latin culture, in my music, in my friends, the relationships I have, food and art," said Madonna. "A lot of people have told me I could have been Latin in another life. Everything is connected. Life gives us symbols and it's up to us to follow them."

# STING: UFO TRUTH-SEEKER

Sting is eager to learn the truth about UFOs and the origin of the crop circles, particularly the one that mysteriously turned up on his property. Together with a friend, Sting witnessed a UFO while on a skiing vacation in Switzerland. They saw what looked like the top of a mountain "lit up like a Christmas tree." The light then sped away at high speed. Sting's wife, Trudie, discovered the crop circle on the couple's estate in England, in the same area where most of the crop-circle formations have appeared. In some cases UFOs have been seen and photographed hovering above crop-circle sites. The video for Sting's song, "I'm So Happy" from his *Mercury Falling* CD shows little, dancing gray aliens of the type generally associated with UFO abductions.

A devoted practitioner of yoga, Sting said that he hears music all the time and can't turn the music off. "Sometimes it drives me crazy. In absolute silence I hear music. I hear music, I hear rhythms, I hear birdsongs. I live in an aural world. It's never totally empty. The yoga can induce that state."

Sting said that for most of his life he has been skeptical of paranormal phenomena, despite his having had some experiences that he can't readily explain, most notably the sighting of ghosts. "I've actually seen an apparition," said Sting. "It was quite something. I was terrified. I saw a woman and a child in my bedroom. My wife saw it too. We both woke up. At first I thought it was her with one of the kids until I reached over and realized she was still in bed with me. I was absolutely terrified. I now believe those things are out there, but I have no explanation for them." Asked if he wanted to do a little haunting in his next lifetime, Sting replied, "I would hope my music will do the haunting for me. I don't want to be a ghost at the feast—

Sting witnessed a UFO in Switzerland that looked like the top of a mountain "lit up like a Christmas tree." His wife, Trudie, discovered a crop circle on the couple's estate in England. They have also seen ghosts, although for most of his life Sting has been skeptical of such phenomena.

but a little of my music wafting in the ether now and then would do me."

The former member of the Police—one of the most influential pop groups of the 1980s—called in a professional ghostbuster when he discovered that his home in Highgate, north of London, was haunted. "Ever since I moved there, people said that things happened—they were lying in bed and people started talking to them, or things went missing," said Sting. "I was very skeptical until the night that my daughter Mickey was born. She was disturbed and I went to see her. Her room is full of mobiles and they were going berserk. I thought a window must be open, but they were all shut."

Sting has often been on the front lines of environmental and social causes, raising millions of dollars for organizations like the Rainforest Foundation and Amnesty International. The Rainforest Foundation is responsible for saving millions of acres of endangered rain forest in Brazil.

# BOB DYLAN: END TIMES PROPHET

Bob Dylan characterized the 1960s this way: "The sixties was like a UFO landing. A lot of people heard about it, but very few actually saw it." While that comment was meant as a joke, some of Dylan's lyrics, indicate rather vivid UFO imagery.

Sean Casteel, a UFO journalist and lifelong Dylan fan, pointed out that one line in Dylan's celebrated song "Sad-Eyed Lady of the Lowlands" resonates with the 1947 Roswell UFO crash-type scenario, where local officials covered up the bodies of dead aliens strewn nearby. Dylan sings, "The

Bob Dylan predicted fifteen years ago that the Middle East was going to explode into a terrible war. The Prince of Protest believes that we are living in the End Times referred to in the Bible. Dylan's song "Sad-Eyed Lady of the Lowlands" contains a key line that some experts think could be connected to the 1947 Roswell UFO crash-type scenario.

farmers and the businessmen, they all did decide, / To show you the dead angels that they used to hide . . ."

Dylan's trademark 1964 song, "The Times They Are a-Changin'," is rich in millennial imagery, but his comments on the so-called End Times predicted in the Bible have now cast the former Prince of Protest in the role of Millennium Prophet—a prophet who correctly predicted fifteen years ago that the Middle East was going to explode in a terrible war. Whether by coincidence or by design, Dylan's preoccupation with a long-prophesied War of Armageddon, which some people think could be a consequence of the present United States war in Iraq and the ongoing bloody conflict between Israel and Palestine, underscores messages received by many UFO abductees about the end of the world as we know it. "You know we're living in the End Times," said Bob. "I don't think there's anybody . . . who doesn't feel that in his heart."

Dylan caused a huge uproar among his fans when he converted from Judaism to Christianity after having a so-called born-again experience in November 1978 that had supernatural qualities. "There was a presence in the room that couldn't have been anybody but Jesus," said Bob. "Jesus put his hand on me. It was a physical thing. I felt it. I felt it all over me. I felt my whole body tremble. The glory of the Lord knocked me down and picked me up." He claims that the windows in the house shook.

Some researchers believe that Jerusalem's Wailing Wall, the holy site that Dylan once visited and prayed at, may actually have been part of a sprawling ancient spaceport used by humanlike gods called Anunnaki for their trips to Mars on their way back to their home planet, Nibiru, also known as Planet X. The nearby Temple Mount, which once was the site of King Solomon's Temple, is built around a section of exposed mountaintop that still bears the imprint of some type of mechanical equipment that may have been used to launch rockets to the heavens. Present-day Iraq, which has served as a tinderbox for the entire Middle East, traces its roots to Sumeria, Earth's first civilization, which some believe to have encountered advanced extraterrestrial beings thousands of years ago.

Meanwhile back down here on Earth, Tom Petty of Tom Petty and the Heartbreakers, who toured with Dylan, George Harrison, Roy Orbison, and Jeff Lynne as a member of the 1980s supergroup the Traveling Wilburys and more recently with Dylan himself, spotted a UFO flanked by helicopters while cruising up the Pacific Coast Highway in Malibu, California, in 2003. His wife saw the otherworldly object too. "I thought, they're landing in Malibu!" Tom later told reporters. Petty was so shaken by the incident that he lost control of his car and nearly plowed into a bunch of press photographers who had gathered to cover actor Adam Sandler's wedding reception nearby.

# MOBY: EXTRATERRESTRIAL BEING

Techno-pop sensation Moby is all dressed up and ready to be beamed up to Mars or some other planet in a galaxy far, far away. His album *18*, released in 2002, shows him standing on a barren extraterrestrial landscape, wearing a silver space suit and smiling. He chose the title *18* for three reasons: the album has eighteen songs, the Hebrew word for eighteen is also the word for life, *chai*, and last but certainly not least, "after the space aliens crashed in New Mexico, they were taken to Hangar 18 in Roswell [New Mexico]." For the record, Hangar 18 is actually at Wright-Patterson Air Force Base in Dayton, Ohio, where the Roswell aliens were allegedly put on ice.

Moby's CD titled *18* was the techno-pop star's tribute to legendary Hangar 18 at Wright-Patterson Air Force Base in Dayton, Ohio, where the bodies of dead aliens were allegedly kept on ice. Moby wants to learn how to transport himself at will through time and space.

Moby's first single, "We Are All Made of Stars," is about quantum physics. "It's reminiscent of David Bowie's 'Berlin' period," said Moby, who produced the Area2 extraterrestrial concert tour that costarred Bowie and Busta Rhymes. Moby described "We Are All Made of Stars" as "an uplifting new-wave song" but also "a song about the fact that all of the matter of our planet comes from the furnace of a star."

Indeed Moby's head is so chock-full of stars that he mixed the music for the mind-blowing "Sonic Vision" shows at New York City's renowned Hayden Planetarium on Friday and Saturday nights. Music selected by Moby includes Radiohead, U2, Bowie, Coldplay, Queens of the Stone Age, Prodigy, the Flaming Lips, Fischerspooner, Spiritualized, Audioslave, Stereolab, Boards of Canada, David Byrne and Brian Eno, Goldfrapp and Zwan. Hypnotic visuals created by digital technicians transport viewers into a fantastic dreamspace.

Two Moby videos focus on the recurring alien theme. "In This World" has tiny aliens coming down to Earth to make contact with humans, but unfortunately the spacemen are too small to be seen by anyone. For "Sunday (The Day Before My Birthday)," the same small aliens return for a visit, only this time they are armed with a bigger sign and everyone welcomes them with open arms. "They become celebrities and start going to sleazy parties and hanging out at celebrity nightclubs," explained Moby. "The aliens do an endorsement deal where they start selling out to different corporations. They all become fat and drunk, and in the end they all look at each other like, 'Well, what happened? We've come to Earth and we've been awful.' So they get back in their spaceship and go home, and they have a picnic and play Frisbee with their dog." Moby is a kidder. He called the MTV Video Music Awards, which attracts punk rockers, aging pop stars, and hip-hop artists, "an extraterrestrial freak show."

But Moby is totally serious when it comes to space exploration. He jumped at the opportunity to spend a day at the space camp run by NASA in Houston, Texas, where he flew a space shuttle simulator, came in for two successful landings, examined a prototype for the International Space Station Freedom, and came face-to-face with several sophisticated robots. He also saw the world's largest swimming pool, where NASA conducts quasi-weightlessness experiments to prepare astronauts for work in the zero gravity of outer space.

"I would like to learn how to transport myself at will through time and space," said Moby. "It would be nice to spend a day seeing the far-flung reaches of the universe, don't you think?" Like Michael Jackson, he is also interested in unlocking the secret of immortality.

Moby's nemesis, Eminem, expressed concern about space aliens with his rap line "I'm Slim, the Shady is really a fake alias, to save me in case I get chased by space aliens."

# TINA TURNER: ROCK GODDESS

Rock's superwoman, Tina Turner, has a secret of cosmic proportions. Tina reportedly is a devotee of Zecharia Sitchin, the distinguished biblical scholar who has studied the Sumerian, Babylonian, and Egyptian civilizations and concluded that humanity owes its very existence to ancient space travelers who may be returning to Earth in the near future—quite possibly within our lifetime.

Tina, who taught Mick Jagger many of his famous dance steps, could have told Mick and the rest of the Rolling Stones that they had nearly stumbled upon the outer space Holy Grail when they picked *Bridges of Babylon* for the title of their 1997 album and tour. The fierce lion reared upon his haunches on the *Bridges to Babylon* CD cover is virtually identical to the proud-lion sculptures that guarded that ancient city. Babylon's "cult of Marduk" held that superbeings who looked human came down from Marduk, a planet often identified as Planet X, situated way beyond Pluto, and

Tina Turner will play the Hindu goddess Shakti, a recycler of souls, on the big screen in a new picture called *The Goddess*. Rock's superwoman reportedly is a follower of biblical scholar Zecharia Sitchin, who claims that humanity owes its very existence to ancient space travelers who may be returning to Earth in the near future.

jump-started the human race by combining their DNA with the DNA of primitive man.

The space gods notwithstanding, Tina, who has been a practicing Buddhist for the last twenty years, is slated to play the Hindu goddess Shakti in a new film titled *The Goddess*. But Hindu groups are upset that Turner was chosen for the movie role due to her status as a "sex icon" and have threatened to picket movie theaters in India. Film director Ismail Merchant steadfastly defended Tina, calling her an artist of international stature who should be welcomed to India. "Contrary to the accusations of the objectors, nobody is going to sing and dance on the back of a tiger, and the goddess is not going to be half-naked or a sex symbol," said Merchant. Shakti is the Hindu symbol of female power and energy—perfect typecasting for the veteran show business dynamo.

Tina, who is now lives in Zurich, Switzerland, said that the "cosmic energy of Shakti" attracted her to the film. She was also attracted by the music. "In the last two years I have got into the New Age sound," said Tina. "I like the emotions that go with this music." To warm up to the role, she watched Hindu religious rituals in the temple town of Benares and is studying Indian classical music and Hindi.

Merchant picked Tina to play the Indian goddess and recycler of souls when he witnessed her electrifying performance at New York City's Radio City Music Hall: "She was suspended over the audience and had them mesmerized, and I thought that spiritual connection, that's Shakti." Tina may be playing an Indian goddess on the big screen, but in real life she is convinced that she is the living reincarnation of an ancient Egyptian princess.

# DAVE GROHL OF FOO FIGHTERS: ROSWELL RECORDS SUPERSTAR

Dave Grohl named his immensely popular group the Foo Fighters after what pilots dubbed the strange balls of light that followed Allied aircraft during bombing raids in Germany in World War Two. The Foo Fighters' Roswell Records label was named in honor of a UFO crash in New Mexico that made headlines around the world and touched off the flying saucer debate that is still going on to this day.

"I used to have freaky dreams about UFOs," confessed Dave. "When I was a kid, I really wanted to see one, so I would just sit in my front yard and go, 'Take me, I'm here. Can you hear me?' In the fifth or sixth grade I found out about Project Bluebook [the U.S. air force's official probe of flying saucers], so I got really into being an investigative UFO expert." Grohl would go around to friends' homes to see dead grass and tell them, "See, that's definitely an indication of some sort of life-form landing in your backyard."

Dave admits, "I've seen some weird stuff, actually. On a Foo Fighters tour when we were driving through Arizona, we saw what looked like weird little explosions going in a circle moving through the sky. Even as a child I just couldn't understand why anyone would want to be so closed-minded as to think there was no life anywhere but our tiny ignorant planet."

Grohl believes that many crop circles may be the work of space visitors. He compares them to "alien graffiti . . . they're coming and putting tags on cornfields." And what about unexplained phenomena? "People are sort of looking back at ancient religions and starting to realize that they have a lot more to do with the unexplained than they could ever explain before," said Grohl.

Dave once had a walk-on role in *The X-Files*, filmed in Van-

Dave Grohl founded the Foo Fighters and established the Roswell Records label. The name *Foo Fighters* derives from the strange balls of light that pursued Allied aircraft during bombing raids in Germany in World War Two. While driving through Arizona on a Foo Fighters tour, Dave saw "weird little explosions going in a circle moving through the sky."

couver, Canada. "But I didn't get to see their big warehouse where they keep all of their UFOs and stuff," he said. But Dave did discover that his home in Seattle, Washington, was haunted by the ghost of a Native American woman who'd murdered her baby more than a century ago and was waiting for the child to be given a proper burial. His wife,

Jennifer, consulted the Ouija board to find out if any spirits were in the house. Dave said that the glass of the Ouija board moved itself. It spelled out the letters Y-E-S.

# DAN AYKROYD: PARANORMAL DETECTIVE

Surviving Blues Brother Dan Aykroyd once took on comedian David Letterman, who was trying to poke fun at UFOs. Dan brought a copy of British author Timothy Good's best-selling book *Above Top Secret* to Dave's show in a plain black bag and planted it squarely on Letterman's desk so the camera could get a good shot of it. The former star of *Saturday Night Live* told Dave that many military people and professional pilots told their accounts of encounters with UFOs in the book, which Dan called "the definitive UFO bible."

Dan, who is currently the number one celebrity UFO advocate in the nation, was recently appointed Hollywood consultant to the Mutual UFO Network (MUFON), the largest UFO organization in the United States. Dan said that what he likes "about it [the UFO field] is that it's entertaining and now the little alien head you see everywhere. It's as big as the Easter Bunny, Santa Claus, the Tooth Fairy. It's entered our mythical culture in a very strange way. Kind of almost replacing elves and fairies from the turn of the century, so that's what really fascinates me." But there is a serious side to the UFO puzzle.

The Blues Brothers outfits worn by John Belushi and Aykroyd on *Saturday Night Live* and in the *Blues Brothers* movie were modeled after the black suits worn by the real Men in Black who terrorized UFO witnesses in the 1950s and 1960s. Some witnesses believe that MIBs are government agents. Others believe that

Dan Aykroyd and John Belushi carry on as the Blues Brothers in outfits that were based on real Men in Black who terrorized UFO witnesses in the 1950s and 1960s. Ironically Aykroyd encountered two latter-day MIBs last year while standing outside a studio in New York City where he was taping his UFO show, *Out There,* for the Sci Fi Channel. Two hours after the encounter, Dan's show was inexplicably canceled.

they are extraterrestrials disguised as humans. It certainly wasn't a laughing matter when Dan encountered two alleged MIBs outside the New York City studio where his no-holds-barred TV series *Out There* was being filmed for the Sci Fi Channel. The scenario that unfolded had all of the earmarks of a Hollywood science fiction movie complete with a surprise ending, but the players were real and Dan was caught right in the middle of the action.

Dan's chilling encounter with the MIBs is described on a new DVD produced by David Sereda titled *Dan Aykroyd Unplugged on UFOs*, in which Aykroyd displays an encyclopedic knowledge of UFOs and extraterrestrials. Dan recalled receiving a call on his cell phone from Britney

Spears inviting him to go on *Saturday Night Live* with her. Just at that moment Dan noticed a black Ford sedan parked across the street at Forty-second Street and Eighth Avenue with two tall men wearing black suits sitting inside. One of the MIBs got out of the car and stared daggers at Dan from across the street. Dan couldn't read the license plate. Aykroyd turned away for a matter of seconds, and when he turned his head back, the car and the men had inexplicably vanished. Dan said that the car would have needed to make a U-turn to get away and he would have seen it drive off. Dan thinks that the MIBs might have used some type of "cloaking device" to make themselves and the car invisible. Next came the surprise ending: Dan went back inside the studio. Two hours later he was told to discontinue taping the show. The controversial series *Out There* had been canceled.

The world-recognized actor believes that the U.S. "Star Wars" program, which was originally designed to target incoming enemy missiles, now has a secret agenda: firing at UFOs. He is upset that Star Wars weapons could be deployed offensively against incoming extraterrestrial spacecraft without provocation. "There are no projectiles being used [by UFO pilots], no weapons of mass destruction against humanity," Dan pointed out on his *Dan Aykroyd Unplugged on UFOs*. Some researchers have warned that such an attack could lead to a real-life "War of the Worlds."

Dan counts himself as one of thousands upon thousands of UFO eyewitnesses every year from all parts of the world. Dan and his wife, Donna, observed three small "perfectly rounded, luminous bodies" track across the night sky at an altitude of about one hundred thousand feet moving at a terrific speed "doing maneuvers that F-18s wish they could do."

Aykroyd said, "There is no question as to the existence in multiple of these advanced machines and in diverse forms—discs, crosses, wedges, triangles, cigars—and their respective occupants in various manifestations—grays, blues, humanoids, reptilians, and Mothmen, and so forth. The question is not whether they exist, but rather are some of them here to do our species harm or good?" Dan thinks, "There is at least one species of extradimensional/terrestrial entity which is very interested in our well-being and survival in a most profound and wonderfully positive way." Hardly the type of beings you would want to shoot down.

Aykroyd played a Robert Stack–like host on the paranormal television series *Psi Factor*, which he also produced. One episode was tagged "The Gray Man," a reference to stereotypical gray aliens who are believed to pilot some flying saucers.

Dan said, "The United States government has never concealed interest in UFOs . . . the air force sponsored Project Sign, Project Grudge, [Project] Bluebook, and amassed thousands of files. So there must be some material which they felt would panic the population, and therefore various agencies have chosen not to release many pieces of information."

Aykroyd took the unusual step of endorsing a videotape called *Evidence: The Case for NASA UFOs*, containing official footage of the so-called Space Tether incident encountered by NASA astronauts during the STS-75 mission. The footage shows discs swarming toward a tether that accidentally broke loose from the space shuttle *Columbia* in February 1996.

David Sereda, a former defense analyst who produced *Dan Aykroyd Unplugged on UFOs*, also produced the groundbreaking *NASA UFOs* video, which could provide the first important smoking-gun evidence of extraterrestrial visitation. The first impression of some of the scientists quoted on the tape is that the UFOs are actually an optical effect, known as airy discs, produced by the space shuttle's CCD cameras. But Sereda shows rather conclusively that the disc-shaped objects pass *behind* the twelve-mile-long tether, which was between 77 and 110 nautical miles away from *Columbia* when the break occurred. That would mean that the UFOs are unbelievably large—some two to three miles in diameter, similar in size to the huge mother ships that attack Earth in the hit film *Independence Day*.

# REG PRESLEY OF THE TROGGS: CROP CIRCLE ACTIVIST

Reg Presley of the 1960s British rock group The Troggs has emerged as a leading figure in the worldwide crop circle movement. Best known for producing "Wild Thing," "Love Is All Around," and "With a Girl Like You," Reg has spent an extraordinary amount of time and money investigating crop circles and extraterrestrial phenomena.

"Love Is All Around" was originally a big hit for The Troggs in 1967, but soared to number one on the U.K. charts and stayed there for fifteen weeks after a cover version by Wet Wet Wet was featured in the British film *Four Weddings and a Funeral* in 1994. The song sold 1.72 million copies. According to Larry Page, manager of The Troggs, Reg pumped some of his multimillion-dollar profits from the song into crop circle research. "Reg has been fascinated by UFOs and crop circles ever since I've known him," said Page. "He's always there at night with his video looking out for UFOs and waiting for crop circles to form."

Reg said that he was on a crop circle watch in 1992 when he saw an object "about the size of a star, which crossed the valley, turned orange, and stayed there for about three minutes. The next day we went to where we'd seen the object, and there was a crop circle formation." But Presley admits that it would be hard to prove that the UFO made the crop circle.

Astronomer Gerald Hawkins thinks that crop circles are actually a means of creating music. After studying various precise diatonic ratios present in crop circle design, Hawkins found that they corresponded to the same mathematical ratios found in music. Stephen Smith, a paranormal investigator and amateur composer, used a fractal music-generating computer program to obtain music from the crop circles. He said that the music resembled "an ambient space quality" and was "very relaxing."

Reg has spotted unexplained lights in the sky on no fewer than eleven occasions. He said that in 1993 he saw "a phenomenal thing. There were five of us. It was a full-blown rain and we were thinking of leaving. . . . An object came from one horizon so fast that it must have been [traveling at] six or seven thousand miles per hour."

Presley said that Marina Popovich, the Russian cosmonaut, told him an astonishing story about a UFO that was photographed seconds before their *Phobos 2* probe of Mars vanished into thin air. The picture showed a thin, cigar-shaped object of unknown origin. Reg said, "They [the Russian scientists] were able to see a shadow on Mars from which they worked out that the object was fifteen miles long [approximately the length of New York City's Manhattan Island]. This is a cosmonaut talking, not just anybody."

Reg subscribes to Zecharia Sitchin's theory that highly advanced beings called the Anunnaki came to Earth and altered the DNA of primitive man to help them mine gold. "Using a special process, they [the Anunnaki, from a planet beyond Pluto] turned the precious metal to a powder, which when consumed over forty days and forty nights increases intelligence and cures fatal diseases and hereditary defects."

Reg Presley of the Troggs, who produced "Wild Thing," has spotted unexplained lights in the sky on more than eleven different occasions. Reg is a passionate crop circle researcher and believes that some of them were created by extraterrestrials visiting Earth.

How does Reg know for certain that humans are descended from outer space? He answers the question this way: "When you get up in the morning, you go outside and you squint 'cause it's sunny. Have you ever thought why you squint? Have you looked at the other animals? You can shine your car lights into somebody's eyes and you will blind them. . . . Bloody deer doesn't, rabbits don't, nor do cats. Why's that? We are not from here. We are not from here!"

Reg admitted, "For the first fifty years of my life, I was sure that aliens were a figment of some people's imaginations. This was cemented in my mind by the belief that if there were such things as alien craft around the Earth, our technology would have picked them up, and it would have been broadcast around the world in an instant." He now thinks he was naive to think that way: "I did not take into account that our government, or any other, could possibly want to hide information from its people. It wasn't until I saw an alien spacecraft . . . that I knew our government had to be withholding information."

Presley was surprised by how many people told him they had seen similar craft. "Knowing they would not be ridiculed by me, they openly confessed and felt relieved by doing so." He now claims to hold the answer to one of the biggest UFO secrets of all:

"There have been several crashes of alien craft throughout the years, the most notorious at Roswell, New Mexico, on July 2, 1947, which had at least three hundred witnesses. I believe the craft is being kept at a secret U.S. base called Area 51. The technology being gained from this and other craft is one reason for the secrecy."

Reg said, "I think they [the aliens] are trying to tell us something. We are very close to screwing up this planet, and maybe they are trying to help, to wake us up in some way." Presley believes that governments have steered away from finding free energy because it would close down the oil industry and have avoided finding cures for diseases because it might be fatal for the drug industry.

Presley and The Troggs have been back on tour with fellow 1960s rockers Spencer Davis, The Yardbirds, and Manfred Mann. Peter Lucas, The Troggs' bass player, has also seen a UFO. "I noticed a light in the sky which was slowly headed my way," said Peter. "When it came closer, I realized it was a craft and that a shaft of light was coming from it, pointing towards the ground."

# MARC BOLAN OF T. REX: GLAM ROCK'S MUSICAL WIZARD

Pretty boy Marc Bolan of the heavy metal group T. Rex ruled England's cosmic rock roost during the 1970s when critics pronounced the glam rock wizard the heir apparent to David Bowie, the Beatles, and the Rolling Stones. In one month, fans attacked eleven cars used by T. Rex, smashing windows and stealing mirrors and door handles as souvenirs. Marc shared a feeling with Elvis, Bowie, and Hendrix that he was from elsewhere. "I really don't know who I am or where I'm from," said Marc in 1972. "I just know that I'm not from here." His life was tragically cut short by a fatal car crash in 1977, putting an end to a cosmic musical career that was on the fast track to the top of the intergalactic charts.

Marc started out as a mod fashion model. He claimed to have met a telepathic wizard living in a castle in France around 1964 who turned him on to the occult and transformed his life. While in Paris, the wizard performed levitation in front of him. "He was standing on the floor," Marc recalled, "and he raised himself about eight feet in the air." Marc also studied yoga and believed that he could make himself invisible. Countless T. Rex songs refer to flying saucers and outer space, including "The Visit," "Ballrooms of Mars," "Space Boss," "Galaxy," and "Interstellar Soul." T. Rex's song "Cosmic Dancer" is about reincarnation. "What I am concerned with," said Marc, "is calling down from the heavens the energy that should go into a song."

Marc and his bandmate Mickey Finn, who joined T. Rex in 1970 and recorded "By the Light of the Magical Moon" and "A Beard of Stars," both encountered UFOs themselves. Marc referred in a book of poetry to a "ship of rhythm" flying around erratically in the sky and then landing "snuggled like an acorn."

Bolan once told a totally bizarre story of how he lay in bed one night with his wife, June, looking at a picture of a tyrannosaurus that was hanging on the bedroom wall. The picture seemed to take shape and move. "I was afraid," said Bolan, "but I knew that it was me that was doing it, that my imagination had brought it to life. I also knew afterwards that if I hadn't turned my mind off, it would have destroyed me. I could feel it and so

Marc Bolan of T. Rex performs on stage during the height of his popularity. Marc proclaimed, "I am not from here" and embraced the outer space theme in his lyrics. He sighted UFOs and claimed to have met a wizard living in a castle in France who raised himself eight feet in the air. Some people think that wizard may have been a nonhuman.

could June. Since then I've been strong. I think nothing can hurt me."

Bolan was as far-out an individual as they come, but T. Rex fans still speculate on the exact identity of the so-called wizard Marc met in Paris who had such a profound effect on the future rock 'n' roll superstar. Bolan commented that he'd encountered some "amazing people" in his lifetime who didn't fit the normal definition of the word *human.* "I don't particularly believe that they come from this planet," he said. Some people today wonder aloud if the wizard himself might have been an extraterrestrial.

# SUN RA: VISITOR FROM SATURN

A brother from another planet named Sun Ra who genuinely believed that he was a Saturnian was the principal inventor of contemporary cosmic music. Sun Ra, whose real name was Herman Blount, was anything but normal. He named himself after the Egyptian sun god in 1952. He dressed as if he had just touched down in a flying saucer and claimed that he was on an extraterrestrial mission to save humanity. His concerts were the ultimate theatrical spectacle for their time, filled with exotic dance, light shows, midgets, fire-eaters, and special chants.

Sun Ra spread the simple gospel that space is the place. "Outer space is a pleasant place, / A place where you can be free," sang Sun Ra. "There's no limit to the things you can do, / Your thought is free and your life is worthwhile, / Space is the place." He predicted, "In tomorrow's world, men will not need artificial instruments such as jets and spaceships. In the world of tomorrow, the new man will 'think' the place he wants to go, then his mind will take him there." Sun Ra's language may have been strictly 1950s, but his thinking was highly advanced.

Over the years, Sun Ra's pioneering jazz group was variously billed as Sun Ra and His Arkestra, the Solar Myth Arkestra, Cosmo Jet Set Arkestra, Myth-Science Arkestra, Intergalactic Research Arkestra, and Astro-Intergalactic Infinity Arkestra. Sun Ra's band members, some of whom had close encounters with UFOs, believed their leader really was from Saturn and that one day they would all be rescued from Earth by extraterrestrials. Saxophonist John Gilmore boasted about having "fans on Mars and Jupiter."

Sun Ra claimed that he was "in contact with something that possibly no one in human form has been in contact with." He thought that "it could possibly be the same thing that the ancient Egyptians called the Nameless One. They had a temple to the Nameless One. The ancient Egyptians had a civilization for five thousand years without a break. No other nation has ever had that. They also gave the world the alphabet and philosophy. . . . I'm sure it's the same force."

Addressing the question of a UFO cover-up, Sun Ra said plainly, "Americans are not that immature to panic because there's more beings in the universe besides them."

Performer Gilmore noticed a strange light flying "sideways" in the sky while driving from San Francisco to Berkeley, California, on October 14, 1984, with fellow Sun Ra Arkestra members John and Peter Hinds and Tyrone Hill. Hinds and Hill observed the strange light as well. Gilmore recalled another sighting he and fellow musician June Tyson had after playing a gig in Watts, California. The two had just exited the club when June said nonchalantly, "Look at that spaceship going across there." John looked up and said, "Damned if it ain't. In broad daylight. It is zooming, you know."

Gilmore then described a frighteningly close encounter he had in Philadelphia, Pennsylvania, with a multicolored flying disc that at one point was maneuvering only thirty feet above his head—a flying machine that he feared might abduct him. The sighting took place at 3 P.M. at a viaduct with a train trestle, said Gilmore. He waited between five and seven minutes for the slow-moving disc to pass over the trestle, but instead the UFO stopped right overhead. "I said, 'Oh, shit! Well . . . I don't want to go to outer space with anyone but Sun Ra! If Sun Ra ain't going, I ain't going! And, man, I lit out like a bat out of hell! I hit the concrete and I was strokin'. I was running, man. I ran . . .'"

In 1973, while traveling aboard an observation car of the Northern Pacific Railroad from Chicago to Seattle, Washington, Gilmore, James Jackson, and drummer Clifford Jarvis spotted at least seven high-flying luminous objects in a V-formation. The objects were seen as the train sped through North and South Dakota. The UFOs kept pace with the train. Then one by one the objects seemed to shoot off into different directions and quickly vanished.

Gilmore and other members of Sun Ra and His Arkestra witnessed an unforgettable sky scene during the UFO wave that hit Westchester County, New York, in the mid-1980s. "One night we were going to New York and we all saw three intermediate ships getting in the mother ship. They were going in and coming out," said Gilmore. "Yeah, it was quite a distance away from us, but you could see them going in and out. I will never forget that."

But nothing could quite match the UFO sighting by long-time Sun Ra musicians Marshall Allen and Pat Patrick in 1964 when they were playing with famed Nigerian drummer Olatunji at the World's Fair in New York. "They saw two hundred UFOs," reported Gilmore. "A squadron of spaceships. Two hundred doing maneuvers! Can you imagine? Two hundred spaceships that could go undetected. This was late one night after the gig. . . . That tops all [the stories] I ever heard."

Sun Ra's musical output was prodigious; he recorded well over two hundred albums in his lifetime and performed years before the Grateful Dead at the Great Pyramid in Egypt. His own movie, *Space Is the Place,* was released in the early 1970s, and he taught an academic course at California's Berkeley University called "The Black Man and the Cosmos." Jerry Gordon, co-owner of Evidence Music, the company that reissued twenty early Sun Ra albums on CD, lamented, "A lot of people never got past the costumes and the mysticism, but Sun Ra was a genius and was not nearly as popular as he should've been."

Sun Ra was bitter about the lack of recognition he received in the United States. But the flamboyant entertainer did get to play a gig on television's *Saturday Night Live* and had a ball jamming in Central Park with Sonic Youth, arguably two of the high points in his musical career. *Downbeat* magazine voted Sun Ra the top big band in a critics' poll. He was also honored by the city of Philadelphia with the coveted Liberty Bowl. A major label, A&M Records, finally released two Sun Ra recordings toward the end of his life.

Sun Ra suffered a stroke in October 1992. He returned to his native Birmingham, Alabama, for urgent medical attention. Upon admission to the hospital, Sun Ra listed his address as "Saturn." His legacy can best be summed up by a poem he wrote: "In some far off place, / Many light years in space, / I'll build a world of abstract dreams, / And wait for you."

# GEORGE CLINTON:
# THE MOTHERSHIP CONNECTION

George Clinton picked up where the late great Sun Ra left off, producing imaginative music with a funky extraterrestrial sensibility for black audiences as well as white. His 1996 album was titled *The Awesome Power of a Fully Operational Mothership* and George, the Grandmaster of Funk, actually had a spaceship constructed at a cost of $300,000 so he could come in for a dramatic "landing" at his concerts. No one can ever accuse George of thinking small.

Clinton's 1975 *Mothership Connection* album borrowed a page from Jimi Hendrix's "EXP" song, where Hendrix had a news announcer telling the audience that a flying saucer had just landed. The first track, "P-Funk (Wants to Get Funked Up)" leads off this way: "Good evening. Do not attempt to adjust your radio, there is nothing wrong. We have taken control as to bring you this special show. We will return it to you as soon as you are grooving. Welcome to station WEFUNK, better known as We-Funk, or deeper still, the Mothership Connection. Home of the extraterrestrial brothers, dealers of funky music. P. Funk, uncut funk, The Bomb." The album's second cut, "Mothership Connection (Star Child)," starts out: "Well, all right! Starchild, Citizens of the Universe, Recording Angels. We have returned to claim the Pyramids. Partying on the Mothership, I am the Mothership Connection."

When not working with his group Parliament, George supervised recording by his other group, Funkadelic, and also took turns in the studio with the P-Funk All Stars, Bootsy Collins, the Brides of Funkenstein, Bernie Worrell, and Zapp. A surprising number of hip-hop groups have shown that they are plugged into the same cosmic wavelength by recording their own cover versions of the

George Clinton, the personification of the *Mothership Connection,* had a space-ship built at a cost of $300,000 to enable him to land at rock 'n' roll concerts. Clinton and his colleague Bootsy Collins encountered a funky UFO while driving in Toronto, Canada. Something came out of the sky and hit the car. Streetlights were knocked out for about eight or nine blocks. George believes that humans are descended from outer space beings.

"Mothership Connection." Among them are Dr. Dre, "Let Me Ride"; Digital Underground, "Tales of the Funky"; Eazy-E, "We Want Eazy"; Infinite Mass, "Mah Boyz"; Run DMC, "Groove to the Sound"; Sweet Tee, "On the Smooth Tip"; Tone Loc, "The Homies"; and Yo Yo, "Make Way for the Motherload."

The appearance of Clinton's mother ship at a major

outdoor event in New York City's Central Park sparked an unexpected response. "Someone had remote-controlled somethings flying around," said George. "Everyone thought we did it, but it wasn't us. We said, 'Wait a minute, they really are here.' I'm thinking someone had remote-controlled things because they were there both nights." Clinton said that people were jumping and saying, "I believe, I believe!" Asked if funk is really a message from outer space, George replied, "I'm sure it's comin' over the right frequency. I'm sure somebody's in touch with us."

Clinton and Bootsy Collins encountered a funky UFO while driving around Toronto. Clinton said, "We saw something. . . . It was like this light that came straight out of the sky and hit the car. It beaded up like oil in water or mercury in a thermometer and rolled off the car. All of the streetlights were out for about eight or nine blocks. . . . We just tried to get down to where the streetlights were. . . . We didn't even talk about [it], we just sat in the car not saying anything. Yeah, I'm sure it came from up there."

George believes that humans are descended from outer space. He and band members often discuss their UFO beliefs aboard a tour bus when traveling across the country from one gig to the next.

A number of other black artists have traveled the same extraterrestrial route. Grammy Award winners OutKast, who hail from Atlanta, Georgia, produced an album titled *ATLiens*, a play on the word *aliens*, complete with extraterrestrial and spaceship sounds. The voices of Dre and Big Boi can be heard on OutKast's production of the song "E.T." The chorus asks, "Are you alien? Out of this world?" OutKast took part in Moby's Area2 extraterrestrial concert tour costarring David Bowie and Busta Rhymes.

Afrika Bambaataa, the self-styled Godfather of Hip-Hop Culture and a member of the Zulu Nation, sighted a bunch of UFOs in 1979. He was sitting on a bench in the Bronx River Houses in

New York City with two friends. Afrika spotted three glittering-white, round-shaped objects in the clear blue sky. The UFOs kept following each other and appeared to be flying at an altitude higher than airplanes from nearby Kennedy and La Guardia airports, Bambaataa said.

On another occasion, while driving on the New England Expressway near Connecticut, Bambaataa and two of his friends noticed strange movements in some black clouds. He abruptly pulled his car to the side of the highway. The objects got smaller and then appeared to be heading straight for them. Afrika and his friends jumped back in his car and tried to get away. He thinks it was the mother ship referred to by Black Muslim minister Elijah Muhummad. Former world heavyweight champion Muhummad Ali, a Black Muslim, has logged over twenty UFO sightings during his lifetime. Ali believes they are a sign directly from God. Veteran black rapper Rakim used the title track on his 1988 album, *Follow the Leader,* to invite listeners to "travel at magnificent speeds around the Universe." Rap artist Canibus mentioned the Drake equation, a formula designed to determine the number of intelligent civilizations that may exist in our galaxy, in his song "Channel Zero."

Killah Priest, a member of rap music's multiplatinum Wu-Tang Clan, proclaimed, "Black people come from space. When you look at the sky, it's black. Without the sunlight—forget it, it's black. In the beginning, there was darkness." Killah Priest is right on the money. The overwhelming majority of space contains dark matter and dark energy, which cannot be observed even by the powerful Hubble telescope. John Percy, an astronomy professor at the University of Toronto, estimates that 95 percent of the known universe is composed of dark matter and dark energy. Stars and planets represent only about 5 percent of what is floating out there in space cloaked in darkness.

The Shapeshifters, an underground hip-hop group

from Los Angeles, issued a CD with the novel name *Adopted by Aliens*. One of the tracks on the album is "Planet Rock 2012." The name *shape-shifter* generally refers to UFOs that change shape in midcourse, but the term can also apply to extraterrestrials who can alter their appearance. Many of the Shapeshifters' songs are twelve minutes long and deal with topics ranging from alien abductions to doomsday predictions. The year 2012 is the last year recorded on the Mayan calendar, leading some to speculate that the world will end then.

# MERLE HAGGARD AND WILLIE NELSON: ROSWELL COUNTRY MUSIC REBELS

Country music legend Merle Haggard has hitched his star to the Roswell UFO Festival, held annually in Roswell, New Mexico, for the last ten years to commemorate an event that some people say changed the world forever—the crash landing of a spaceship from an unknown world.

Merle makes no bones about the importance of what may have happened over a half century ago in the small rural community that has become a household word and spawned a network television show. "If that thing [a flying saucer] came down in Roswell, then it is the biggest thing to happen since Christ," he said.

Shawn Hughes, head of the Roswell Chamber of Commerce, is ecstatic that Nashville celebrities are rallying behind the town's cosmic event. The first Merle Haggard UFO Music Festival, held in

2003, featured Merle sharing the spotlight with country singers Marty Stuart and Pam Tillis. Merle's 2004 concert, which was moved to the Eastern New Mexico State Fairgrounds, costarred beloved country-music icon Willie Nelson and drew a crowd of up to ten thousand enthusiastic fans. Lacy J. Dalton and Michael D. opened the rip-roaring, foot-stomping show. Merle announced that the Eagles had expressed interest in appearing at a future UFO Festival in Roswell.

Beginning in 1967, Merle scored a string of thirty-seven top-ten country hits. Haggard is perhaps best known for his redneck song "Okie from Muskogee." Willie Nelson's signature song is "On the Road Again." Willie recorded it for the film *Honeysuckle Rose*. He founded Farm Aid in 1985 with singers Neil Young and John Mellencamp. To date the charity has raised more than $12 million for various rural causes.

Merle and Willie are regular listeners to Art Bell's and George Noory's late-night paranormal/UFO radio shows. Willie believes in psychic healing and reincarnation and is a devotee of Edgar Cayce, the so-called Sleeping Prophet, who predicted that massive earth changes would virtually wipe out California and parts of America's East Coast. Acknowledging that he is mortal (at least this time around), Willie said, "It's kind of like you stopped a big train for a minute. It gives everybody a time to stop and think, 'Whatever this is, it is not going to last forever.' So we might as well enjoy the rest and take it as far as we can."

Meanwhile, the Roswell festival that Merle Haggard and Willie Nelson have lent their names to keeps gathering momentum. New Mexico governor Bill Richardson is the latest person to call for a reopening of a government investigation into the Roswell case. "People can handle the truth—no matter how bizarre or mundane," said Richardson. "We've become a tourist attraction by chance, not design," said Julie Schuster, executive director for the UFO Museum and

Country crooner Willie Nelson belts out a tune at the Merle Haggard UFO Music Festival held in Roswell, New Mexico. Willie is a regular listener to Art Bell's and George Noory's late-night paranormal/UFO radio show. He believes in psychic healing and reincarnation and is a devotee of Edgar Cayce, the so-called Sleeping Prophet.

Research Center in Roswell. A flying disc reportedly crashed in the desert near Roswell around July 4, 1947. Newspapers across the country soon reported that the Roswell Army Air Force Base had announced that they had captured a flying saucer. The next day the base claimed that the saucer was actually a weather balloon. But that explanation didn't sit well with many who believed that a flying saucer actually came down in the middle of the desert one stormy night. Tens of thousands of people who are curious about what actually transpired have flocked to the small community of Roswell ever since to express their belief in space aliens. The festival includes a parade, films, lectures, and an extraterrestrial marketplace. The Platters, the Coasters, and the Temptations performed their hits at 2004's gala celebration in Roswell.

After his death in 2003, legendary country singer Johnny Cash was buried along with a commemorative guitar pick from Roswell's first Merle Haggard UFO Music Festival, said his close friend Marty Stuart. "John would have appreciated the gesture—most people didn't know that side of him," said Stuart. "Every December he and I would go visit Luther [Perkins, Cash's original guitarist] and bring him a cigarette. We would lay down on the grave, smoke, and talk to Luther." Rick Rubin, who cofounded the Def Jam record label and produced Cash's final five albums, claimed that he has been able to communicate with his late friend. "As time goes on, it's a little harder to do," said Rubin. "But I still do it." An intriguing twenty-five-year-old photograph has surfaced showing a young Cash looking skyward at a daytime flying saucer that appears to be hovering overhead. UFO researchers are divided on whether the saucer is real, but few will argue that Johnny was the original Man in Black, making a fashion statement years before shadowy government agents investigating UFOs earned the same title.

As fate would have it, fellow country singer Lefty

Frizzell was sitting behind bars in the Roswell jail at the time of the Roswell incident. Frizzell, who was then twenty-one and had made guest appearances on Roswell radio station KBFL, was serving a sentence for statutory rape when he witnessed the town's sheriff dealing with fallout from the UFO crash. Frizzell's song "I Love You a Thousand Ways" was written during his jail term in Roswell. In the summer of 1994 country singer Dwight Yoakum costarred with Kyle MacLachlan and Martin Sheen in the landmark Showtime-televised docudrama *Roswell*, which told the true story of the event that has become a cause célèbre for the UFO movement. Dwight played Mac Brazel, the farmer who made the initial discovery of debris from a crashed UFO and reported it to the sheriff. Analysis of pieces of Roswell crash debris showed that material was unusually light, yet couldn't be dented with a sledgehammer. Strange hieroglyphic markings were found on an I beam picked up at the crash site, lending credence to the extraterrestrial explanation for the Roswell incident, which continues to have worldwide repercussions.

## DEBORAH HARRY: ALIEN SONGSTRESS

Punk princess Debbie Harry of Blondie takes being an alien as seriously as she takes her music. She happily endured hours in the makeup chair having her entire face and body reconfigured into those of an extraterrestrial creature for a video, filmed in Switzerland, promoting the song "Now I Know You Know." Blondie hired H. R. Giger, the artistic master of the macabre behind the blockbuster film *Alien,* to work his magic on Debbie, who

Singer Deborah Harry plays a biomechanical alien on the rock video "Now I Know You Know," directed by H. R. Giger, who created the artwork for the film *Alien*. The former Playboy bunny may have spotted UFOs over New York's West Side Highway many years ago when her father was at the wheel. She saw red lights that seemed to be hovering over the cars and then disappeared.

donned a full-body suit and allowed herself be spray painted. The results were absolutely astonishing. The former Playboy bunny was turned into a biomechanical creature from another planet.

Blondie also called on Giger to design the bizarre cover for the 1981 *Koo Koo* album, which had Harry's face pierced by four giant needles. Giger got the idea for the piercing artwork when he visited his acupuncturist for a routine treatment. "The idea of the four needles came to me," said Giger. "I saw symbols of the four elements [earth, air, fire, and water] to be combined with her face."

The singer defended Giger, saying, "He is a man easily misunderstood." Well-known for his exceptionally dark images, Giger "even scared himself one night when he went to brush his teeth and ran into his alien model in the dark," said Harry. Harry's husband, Chris Stein, owns a collection of occult artifacts obtained from well-known magicians that would scare the pants off Harry Potter. "Chris thinks that I'm definitely an alien because I fit the description of a race of females who were put on this planet from space," she said jokingly.

Stein commissioned Tom Lieber of Lieber Guitars, who has designed instruments for leading entertainers like Paul McCartney, Tom Chapin, Jerry Garcia, and Phil Lesh, to produce a macabre guitar based upon Giger's artwork. The bone-chilling alien guitar has a biomechanical body carved of wood and is adorned with carbon graphite and is complete with bronze castings. The neck of the guitar has a six-fingered alien hand. Called the Gigerstein guitar, the instrument carries a price tag of $57,000.

Blondie's well-known hit tunes through the years have included "Heart of Glass," "The Tide Is High," "Rapture," and "Call Me." Deborah Harry may have spotted a UFO over New York City's West Side Highway many years ago. "My father was driving me somewhere and there was a lot of traffic, and I saw these red lights that seemed to be hovering over the cars, and then all of a sudden it just popped into a billboard and disappeared," Harry said. What does the pop star who sings about the "man from Mars" think about real extraterrestrials? "I'm going to let them come for me," she said unabashedly.

# LANCE BASS OF *NSYNC: ASTRONAUT WANNABE

*NSync star Lance Bass came exceptionally close to becoming the first pop star in outer space, but unfortunately his backers couldn't come up with the full $20 million required to launch him aboard a Soyuz rocket ship to the International Space Station, disappointing millions of Lance's fans around the world.

Lance, who attended space camp near Titusville, Florida, in 1992 at the age of twelve, traveled to the Star City astronaut-training center in Russia and underwent a series of stringent health tests in his no-nonsense bid to qualify for the out-of-this-world mission. "You had a different doctor for every part of your body," noted Bass, "and to make sure it all works from your eyes, nose, ears, whatever, every internal organ, so I know I'm very healthy."

When Russian doctors eventually found that Lance had a heart murmur, he elected to have heart surgery to correct an irregular rhythm so he could be in top shape for the mission. The blond heartthrob was determined that nothing, absolutely nothing, was going to stop him from reaching his cosmic goal. He faced a six-month intensive training program that would have included time in a centrifuge machine that spins astronaut wannabes around the room hundreds of times a minute. Candidates have been known to pass out because of the punishing g-forces exerted on the body.

Bass called his planned trip to the International Space Station the fulfillment of "a lifelong dream." He said, "I feel like a pioneer creating something new. I am glad we are bringing interest to the space program. All I want to do is to be an astronaut."

Lance Bass of the boy band 'N Sync basks in the international media spotlight after announcing plans to fly to the International Space Station aboard a Russian
Soyuz rocket ship. Lance's dreams were derailed when his backers were unable
to raise the $20 million needed to complete the out-of-this-world mission.

'N Sync's 2001 song, "Space Cowboy," captured the space-
faring spirit: "I've got my eyes on the skies, / The heavenly bodies of light, / And if you're in the mood to take a ride, / Then
strap on the suit and get inside." The whole world was watching
to see if Lance would succeed.

David Krieff, president of Destiny Productions, had planned to produce a television special about Lance's rocketship ride into the stratosphere called "Celebrity Mission: Lance Bass" and to welcome him back to Earth with a live television concert. But plans came to a screeching halt because of a lack of deep-pocketed sponsors.

Millionaire Dennis Tito was the first space tourist to blast off on an eight-day trip to the International Space Station in 2001. The next tourist to travel to space was an Internet tycoon from South Africa, Mark Shuttleworth. Although space tourism is still very much in its infancy and ultrapricey, it is expected to flourish during the coming decade with private companies competing for shares of a multibillion-dollar market. Real estate mogul Robert Bigelow, the head of Bigelow Aerospace in Las Vegas, Nevada, has announced plans to build a floating hotel in space to accommodate space tourists. A controversial figure, Bigelow has also invested substantial funds in UFO and paranormal research.

Richard Branson, CEO of Virgin Airlines and Virgin Megastores, a leading purveyor of rock and pop music, has set 2007 as the year that people will be able to ride eighty miles into space—about nine times higher than commercial jets fly—aboard a futuristic space plane from Virgin Galactic at a cost of $198,600 per ticket. "Within five years, Virgin Galactic will have created over three thousand new astronauts from many countries," crowed Branson, who also has designs on a floating hotel in space. Branson pulled off an elaborate April Fools' stunt in 1989 near London that had that many convinced that a flying saucer had landed. British policemen sent to investigate a glowing flying saucer that touched down in a field in Surrey didn't know what would happen when a door opened in the bottom of the spaceship and out walked a small figure wearing a silver space suit. The bobbies were scared to death and ran like hell in the opposite direction. It turned out that Branson had piloted the balloon and the alien was a midget hired by the rebel billionaire for an out-of-this-world April Fools' joke.

Lance Bass's rival Nick Carter of the Backstreet Boys thinks that "aliens are real." Nick said that he used to go hunting for flying saucers. "I'd get back from a tour and couldn't go to sleep," he said. "I'd go out in my car with friends late at night in the middle of Florida and look for UFOs."

# PATTI LABELLE, JUDY COLLINS, LAURIE ANDERSON: SPACE DIVAS

Soul diva Patti LaBelle is America's reigning Space Queen. Patti, whose soul hits include "Lady Marmalade" and "New Attitude," was chosen by NASA to record "Way Up There," a soaring spiritual number celebrating the one hundredth anniversary of the Wright brothers' first flight, a release that won her a Grammy nomination.

"Way Up There," which was penned by LaBelle's longtime collaborator, Tena Clark, is now NASA's official theme song, assuring that the rhythm and blues singer's name will always be identified with America's brave space exploration efforts. Clark has previously written hit songs for Dionne Warwick and Gladys Knight.

Space pioneers John Glenn and Neil Armstrong were among the celebrities on hand when LaBelle hit the high notes at the song's premier performance. Disc Marketing has released a commercial version of "Way Up There," recorded at the Firehouse Recording Studios in Pasadena, California.

Folksinger Judy Collins, a contemporary of 1960s legends Bob Dylan, Phil Ochs, and Tom Paxton, composed a song titled "Beyond the Sky" for NASA to honor Eileen Collins, the first woman to command a space shuttle flight. Judy performed the number at a preflight briefing on the thirtieth anniversary of the Apollo Moon landing. The song ends, "Beyond the stars beyond the heavens, / Beyond the dawn we'll carry on, / Until our dreams have all come true, / To those who fly we sing to you, / Into the sky, / Beyond the Stars, / We'll reach our dreams."

Performance artist Laurie Anderson has the honor of being named NASA's artist-in-residence. A classically trained violinist and avant-garde performer, Anderson plans to produce a film on the moons of the solar system that is scheduled to debut at the 2005 World Exposition in Japan. She called the greening of Mars an "unbelievable aspiration" and would love to be launched into space. She currently lives with rocker Lou Reed, formerly of the Velvet Underground.

A contemporary of noted avant-garde composers Philip Glass and Brian Eno, Anderson is famous for her multimedia productions rich in storytelling. She scored a hit in 1981 with her song "O Superman" from her album *Big Science*. She has also designed a wireless musical instrument called the Talking Stick in conjunction with California's Interval Research Corporation.

# JAMIROQUAI: THE SPACE COWBOY

British pop star Jamiroquai (aka the Space Cowboy aka Jason Kay) can't seem to get outer space out of his mind. It has helped him sell 16 million albums worldwide. "I'm fascinated by space because I'm in it—the concept of getting up and looking at the stars and seeing a million places you could never go in this lifetime. I just want to go there. . . . Let's face it, we're all from space. All made from space dust." He must be listening to Moby or vice versa.

Jamiroquai, whose albums include *Emergency on Planet Earth, The Return of the Space Cowboy, Traveling Without Moving, Synkronized,* and *A Funk Odyssey* (named after Kay's favorite film, *2001: A Space Odyssey*), combines elements of jazz, funk, disco, and soul music.

He is presently concerned that a giant asteroid may hit Earth in 2028 and wipe out the entire planet. "They sent out probes that made that calculation," said Jamiroquai. "It [the asteroid] will miss us by less than six hundred thousand miles; on such a massive scale, that's nothing. We should pay more attention to space. You never know when the end will come."

# 6

# ROCK 'N' ROLL'S SECRET X-FILES

JERRY GARCIA, DAVE
DAVIES, SAMMY HAGAR,
RICK WAKEMAN, NINA
HAGEN, OLIVIA NEWTON-
JOHN, ACE FREHLEY, CAT
STEVENS, PHOEBE SNOW,
JOHNNY ROTTEN, MARILYN
MANSON, AND OTHERS

**R**ock 'n' roll stars and pop performers all over the world have had unusual encounters with flying saucers that in some cases have involved alien abductions and other chilling scenarios that rival *The X-Files* for heart-pounding action.

Jerry Garcia, leader of the beloved Grateful Dead; Dave Davies of The Kinks; members of the legendary Moody Blues; German pop diva Nina Hagen; Sammy Hagar, formerly of Van Halen; Rick Wakeman, keyboard genius for Yes; singer-songwriter Cat Stevens; and pop singer Phoebe Snow are among a small fraternity of well-known musicians who believe that they have been contacted by extraterrestrials.

Hundreds of thousands of people who reside in nearly every country on Earth have undergone similar experiences with alien intelligences. Alien abductions and close encounters are now so commonplace that Sheryl Crow, Foo Fighters, Frank Black, and many others of today's top artists have recorded songs about the strange phenomenon, where a person's body is usually teleported through the closed window of his or her home or apartment by alien beings intent on performing some type of medical experiment on board a UFO before releasing him or her relatively unharmed. Sheryl's tune "Maybe Angels" moves from Holy Roller meetings in Pensacola to secret UFO bases in New Mexico. She sings, "I swear they're out there" and "My bag's all packed in case they come for me . . . I'm headed down to Roswell . . . I believe they're coming back for me . . ."

Celebrated British guitar legend Eric Clapton composed the instrumental sound track for the spooky 1989 film *Communion,* starring Christopher Walken, based on best-selling author Whitley Strieber's well-publicized alien abduction from a cabin in upstate New York. Many rock stars have enthusiastically jumped on the extraterrestrial/paranormal bandwagon, recording music for *The X-Files* movie and television show and the TV series *Roswell,* which depicts teenagers from outer space hanging out in Roswell, New Mexico—ground zero for the UFO movement.

Travis, the popular Scottish group, produced the ultimate alien-abduction rock video, which takes verisimilitude to a whole new level, showing members of the group being beamed aboard a flying saucer in a stunning scene that in some ways outshines the saucers from *Close Encounters of the Third Kind* and *Independence Day.* The UFO video promoted their single "Side" from *The Invisible Band* album released in August 2001. MTV got in on a recent outbreak of UFOria by broadcasting an unprecedented "Abduction Special," featuring a profile on the Ark Alliance, a Los Angeles rave group that is trying to use their music to establish contact with ETs.

Alien abduction is in vogue. Pop star Britney Spears, responding to a question about how she would react if aliens landed outside her home and invited her to stay on their planet for five years, said that she might agree to go if she could bring her parents along for the ride. Britney admitted that she might be "a little afraid," but quickly added, "The way life is lived on other planets would be of burning interest to me." She volunteered, "There are spirits around us, good angels and bad angels." Britney hinted that she once ran into one of these spirits in a castle in Germany. Britney boogied with Martians and an astronaut in an outrageous video for her hit song "Oops! . . . I Did It Again" and told students at the Michigan Institute of Technology how delighted she was that the NASA rovers had discovered significant evidence of life on Mars.

Radiohead singer and guitarist Thom Yorke said, "I'm like most people. I'd love to be abducted. It's the ultimate madness." Radiohead's song "Subterranean Homesick Alien"—a spoof of Bob Dylan—is on their *OK Computer* album. The Blue Oyster Cult's song "Take Me Away" from the *Extraterrestrial Live* album depicted a bored man who asked to be abducted by space aliens. The album cover shows a landed flying saucer with a humanoid figure and two dogs coming down the ramp. Graham Parker's hit song "Waiting for the UFOs" on his *Squeezing Out Sparks* album demonstrated just how much the subject of flying saucers and their imminent arrival is on people's minds.

# JERRY GARCIA'S TWO-DAY ORDEAL

On the other end of the spectrum, Geezer Butler of Black Sabbath warned on the *Black Science* album, "The aliens are coming/ and the world is succumbing/ Flying saucers have landed on Earth/ the invasion is coming." Dave Grohl of Foo Fighters acknowledged that he was aware of "horrific tales of abduction." He could have had the Grateful Dead's Jerry Garcia in mind. Talk about "a long strange trip." Although it lasted only forty-eight hours, to Jerry it must have seemed like an eternity.

Garcia admitted that for two days he was locked in a "tremendous struggle in a sort of futuristic, spaceship vehicle with insectoid presences." Large insectlike beings, often described as praying mantises, have been encountered before by UFO abductees. Asked whether he had ever been in contact with higher intelligences, Jerry said, "I've had direct communication with something which is

Jerry Garcia of the Grateful Dead reported that he experienced a grueling, two-day ordeal trapped inside a futuristic spaceship with "insectoid presences." Jerry said that he had contact with higher intelligences and out-of-body episodes.

higher than me! I don't know what it is. It may be another part of my mind. There's no way for me to filter it out because it's in my head." Garcia said that the experience was similar to the effect of DMT, the "spirit molecule," one of the most powerful psychedelics that exist, but it lasted longer than DMT.

From 1990 to 1995, Dr. Rick Strassman, a clinical associate professor of psychiatry at the University of New Mexico School of

Two insectoid-type aliens of the kind seen by Jerry Garcia are joined by a smaller gray alien in this detail from a painting by noted UFO artist David Huggins. Some of these aliens resemble praying mantises.

Medicine, conducted DEA-approved research in which he injected sixty volunteers with DMT. A plant-derived chemical that is also manufactured by the human brain, DMT consistently produced near-death and mystical experiences. "Many volunteers reported convincing encounters with intelligent nonhuman presences, especially aliens," said Dr. Strassman. "Nearly all felt that the sessions were among the most profound experiences of their lives."

Dr. Strassman's research connects DMT with the pineal gland, considered by the Hindus to be the site of the seventh chakra and by René Descartes to be the seat of the soul. Dr. Strassman's book, *DMT: The Spirit Molecule,* makes the case that DMT naturally released by the pineal gland facilitates the soul's movement in and out of the body and is an integral part of the birth and death experiences as well as the highest states of meditation and even sexual transcendence.

The Dead's Jerry Garcia said that he received messages "as clear as someone speaking in my ear. They're that well expressed and they have all the detail that goes along with it. Sometimes it comes in the form of an actual voice, and sometimes it comes in the form of a hugeness, a huge presence that uses all of the available sensory material to express an idea." In addition to his strange UFO encounter, Garcia said that he "once slipped out of my body accidentally. I was at home watching television and I slid out through the soles of my feet. All of a sudden I was hovering up by the ceiling looking down at myself." Garcia's OOB experience is typical of near-death episodes where patients find themselves looking down from above and seeing themselves on an operating table.

According to a special report in the *Fortean Times*, the Dead hosted the world's largest telepathy experiment in February 1972 at a concert held at the Capitol Theatre in Port Chester, New York, with somewhat encouraging results. Parapsychologist Dr. Stanley Kripner, director of the well-respected Maimonides Hospital Dream Laboratory in Brooklyn, New York, was in charge of the elaborate ESP experiment. Two "psychic sensitives," Malcolm Bessent and Felicia Parise, were chosen for the assignment. Bessent was observed under strict laboratory conditions while sleeping at the Dream Laboratory forty-five miles away from the Capitol Theatre. Parise slept in her home, where she was telephoned several times during the night and asked to describe the content of her dreams. Various slides were projected on the Capitol Theatre's stage backdrop during six shows involving thousands of people. Bemused concert-goers were told that they were about to participate in an unusual ESP experiment. They were instructed to try to use their ESP to "send the picture" to the receivers. One image was a painting called *The Seven Spinal Chakras* and showed a male sitting in the lotus position, deep in meditation. Another image was a surrealist painting by Magritte called *Philosophy in the Boudoir,* which showed a headless woman wearing a transparent robe.

Dr. Kripner, who was a longtime Dead fan, pronounced the experiments a success, meaning that there were many more matches of images than might be expected to occur at random, but the results were open to broad interpretation.

Years later Jerry and his bandmates found themselves inextricably drawn to perform three live concerts in September 1978 at Egypt's Giza Sound and Light Theatre, an open-air auditorium with the awe-inspiring Great Pyramid and the Sphinx as an eternal backdrop. "It totally blew my mind," said Jerry. "For me it was one of those before-and-after experiences—I mean, there's my life before Egypt and my life after Egypt. It expanded certain levels." Jerry was amazed that the Egyptian Ministry of Culture agreed to the concerts in the first place: "If we had asked to play the Washington Monument, we know damn well what they'd say." While most mainstream archaeologists have declared that the Great Pyramid at Giza is a funerary monument for the pharaoh Cheops, others have seen the oldest magical building in the world as an encyclopedia of stone storing the secrets of the universe—the perfect setting for the world's most unusual band.

The final night of the concert in front of the floodlit Great Pyramid saw the band performing during an eclipse of the full moon, and the music didn't stop until after 3 A.M. Promoter Bill Graham had horses and camels standing by to carry members of the Dead and members of their entourage to a lavish party at a nightclub in Sahara City about an hour away. Most Egyptians had never heard of the Dead. "We would've played [Egypt] whether there was an audience or not," said Jerry. The band spent $500,000—"all the money we have in the world for the next two years"—to make the venture happen. Part of the proceeds from the concerts went to the Egyptian Department of Antiquities.

The Grateful Dead performed live on location at the Giza Sound and Light Theatre with the Sphinx and the Great Pyramid as an eternal backdrop. Jerry Garcia and members of his band camped out in the King's Chamber in the Great Pyramid and took turns lying down and singing in a giant open sarcophagus.

Dead drummer Mickey Hart recounted the group's behind-the-scenes adventures in Egypt in a lengthy conversation recorded by Cookie, a longtime member of the trippy musical family who came along for the journey: "I had always been intrigued by the acoustical properties of the King's Chamber [located in the Great Pyramid] because of its size and shape and because it doesn't conform to the physics formulas Western science has developed for determining the sound qualities of a given room."

The Dead decided right there on the spot to conduct an acoustic experiment inside the King's Chamber, a perfect rectangular box about sixty feet long and forty feet wide, made of polished stone with perfect seams and edges. "No building could be built that perfectly today," marveled Mickey. "Notes resonate in ways that defy the laws of physics."

Garcia and his wife, Mountain Girl, together with band members David Freiberg, John Cutler, and Hart, secured permission from one of the guards to spend some time after 5 P.M.—the regular closing time for tourists—by telling him that they wanted to test the musical qualities of sound in the King's Chamber. What Jerry didn't tell the guard was that they were going to actually climb into the king's giant open sarcophagus, the chamber's only surviving artifact. Garcia and his friends spent the whole evening singing inside the chamber. One by one they took turns lying down in the sarcophagus.

"We made up little choral groups and divided up into different vocal parts and just sang," said Hart. "The sound was incredibly rich and full." What happened inside the sarcophagus was a different story altogether. The sarcophagus had its own particular resonance. "When you found the resonant note, the softest you could hum would reverberate so much in that frequency that it would massage your whole body. And if you hummed at the level of a reasonable talking voice or louder, it actually hurt your ears," said Hart. The Dead wanted to run wires from the King's Chamber to the outside of the monument for their live show, but they didn't have sufficient cable to do the job.

Hart said, "The crowds [in Giza] were open, they wanted to hear what we had to say, and they wanted to boogie. You could tell that they were ready for electric music. But they'd never seen that much equipment or heard music that loud or experienced the intensity of this sort of live performance. They'd heard Western music on cassette machines in Cairo—mainly disco—they'd never faced this kind of concert situation."

Asked about the future of the human race, Jerry said that he believed that "everything tops out" in 2012. The Mayan calendar—the most accurate calendar ever invented—inexplicably stops in 2012, leading some scholars to conclude that it may be the end of the world as we know it and the beginning of a bold New Age. "I've always thought that the thing to do is something really chaotic and crazy, like head off into space," said Jerry. "That's something that would keep everyone real busy and would also distribute more bodies out there." Also out there is a minor planet named Garcia in Jerry's honor. Minor planet number 4442 became official on November 7, 1995. It was discovered on September 14, 1985, by a spacewatch at the Kitt Peak Observatory. Little is known about the physical properties and size of the planet, but Deadheads will be happy to know that it can be seen through a telescope and is located in the inner solar system.

For three years in the mid-1990s, Wendy Weir, sister of former Dead guitarist Bob Weir, claimed that she received messages from Jerry's oversoul or "JO." Wendy described JO as that "advanced spiritual being or expression of All That Is who exists in the higher spiritual dimensions, aspects of whom have been or are incarnated on Earth or other dimensions." Wendy was fourteen years old when her brother formed the rock band that eventually became the Grateful Dead.

When Garcia died, Bob Weir wanted to communicate with him from the other side, but was unable to establish a link. He asked Wendy for help. At first Wendy, too, had difficulty reaching Jerry, but eventually she was able to contact Jerry's oversoul by using breathing and meditation exercises. "Almost instantly I see Jerry's spirit," she said. "It looks like a brilliant white-gold beam radiating from the center of pure light. Free at last from the weight and pain of his physical body, he is in a powerful state of ecstasy." Jerry's message to Bob Weir and other surviving members

of the Dead was to keep making music because it represents a connection to All That Is. "There is a flow of energy in all that you do,"
said Jerry's oversoul, directing Wendy to convey that the band's
greatest and most important work was still to come.

# THE KINKS' DAVE DAVIES HEARS VOICES

Former Kinks star Dave Davies, who now performs backed up
by his own four-piece band, said that his latest album, called
*Bug* (as in alien implant), was inspired by personal contact he
had with extraterrestrials in 1982. Dave was preparing for a
concert with the British rock group the Kinks when he heard
strange voices that struck up a telepathic conversation with
him. "The intelligences did not tell me who they were," he
said, "but two of them said that they had always been my
spirit guides, and two others were entities who were not of
this Earth, but were involved in missions here as watchers or
nurturers of our race.

"The intelligences showed me, by some kind of thought
projection, things which they have on their spacecraft," said
Dave. "They showed me crystal computers that monitor the
actions of every single person living on Earth." The extraordinary close encounter constituted an "epiphany" for Davies.
"I was fortunate to have been given a lot of information all
at once. It takes a long time for some of this stuff to actually seep into the unconscious mind. . . . It's all related to my
personal growth, to a consciousness shift."

Davies told me that he thought it was a "cool idea" for
rock stars to join forces in an attempt to contact ETs—especially at this challenging time in Earth's history. He said

Dave Davies, formerly of the Kinks, said that he was telepathically contacted by extraterrestrials in 1982. Dave has had other rock musicians coming to him seeking answers to their questions about alien encounters. He favors rock musicians joining forces in an attempt to contact entities who are not of this Earth, but are nurturers of our planet.

that spiritual messages received during genuine contacts are "the most important and revolutionary aspect of UFOs and close encounters with ETs. . . . Many people seem to be coming out of the closet and coming to me for answers and opening themselves up with all kinds of stuff. These are very important times . . . times that I have been waiting for and preparing for my entire life. There is a way out of this misery, hatred, and confusion. The answers are as old as time, yet so strange and mind-boggling to 'conscious' consciousness." A reasoning factor in our mind, he said, "creates the four walls to our three-dimensional prison cell."

# THE MOODY BLUES' REALLY CLOSE ENCOUNTER

The beloved British rock/pop band the Moody Blues had a really close encounter with a cigar-shaped spaceship and possibly small alien grays late one autumn night in 1967. "We were returning to London after a concert in Carlisle," said Moody drummer Graeme Edge. Riding in the car with Graeme were band members Denny Laine, Mike Pinder, Ray Thomas, and Clint Warwick. The UFO passed over the car and then landed in a nearby field.

"It was quite uncanny and we were mesmerized as if in a dream," said Graeme. "We could see the object . . . it was shaped like a fat cigar with a low protrusion on top, with seven dull red lights on it. . . . The upper half of the object appeared metallic, whereas the lower half was red and pulsed from left to right.

"Suddenly all five of us were gripped simultaneously with dread and panic," said Graeme. They drove off. "As we looked back, we could still see the object pulsing away in the field." Years later when somebody asked Graeme kiddingly what the aliens looked like (Graeme never mentioned aliens in his original account), he made a sketch of a small gray extraterrestrial and said that the sketch "seemed to come from the inside" of his mind, raising the possibility that the Moodys had actually encountered a being or beings not of this Earth. After their experience the group started to record cosmic albums such as *Days of Future Past* and *In Search of the Lost Chord*. The Moodys' first track, "Procession," on their 1971 album, *Every Good Boy Deserves Favour*, broadly hints that extraterrestrials were at the

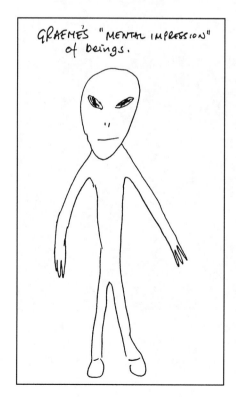

GRAEME'S "MENTAL IMPRESSION" of beings.

Moody Blues drummer Graeme Edge drew this picture of a small humanoid with a large head and eyes and tiny nose when asked to recall years later what the aliens looked like who buzzed the band's car in 1967 and landed in an adjacent field. Edge said that all five of the Moodys were gripped with fear at the time of the incident.

People standing on a New York City rooftop are beamed aboard an extraterrestrial spaceship in this virtual simulation by special effects artist Michael Sullivan. Scores of well-known rock and pop musicians consider themselves to be UFO abductees and contactees.

origin of life on this planet. The three key words used in the song are *desolation, creation,* and *communication.*

A group of six well-known Chilean pop stars were on a concert tour in the mining town of Maria Elena in northern Chile on August 16, 1974, when their van was buzzed by a UFO on a desolate stretch of desert highway known as Pampa Soledad. The singer Marcelo said that the performers were driving toward the city of Antofagasta around midnight when he spotted "this light following us for about half an hour." All of the musicians in the group, including Gloria Benavides, Tito Fernandez, Jorge Cruz, and Patty Chavez, witnessed the phenomenon.

Fernandez explained later, "We saw a shape. I can draw it. There was definitely something there . . . suddenly I found myself in front of a very tall figure about two and a half meters [seven and a half feet] tall . . . it was pure light." Seventeen years later on the night of June 23, 1991, another van driving on the same lonely stretch of highway in Chile's Atacama Desert encountered a similar light following their vehicle. This time the witnesses were able to videotape it.

Ray Dorset, the singer from the British group Mungo Jerry, was traveling home near Guildford when his car headlights picked up "between eight and ten small gray aliens" scampering across the road. Ray jumped out of the car and pursued the aliens on foot. The aliens vanished. Fellow British rocker Clem Curtis of the Foundations noticed that something was moving in the room where he was sleeping and tried to move his head to see what it was. He then realized that he was paralyzed. Fortunately he was able to snap out of it.

# NINA HAGEN'S "LIGHT MACHINE"

Nina Hagen, the 1980s Queen Mother of Punk from East Berlin, Germany, reported that she was temporarily paralyzed when a flying saucer "light machine" appeared in the middle of the night only thirty feet outside the window of her home in Malibu, California, in January 1981, close to the same beach where Barbra Streisand and Bob Dylan also have their homes. "I couldn't tell my friends who were sleeping on the side because I couldn't move," she explained.

At the time of her really close encounter, Nina was four months pregnant with her daughter, Cosma Shiva, "so there was no alcohol or any kind of substance to impair my judgment," she remarked. The lights she saw "were stronger than anything I have ever seen on this Earth, but it didn't hurt the eyes. And the blue and the red, the purple and the orange, and the turquoise and the green, every single color had, ahhh, such a loving energy and was extremely ecstatic." Her experience was totally positive.

Nina was able to peer inside the glassy spaceship, which she said "looked like a cool little recording studio." Nina said, "I saw beings like us working on the interior." One she said was female and two were male ("Please don't ask me how and why I know"). They all wore identical tight overalls. Nina thinks that the space visitors she observed were "us in the future."

Nina's first experience with UFO contact was in 1979. She said that she came into contact with a space being while on an astral trip out of her body. Nina believes that ETs are here to help earthlings survive the present situation, which she called "dangerous." "They cannot intervene with Earth beings, but could help if we ask for it," said Nina. "They would inspire us to substitute the gasoline pollution with magnetic cars, how to avoid the violence over eco-

German punk diva Nina Hagen was blown away by a flying saucer "light machine" that temporarily paralyzed her in 1981 in Malibu, California. The spacecraft resembled "a cool little recording studio." Nina said that she saw humanlike beings working in the ship's interior. She thinks that the space visitors may have been "us in the future."

logical systems. They would avoid the physical deterioration by creating better-adapted machines. They would facilitate our friendship with our friends in the cosmos."

Nina believes that extraterrestrial mother ships are enormous—"one hundred miles in diameter, and in there are hundreds of small ships. Those are the spaceships which we see time and time again hovering over the Earth."

Nina has always tried to link her singing career with UFOs. In 1985, for example, she descended over a concert crowd of fifty thousand people at the Couto Pereira Stadium in Curitiba, Brazil, in a spectacular flying saucer. A song titled "Witness," written and composed by Nina together with Sascha Konietzko and Tim Skold, urges people to "escape the destruction, enjoy the abduction." Nina is also a practicing Hindu and performs Indian spiritual music. She has often visited India and produced an independent movie titled *Om Gottes Willen—Om Namah Shivay.*

# OLIVIA NEWTON-JOHN'S UFO SHAPE-SHIFTER

Australian singer Olivia Newton-John, universally loved for her starring role in the musical film *Grease*, encountered a shape-shifting UFO in 1974. She and her friend were riding in a car on a desolate road. Olivia suddenly had a weird sensation that something was nearby. "It was a prickly feeling, rather than static electricity," she recalled. She looked around and couldn't see anything. Then something she couldn't explain made her look up into the clear sky.

"I was stunned by what I saw," said Newton-John. "The object seemed fairly small at first, but increased in size with amazing speed. It was brilliant silver, yet seemed occasionally to glow with the halo of different colors. It moved at a terrific pace and seemed to change direction very quickly. It would hover motionless for a while like a bright star, before moving across the sky again. The shape changed as I watched. First it was triangular, then it changed into a ball." Before her highly unusual encounter Olivia didn't believe in UFOs, but she does now. Her only regret is that someone else didn't come along "to share the experience with us."

Film buffs will be amused to learn that Olivia played the lead role in a seldom-seen 1970 science fiction film titled *Toomorrow*. The campy plot has Olivia and members of the Toomorrow rock group being abducted by the Alphoids, a race of extraterrestrials hell-bent on bringing "grok 'n' roll music" to their home planet.

A close encounter of the musical kind occurred during the summer of 1970 in the Fujian province in China. Around 10 P.M. a local peasant from the Taining district observed a metallic, disc-shaped flying object descending over a hill. The object emitted a brilliant green light. As it touched the hill, it started to play incomprehensible "music." The eyewitness informed the chief villager, who promptly called in the army. Hundreds of soldiers were rushed into the area and circled the hill and waited. About an hour later the flying object emitted a powerful white light, broke the circle of soldiers, and ascended rapidly into the sky. Other UFO sightings were reported in the same district of Taining in September 1972 and December 1976.

An obscure Japanese folk story relates how music—in this instance, a whole orchestra of "harps and guitars, flutes and horns, bells and drums of all kinds"—descended from the sky. This cosmic band was composed of "five celestial maidens," fairies or muses referred to in Japanese folklore. One version of the story holds that Emperor Temmu, who ruled in the seventh century, was playing the koto, a classical Japanese string instrument, at his palace festooned with cherry blossoms when five fairies appeared in the sky, playing on their instruments in harmony with the emperor. They performed the dance of the Five Tact based on the five senses, also known as the Azuma Dance.

The lyrics of the Azuma Dance exclaim, "Oh, what a wonder! Music is heard in the sky. Miraculous perfumes fill the air. Petals fall from heaven like raindrops! . . . To the accompaniment of heavenly music, celestial maidens dance, hovering in the air, fluttering their sleeves of feathers, flying and wavering among the cherry blossoms."

Flying saucers rarely produce sounds, but in a relatively small number of cases sounds ranging from violent noise such as a bang or blast, a low-pitched sound like humming or buzzing, a rush of air like hissing or a whoosh, a high-pitched sound like shrieking or a piercing whistle, and signals like beeping or strange pulsations have been heard. The U.S. air force's Project Bluebook reported that a musician who worked at a radio station and was considered a reliable witness saw a seventy-five-foot-long, metallic saucer with a window in which he could observe the head of an occupant. The spacecraft made a deep throbbing sound while hovering and a wild whirring sound when ascending.

# SAMMY HAGAR'S MULTIPLE CONTACTS

Rock 'n' roll singer Sammy Hagar, former front man for Van Halen, claims not only to have had repeated contacts with extraterrestrials, but also thinks he knows where they originate. Sammy said that in 1968 he had an "unbelievable experience" in Fontana, California. "I'm a firm believer that I have seen, have felt, been contacted [by space aliens] two or three different times," Sammy told *Guitar World* magazine. "I have reviewed information that has been valuable in my life from those people, and they have used me in an experimental fashion.

"When I was about eighteen or nineteen, they downloaded everything that was in my head," said Hagar. When he awakened at around 3 A.M., "my whole room was so bright that I could hardly keep my eyes open. When it was over, I was shaking. I almost passed out. I was sick to my stomach. . . . It was so scary." The aliens communicated via mental telepathy; not a word was spoken. When pressed for a description of the aliens, Sammy said that they were "just energy." He emphasized that he wasn't doing drugs when the encounters happened.

The experience sent Sammy on "a course of curiosity." He bought a telescope and started reading UFO books. Since then he has had three or four other contacts. "I have narrowed them down to a people called the Nine, who are called that because they're from the Ninth Dimension," said Sammy, who has named his publishing company Nine Music in honor of his extraterrestrial friends.

"Anyone who thinks we're the only ones here, despite the vastness of the universe, is crazy," he said. "These people [who don't believe in extraterrestrials] gotta be put away, not the group having these contacts," Sammy jested.

Singer Sammy Hagar, former front man for Van Halen, claimed that he has had multiple contacts with space beings. Sammy said that he has narrowed down the space visitors to a people called the Nine from the Ninth Dimension. Sammy has named his company Nine Music in honor of his extraterrestrial friends.

# RICK WAKEMAN'S MISSING TIME

Keyboard player extraordinaire Rick Wakeman, who has sold 100 million records as a member of the progressive 1970s band Yes and as a solo artist, disclosed that he had a harrowing missing-time experience while he was recording his LP *No Earthly Connection* in France in 1976 and was also allegedly busted for trying to sneak into an airplane facility where some kind of unusual spacecraft was stored.

It began with a UFO sighting that Rick had at 3 A.M. while he was writing a song for the album on the veranda of a beach house in Miami, Florida. When Rick first noticed the object, he thought it was a shooting star. "But no shooting star falls across the sky, stays still for an hour, and then shoots off in the other direction," said Rick. A local newspaper reported that other people had seen the UFO, which made zigzag movements. Rick expressed concern that "everyone would explain it [his UFO sighting] away by saying that the pressure of writing the album was getting me down, making me imagine things."

During the recording of *No Earthly Connection* at France's Château d'Herouville (the same place where Elton John recorded his *Honky Château* album), Rick found himself sitting on a wall in a small French village located miles from the château, crying his eyes out. "I still don't know how I got there or why I was crying," said Rick. "It was as if my mind had blown a fuse." He couldn't account for some missing time, a condition that is frequently associated with UFO abductions. Wakeman said that he wrote the album "based on my thoughts that music was a sixth sense." The main song is titled "Music Reincarnate." The lyrics state, "Music is the spaceman's time, / A travel form of moving love, / Music is the spaceman's time, / Placed on Earth for man to find."

Rick Wakeman, keyboard player for Yes, has earned his wings as the "Caped Crusader." Rick had a missing-time experience during the recording of *No Earthly Connection* at France's Château d'Herouville. He was also allegedly busted for trying to break into an aircraft hangar that purportedly housed "unspecified craft" that may have been alien in origin.

Following his UFO experiences, Rick spent a year talking to people who claimed to have met aliens and was arrested when he tried to enter an aircraft hangar that purportedly housed "unspecified craft"—a first for any rock star. He called the hangar incident "an adventure." His latest album, *Out There*, is about a spaceship made out of musical instruments that collects different types of music from around the universe. Cuts on the album include "Universe of Sound" and "Cathedral of the Sky." A mysterious UFO is pictured on the cover. Wakeman has played keyboard on some two thousand tracks, including for David Bowie ("Hunky Dory," "Life on Mars," and "Space Oddity"), Elton John, Lou Reed, and Cat Stevens. He has worn a trademark silver cape during many of his live performances, earning him the nickname of Caped Crusader.

# ACE FREHLEY'S ALIEN SPACESHIPS

Ace Frehley, former guitarist of the veteran heavy-metal group Kiss, always wanted to see an extraterrestrial spacecraft, ever since he was a kid growing up in the Bronx, New York. Ace, nicknamed The Spaceman, got much more than he bargained for when a UFO purportedly landed one night in the garden of his estate in Westchester County, New York, in 2002. Westchester County and the surrounding Hudson Valley area in upstate New York has long been a UFO mecca.

"I had an alien ship land in my backyard," Ace excitedly told radio interviewer Eddie Trunk, adding that he had videotaped the encounter. The flying saucer that may have abducted Ace and then deposited him back on Earth with no conscious recollection of what happened left a cosmic calling card: a circular burn mark twenty-seven feet in diameter on the ground. "Don't ask me how, but I remember, vividly, taking off," recalled Ace. The rock star has also claimed that he can foresee the future. "I know for a fact that I'm going to take a ride on the space shuttle before I die," Ace said.

Ace's hair-raising close encounter with the UFO in his garden was not the first time that Frehley had sighted what appeared to be an alien spaceship at close range. Toward the end of July 1974, well after midnight, Ace sighted an object that he described as "an enormous baseball" staring at him outside the window of a 747 airplane flying from Los Angeles to New York.

Kiss had just completed their second album when the encounter happened. "It was very strange," Frehley said in an interview with UFO journalist Timothy Green Beckley. "As I was about to shut my eyes, I noticed a bright ball of light out the window to my right. I blinked once or twice to make certain it wasn't some sort of an illusion, but sure enough, this 'thing' was still there."

Ace said that he couldn't make out any great detail. "It looked like an enormous baseball, and its actions were completely erratic, moving from side to side," he said. "The UFO remained in view for a brief period and then darted off, traveling quite rapidly. We were pretty high up when it appeared, leaving me to conclude it was a UFO." The sighting made a great impression on Frehley, moving him many years later to create a series of computer-generated pictures that included Elvis Presley and a flying saucer. The Elvis UFO picture was displayed at the first UFO Festival held by this author at New York City's Village Gate. Artists from around the Big Apple showed their extraterrestrial-themed paintings and alien sculptures at the festival.

In 1984, while still under contract to Kiss, Ace formed Frehley's Comet, which lit up the sky with a formidable display of musical pyrotechnics but then burned out in 1989. He was the group's vocalist and lead guitarist. Frehley hit the road again in 1996 for Kiss's world tour, joining all of the original band members, but has recently again opted for a solo career. Way before he was a member of Kiss, Frehley was a roadie for the Jimi Hendrix Experience for what proved to be Jimi's final appearance in New York City.

Ace Frehley, formerly of Kiss, claimed that he filmed a UFO landing on his estate in Westchester County, New York, in an area that has long been a UFO hot spot. Ace said that the flying saucer left a circular burn mark in his garden twenty-seven feet in diameter.

New York UFO researcher John Ostrosky performed on *Return of the Comet,* an Ace Frehley tribute album. Recording under the name of Ostronomy, John released his own single in 1998, titled "Disturbing Abduction." He regularly performs with silver makeup and seven-inch heels, is a devoted Kiss fan, and has been featured on a number of VH1 television specials.

# CAT STEVENS "SUCKED UP" BY A SAUCER

Singer-songwriter Cat Stevens was unceremoniously "sucked up" by a flying saucer that obviously left an indelible impression on the former American pop icon, who many years ago converted to Islam and formally changed his name to Yusuf Islam. Cat, who presently lives in London, said in 1973 that "one night I was lying in bed and I saw this flying saucer shoot across the sky and stop over me. And it sucked me up in it. When it put me down, I shot up in bed. I know it wasn't a dream. It was real. I know it was real."

Referring more recently to UFOs and flying saucers, Cat said, "I think there is a higher force watching us . . . and I think they're in a timeless spot. They're just full, concentrated spirit, existing in a pure state, whereas we're undefined and unpolished until we get to that spot. To reach the center of yourself, you have to forget about future and past. It's just an endless staircase; and the way to get off is to take the door marked 'Now.' You don't really know where it's going to take you, but you gotta be ready."

Singer-songwriter Cat Stevens, who now goes by the name of Yusuf Islam, had a rude awakening in 1973 when he was "sucked up" by a flying saucer that shot across the sky and stopped over his bed. Cat said that it definitely wasn't a dream. Before becoming a Muslim, Cat practiced Zen, tarot cards, I Ching, numerology, and astrology.

Cat had a string of hits in the 1970s, including "Wild World," "Morning Has Broken," and "Peace Train." He renounced his musical career after orthodox Muslim teachers convinced him that his lifestyle was forbidden under Muslim law. Stevens was involved in an international incident in September 2004 when his flight from London to Washington, D.C., was diverted to Maine because his name showed up on a terrorist watch list for allegedly giving money to Islamic charities accused of funding terrorism. Both he and British officials vigorously denied the charges.

Cat revealed that his song "Longer Boats" is about flying saucers. The lyrics urge listeners, "Lift up your mind and look around, / You may see them, yes they're looking down." He makes references to UFOs in at least two other songs: "It's a Super (Dupa) Life" and "Freezing Steel." He also wrote a song titled "The Boy with the Moon and Stars on His Head." Before becoming a Muslim, Stevens practiced Zen, tarot cards, I Ching, numerology, and astrology. He doesn't do that any longer. But there are indications that Cat may soon resume his musical career—a move that is bound to please many of his former fans.

# PHOEBE SNOW "TALKS" TO ALIENS

Phoebe Snow, an accomplished jazz, pop, rock, and gospel singer and songwriter, spent time attending an abduction support group in New York City to learn exactly what had happened when extraterrestrials started contacting her and a few of her friends through a Ouija board in 1975. Scores of abduction support groups have popped up throughout the United States and abroad to help abductees cope with the stress and uncertainty brought on by their experience. Many abductees fear that they might be taken again, while others are open to a second encounter or even a third.

Phoebe tape-recorded the intense session with the Ouija board. When the tape was played back, two aliens named Laactiped and Uresi identified themselves and said that they came from an intergalactic civilization based in the inner Earth and the Bermuda Triangle.

Initially Snow was excited to see "the cosmic fireworks," but then things turned rather scary. The aliens started making telephone calls to Phoebe. She heard "tiny, screeching

Singer and songwriter Phoebe Snow became freaked out when aliens with "tiny, screeching voices" started to make telephone calls to her after contacting her through a Ouija board in 1975. For a while she attended an abduction support group in New York City.

voices" on the other end of the receiver. After five months of communication Phoebe and her friends were so terrified that they burned the Ouija board and were forced to contact leading UFO researcher Dr. J. Allen Hynek for advice.

In a separate case, the son of a leading jazz pioneer unexpectedly came face-to-face with a man quite likely not of this Earth. The meeting happened in the sixties in the son's apartment on New York City's Lower East Side. A woman professor at a well-known university showed up for an appointment and brought along a male friend. What struck the musician's son as rather odd was that all of the man's clothing was seamless. The trio spent hours talking, during which time the stranger displayed a great deal of intelligence and said that he was "not from here."

When the two visitors left, the man left behind his jacket, which was hanging in the closet, and he said that it would prove that he was from somewhere else. The owner of the apartment closed the closet door and forgot all about the jacket. Much later that night when he opened the closet door, the jacket was gone. Not only had the jacket disappeared, but there was no sign of anything inside the closet. There were no hangers, no ceiling, and no floor. The inside of the closet had simply vanished as if it were a black hole in space. A bit shaken by the experience, the musician's son slammed the door shut. The next morning, he gingerly opened the closet door again and everything inside the closet had returned to normal, except the jacket was gone.

This same musician's son, who had never believed in UFOs or aliens, sighted a giant delta-shaped spacecraft in the late 1990s at about midnight while looking through the window of his upper-floor apartment on New York's Upper East Side, where he had moved. He said that the object was flat, had tiny lights running along the edges, and was darker than the sky behind it. The UFO floated like a leaf, a motion that has been reported many times by witnesses, and seemed to be under intelligent control and extremely powerful.

Jazz legend Duke Ellington wrote a score in 1969 for a ballet titled *The Ballad of the Flying Saucers*. It is unlikely that this work was ever recorded or performed, but Ellington did lay down a track titled "Moon Maiden," on which he played the celesta.

# ENTIRE CANADIAN ROCK BAND IS ABDUCTED

Across the border in Canada, an entire rock 'n' roll band from St. Catharines, Ontario, claimed to have been beamed up to a spaceship by extraterrestrials. The case was investigated in 1982 by the directors of the Canadian UFO Research Network, a Toronto doctor, and the distinguished New York abduction researcher and psychologist Dr. Aphrodite Clamar, who put "Jack T.," one of the unnamed group's musicians, under hypnosis to find out the truth about this amazing multiple-abduction encounter in 1971. This was one of only a handful of group abductions that have ever been documented.

The four musicians had just finished a gig at a party in Vineland Station and were driving on a road near the Queen Elizabeth Highway close to Charles Daley Park when the driver spotted lights up ahead. "I think you had better take a look at this," said the driver. Sitting smack-dab in the middle of the road was a flying saucer. Not only wouldn't their van turn, but it seemed to be floating sideways toward the spacecraft. The vehicle came to a halt within thirty feet of the saucer. Four aliens with great big bug eyes looked into their van. The aliens asked three of the musicians, including Jack, to come with them. Jack took a bag of recorders (a flutelike instrument) with him. When his friends asked, "Why are you taking them, are you going to do a concert for them?" Jack answered that he thought they would create some social interest.

Once inside the spacecraft, the trio saw three chrome cots on wheels. They were asked to undress and fell into a trancelike state. The aliens checked Jack's fingers, ears, and inside his mouth, taking skin and hair samples, which they put inside plastic bags. Jack said that he felt no fear, only a sense of rapport with his abductors. Later the aliens said that they were from outer space, but maintained bases here on Earth. Some of the bases were underwater, while others were in desolate areas where few people go. Upon exiting the saucer, Jack was suddenly overwhelmed by a feeling of kinship, sadness, and love, all of which emanated from these beings and resulted in tears in his eyes. Further hypnosis sessions revealed that Jack had had several other alien experiences during his childhood, a recurrent pattern in many abduction cases.

In another case, punk rock singer Helen Wheels, who composed best-selling songs for the heavy metal group Blue Oyster Cult, was abducted by a cigar-shaped alien spaceship outside her parents' home in Rockville Center, New York, in May 1961, when she was twelve years old. Her brother, Peter Robbins, who is now a writer and UFO activist, was an eyewitness to the abduction. Helen and Peter first noticed five metallic UFO discs flying in a V-formation. The saucers appeared to have windows. Peter tried to run into the house, but he was struck by a bright blue ray. Next a huge cigar-shaped mother ship, much bigger than a blimp, "absorbed" the five discs, moved four blocks away, and shot up into the sky at a forty-five-degree angle. That was all Helen and Peter consciously remembered. But details about Helen's unusual encounter emerged under hypnosis.

She said that she was "vacuumed up" into the disc that had struck Peter and soon came into contact with a tall, gray being who communicated with her telepathically. For some unknown reason, she wasn't scared. The extraterrestrial led her into some type of a control room. When he moved, he didn't walk, said Helen, but appeared to float. Later she found herself in another room inside the spaceship with "eight or nine tiny guys" and a floating table. Suddenly she found herself on an examining table and was gripped by fear. "Something very painful was shoved up my nostril to the extent that it put a hole in my nose and blood poured out. . . . I felt totally violated . . . and for this reason I do not know if I can ever completely trust them."

A totally different type of abduction by apparently friendly gray aliens occurred during Joe Sofia's vacation in Sedona, Arizona, and led the singer and songwriter to form a group called Planet Blue together with guitarist Frank D'Angelo and to issue an album with the same title. Planet Blue's album cover shows a gray humanoid clutching the Earth in his hand, much like holding a baseball. Sofia, who lives in Oro Valley, California, with his wife, said that he is on a mission to show a lighter side to the abduction phenomenon. The group's first CD featured a song about a little lost gray alien titled "Far Away from Home." "The gray beings are not all negative, there are positive ones visiting and helping us," he said. During a hypnosis session, Sofia learned that his first contact with these beings occurred when he was only seven months old. Repeat abductions are fairly common among some UFO experiencers. Members of the same family have been known to be taken aboard flying saucers at different periods in their life, and some families have been affected literally for generations.

A radical musician by the name of Helios Creed performs techno rock suitable for your next alien abduction and claims that he is possessed by alien beings. "First there's alien abduction, then alien possession," Helios explained nonchalantly. "They just come into your body and you start writing alien music." Not surprisingly he has developed a big cult following.

Helios founded a band called Chrome in the 1970s that was particularly heavy on synthesizers. A few years after the band broke up in 1982, he launched a solo career. Originally from California, Helios said that one year after Jimi Hendrix's *Rainbow Bridge* concert he sighted a UFO in Maui, Hawaii, just as Jimi had. "I was about eighteen or nineteen years old," said Helios. "I was with my friend and it was being very visible, right over my head." He saw strange lights and a saucer-shaped disc. "It was definitely not our technology—human-being-type technology." Helios thinks he may even have had a missing-time experience and has had visions of the future of the world that show continents splitting in half and land coming out of the ocean—visions that he admits are "kind of scary." A good many UFO abductees have also reported apocalyptic visions. Aliens have told them that they should prepare for massive upheavals of the Earth in the immediate years to come.

While in Hawaii in 1989, Helios spotted a triangular-shaped, silver UFO with three lights below. Sightings of triangular-shaped UFOs have been dramatically on the rise over the last ten to fifteen years. If the trend continues, traditional flying saucers could go the way of the intergalactic horse-and-buggy. In 2003, while at Mercy Hospital in Manhattan, Kansas, with his mother, Helios sighted a cigar-shaped object—most likely a mother ship—high up with sun reflecting off the surface. "I want to be the first band to have interplanetary distribution," Helios announced. "I think a lot of people are contacted by aliens and don't even know it." Among his records are *Alien Soundtracks* and *Planet X.*

A rising young punk band from Orlando, Florida, chose the name Hybrid after the human-alien hybrids that some UFO researchers claim are at the heart of the abduction phenomenon. These researchers contend that the ultimate aim of genetic experiments conducted by ETs is to crossbreed with the human race. The band Hybrid, which performed with Ziggy Pop in 2002 at the House of Blues, has a CD titled *7 Hits from Space* with songs about alien abductions, black op conspiracies, cloning, and parallel dimensions. They hang huge banners of UFO photographs from the ceilings at venues where they perform.

*UFO* magazine reported that Hybrid singer and guitarist Denny Schylocke had a hair-raising sighting of a triangular-shaped UFO in 1991 while driving with a friend through the woods of Oviedo, Florida. At one point the object came so close that Schylocke could actually see the metal panels on the bottom of the craft. Dave Scott, Hybrid's former drummer who cofounded another early punk band called Adrenalin O.D., said that he noticed that three hundred people left the auditorium during Adrenalin O.D.'s opening set at a college in Massachusetts in 1984. "In the sky was what looked like a great big cigar," said Scott. "It was huge—maybe the size of two soccer fields. The moon was bright and you could see the craft's metal surface reflecting in the moonlight." Scott added that when he found pictures of cigar-shaped UFOs on the World Wide Web, "it was chilling. There it was. We weren't insane."

Schylocke believes that the angels referred to in the Bible were "the Nordic aliens. It's possible that the gods in Egyptian lore were aliens. It's also possible that Jesus was the first hybrid of human and alien DNA. Genetic engineering could explain the missing link between primitive cave dwellers and modern man."

# GHOSTS HAUNT ROCK 'N' ROLL BAND

Canada's Sci-Fi Prodigy band, based in Toronto, loves to perform at science fiction conventions, but the real-life adventures reported by band members might just give some of the more bizarre science fiction movies a run for the money at the box office. Patrick Cross, the group's leader, is convinced that the Sci-Fi Prodigy band, which specializes in the paranormal, is haunted. "We are followed by ghosts wherever we go," reported Cross. Patrick should know. He just so happens to be a professional ghost hunter.

"We do a lot of special events where we dress up in costumes and act like we're dropping down from another planet," said Cross. "We also have sound recordings of actual ghosts." The band often plays gigs in haunted venues, especially around Halloween. Background vocalist Carolyn Bassel is a psychic and spiritual healer. The group's music has been compared to that of Rush, Yes, Genesis, and Blue Oyster Cult. Releases include "Something Is Out There" and "Going Up."

Cross, who claims to have an implant in his thumb from an alien abduction and owns an alien-shaped guitar with the head of a gray humanoid stuck on the neck, said that some band members have been so freaked out by what has gone on before, during, and after gigs that they have been forced to quit. "All kinds of things happen," remarked Patrick. "Power failures, weird lights, orbs coming out of the band's instruments, sounds, voices, talking and some bad experiences, black-smoke figures, cars going up in flames . . ."

Patrick doesn't know why the ghosts allegedly appear in the recording studio, at different band members' homes, and at performances, but whoever or whatever is behind the weird goings-on just doesn't seem to stop. "It isn't really evil, just ghostly apparitions," said Cross confidently. "Ghosts

Members of the Scottish group C.E.IV (Close Encounters of the Fourth Kind), Brian McMullan, Brian McMullan Jr., and Andrew Morton, are flanked by two alien musicians. C.E.IV aspires to serve as a musical ambassador for the worldwide UFO movement.

are the spirits of people who have died, but either don't know they are dead yet or refuse to go through to 'the other side.' Others are stuck in their dimension because they died tragically or were murdered. . . . They hang around where they are most comfortable."

Patrick said that one of his most intriguing encounters with a ghost occurred in his own apartment in Oakville, Ontario, in 1988 when he had just gotten married. "My wife and I had gotten home late from our wedding honeymoon, and we were sleeping-in the next day when I awoke to the sound of someone in our apartment." Patrick heard what sounded like someone moving wedding gifts and rustling wrapping paper. Then all of a sudden sheets of wrapping paper was tossed in the air five feet in front of him. "I froze," said Patrick. "I was scared so I tried to make sense of this. Then I saw a whitish image moving around

the apartment. It was transparent and had the outline of a man."
Patrick's wife, too, saw the apparition before it vanished. Patrick
later learned that his wife's late brother had committed suicide
several years ago and might have been curious about the two
newlyweds.

As for the alien implant he allegedly has in his thumb,
Patrick said that he tried to have it removed by doctors. "I still
have a one-inch scar around the area. . . . The second time the
doctors tried to operate, it seemed my implant went deeper
into my thumb. They basically said they couldn't operate because it affected my central nervous system."

The Who's John Entwistle insists that he has a ghost living
but not paying rent on his estate in Gloucestershire, England.
"A lot of weird things have happened in the twenty-two years
I've been here," confided Entwistle. Among them were sightings of a lady ghost in nineteenth-century clothes walking the
grounds and the camera of an uninvited photographer falling
apart. Entwistle recalled that a couple of years ago he was
having trouble finding Keith Moon's recording of a never-
used Who song. The rock superstar turned to the alleged
ghost for assistance. "A few hours later when I was about to
give up, the tapes spontaneously fell off the shelf behind me,
revealing the Moon recording, which had been hidden behind them," Entwistle said.

Pet the Pig, an outlandish rock band from Harrison,
North Carolina, may not be haunted, but they do claim the
title of the "the world's only paranormal pop band," which
perhaps is only a slight exaggeration. Pet the Pig's lyrics
normally deal with conspiracy theories and UFO abductions. They recently produced a rock opera based on the
hit fantasy film series *Lord of the Rings.*

Heavy metal group Cobra reported that they were
"spooked" by the sounds of singing nuns whenever they entered the Chapel recording studio on Belmore Road in East-

bourne, England, to lay down new tracks for their next album. The building housing the recording studio once served as a nunnery at the turn of the century. Many rock bands have used the same facilities without divine intervention, but Cobra's brand of loud rock 'n' roll, which has been compared to Led Zeppelin's, seemed to set off the religious fervor.

Guitarist Clive Rogers, who uses the stage name The Axe, couldn't understand why nuns or anyone else would be particularly disturbed by Cobra's music. "There is nothing nasty or unpleasant about our music," said Rogers. "It's just no-nonsense new classic rock. But every time we crank up the volume and really get things moving, we can hear these female voices singing hymns." Studio owner and Cobra band member Vince Von Bastrum said, "It's very bizarre. It's a high-pitched sound which can be heard over the band, no matter how loud they play."

A Scottish rock group known as C.E.IV—the official designation for a Close Encounter of the Fourth Kind, (e.g., abduction by extraterrestrials)—are determined to serve as musical ambassadors for the UFO movement. The group have performed live at numerous UFO conferences throughout the United Kingdom. During their live performances, life-size alien mannequins appear onstage with the band, and unique sound effects and lighting create an eerie atmosphere. Offstage, C.E.IV members have been introduced to eyewitnesses to UFO cases by seasoned paranormal researcher Malcolm Robinson of Strange Phenomena Investigations in Scotland.

Formed in 1984, C.E.IV consists of Brian McMullan on guitar and vocals, his son Brian McMullan Jr. on drums, and Andrew Morton on keyboard. Their music, currently available on their CDs *One Dream, Vision,* and *Abduction,* is absolutely spellbinding. Listening to C.E.IV is probably the closest you will ever come to experiencing alien contact, unless of course you are picked up yourself one lonely night by a strange vehicle that comes darting out of the sky.

Although none of the members of C.E.IV have ever been kidnapped by space aliens, they did have an awesome UFO sighting in July 1985 on a clear night in Glasgow. They spotted a red dot in the sky that grew bigger and bigger, and they weren't the only ones to see it. A small crowd had gathered. Using binoculars, members of C.E.IV saw a classic saucer shape, amber in color. They were immediately convinced that it was intelligently controlled because of the smoothness of its flight and its unusual mobility.

British folk singer Chris Conway makes light of alien kidnappings altogether on a hilarious CD titled *Alien Abduction Salad*. Songs on the album include "Andromeda Bound," "Skyrider," "Space Temple," and "Planet Theremin." The chorus of Conway's title song reads, "Extraterrestrials abducted all the vegetables, / I know it sounds incredible . . . / To take them to their planet and / Create the greatest salads in the galaxy." The liner notes quote Gene Roddenberry, the creator of *Star Trek*. Roddenberry declares, "Humanity will reach maturity and wisdom the day that it begins, not just to tolerate, but to take a special delight in differences in ideas and differences in life-forms. If we cannot learn to actually enjoy those small differences—take positive delight in those small differences—between our own kind on this planet, then we do not deserve to go out into space and meet the diversity that is almost certainly out there."

Blueprint Comedown, a space age group from Sydney, Australia, that specializes in electronica, have dedicated their self-titled album to an alien abduction experience that has taken their music to another dimension. Pixie, Blueprint Comedown's lead singer, and Michael, the group's guitarist, stated, "We have in fact experienced what is commonly referred to as the alien abduction phenomenon. It's as real to us as anything we've ever known and a great foundation for music. This album, musically and lyrically, is a record of our experiences." The Blue Mountains, west of Sydney, are a celebrated UFO hot spot.

# RECORD PRODUCER'S HYBRID SON

Maria Cuccia was a piano teacher living in upscale Commack, Long Island, when she had an alien abduction experience that turned her life totally upside down and led to her writing music, not just teaching it. In a haunting album called *Abduction*, combining music with passionate dialogue, Maria grapples with the meaning of her otherworldly experience and captures the essence of what it is like to be a UFO abductee. Cuccia is pictured on the cover of the CD together with the face of a gray alien and a squad of mysterious black helicopters similar to the helicopters she has seen flying near her home. The album's liner notes state, "The music you are about to hear is an expression of what I have been through. Words alone could not describe the feelings and emotions I have had since my unusual encounter with the unknown."

It all began in 1992. Maria recalled that she was fast asleep in bed with her husband, David, a chiropractor, when she felt a surge of electricity course through her body. Suddenly she found herself being teleported through the window of her home like tens of thousands of other UFO abductees and taken aboard some type of spacecraft. That was only the beginning. Aliens showed her a group of small children, both boys and girls, through a window. They seemed to be boarding some type of school bus. Suddenly one of the young boys waved to her.

Maria felt instant love for the boy. She asked the aliens, "Is that my son?" They replied yes and told her that his name was Elijah. Before she knew it, Maria was back home in bed trying to figure out what had just transpired. For weeks to come, she experienced all kinds of strange things from car radios and computers going haywire to weird sounds over the telephone line. All three of Maria's daughters tried to tell her that they saw strange lights and beings in their room. Life at the Cuccia home had become anything but normal.

In a song called "Isolation," Maria confided, "Ever since I was a child, I have felt a strange coexistence with unseen entities. I sometimes woke in the middle of the night feeling as if there was a presence in my room. I often wondered if others felt the same way I did." For another song, titled "Uninvited Visitors," Cuccia said, "It happened again. The fear, the sense of helplessness, a shadow in the image of a man near the foot of my bed. He did not speak, yet I heard what he was thinking. 'You're not doing what we want you to do.' I asked him, 'What am I supposed to do.' His response sounded like a tape recorder on fast-forward. He then left me with one final message: 'We will send people to you.'"

In "Reunion," the third song on her *Abduction* album, Cuccia said, "What happened last night seemed impossible. I awoke suddenly at 3:15 a.m., a tingling sensation overtaking my body. I felt my soul rising upward, separating from my corporeal self. I was lifted into what I sensed was an enormous spacecraft. Down a dark corridor were many children who appeared half-human. Suddenly a nonhuman form appeared beside me and communicated that one of these children was my son. I wished I could hug the boy, but sadly I have no memory of it. I feel so drained. I have decided to seek out help for myself. I must know what is happening to me." In a more recent song called "Control," Cuccia revealed, "Since I have been heavily involved in UFO research, I am experiencing more disturbances. Like the strange static on my phone, the black helicopters circling my house all too often, and the van with the tinted windows parked opposite my driveway. Friends have tried to warn me about this. I was hoping that they were wrong."

Some years ago, when Maria had a miscarriage, a doctor thought that the fetus was still inside her and had never come out. A doctor who examined her found nothing and declared that she was in good health. However, mysterious fluid-filled objects were found behind her uterus in 1991 that completely baffled physicians. They were photographed, and to this day no one can explain what they are. Maria currently runs Elijah Records, named for the hybrid "son" she has never held in her arms. Maria's music was used for "the making of" a Janet Jackson video and she licenses music for independent artists in Italy, Korea, and Japan.

# JAZZ SINGER'S STRANGE OBSESSION

Los Angeles jazz singer Pamela Stonebrooke has a passionate, ongoing love affair with reptilians from outer space, which is a problem because most UFO researchers feel that it is politically incorrect to talk about them, fearing that it will damage the credibility of the UFO movement. The onetime teenage rock singer turned self-styled Intergalactic Diva, Pamela maintains that she woke up aboard a spaceship during one of many astral voyages that she frequently took. "On this short, metallic table were these four little girls," said the singer. "They were very frail like the grays [the classic description for little gray men], but they had wispy hair. They ran over to me and grabbed my arms and started calling me Mommy. I lost it."

Pamela happily tells anyone within earshot that she was made love to by a scaly humanoid that would make most people's skin crawl. Pamela remembers being awakened one night and finding herself having sex with a "gorgeous blond man." Stonebrooke called the sex "incredible." She felt safe, but then something peculiar happened. "All of a sudden the energy felt different. It felt aggressive and the entity felt bigger—bigger than the person who was inside me." When the blond man transformed himself into another, reptilian being altogether, Pamela was momentarily frightened. "The telepathic communication was so intense and sensual and emotional. It was everything you would want to feel to be able to surrender to in a sexual experience. It was almost like every cell in your body was having an orgasm. . . . It's really hard to explain, but he was definitely in control." Stonebrooke casually displays two unusual scars on her shins, which she claims she has had since the age of about nine and attributes to her out-of-this-world experiences. Pamela thinks that the world is "close to having a global near-death experience" that will be brought about by solar flares, nuclear warfare, or some other catastrophe and that her reptilian friends are somehow preparing the human race for these enormous upheavals. Cole Porter's "I've Got You Under My Skin" takes on a whole new meaning when Pamela performs it. She calls her experiences "profound" and thinks that she was put on Earth to help bridge the communication gap between humans and extraterrestrials.

Aloid and the Interplanetary Invasion arguably stole the show with their bone-chilling song "Abduction" performed at the multimedia UFO Festival held in 1993 at the Village Gate, the world-famous Greenwich Village, New York, jazz mecca. During the song's explosive finale, Aloid struggled with two space aliens, who captured him and dragged him offstage to the crowd's delight.

Aloid's drummer, Casey Conrad, had once encountered a strange ball of orange-yellow light that chased his car for three minutes on the Long Island Expressway in 1976. According to Casey, "The UFO made zigzag movements and appeared to be under intelligent control." Eventually Casey underwent hypnosis, administered by Dr. David Jacobs. Dr. Jacobs, a professor of history at Temple University in Philadelphia, Pennsylvania, found that Casey had been abducted by alien beings. His body had actually been teleported through the closed door of his car. Aloid and the Interplanetary Invasion's song "Missing Time" is based in large measure on Casey's highway abduction.

Lead singer Al Cohen (aka Aloid), who has performed with rock 'n' roll legends Bo Diddley and Ronnie Spector and played guitar in such hit Broadway shows as *Grease, Lion King,* and *Fosse,* raised the roof at the Village Gate with a thundering rendition of "The Inside Truth of Hangar 18," documenting the retrieval of four alien corpses from the crash of a spaceship in Roswell, New Mexico, in the summer of 1947. This author provided the narration in true Orson Welles style.

Hangar 18 is the name of the airplane hangar at Wright-Patterson Air Force Base in Dayton, Ohio, where the alien bodies and spacecraft were purportedly stored. A camera crew from the *In Search of . . .* television series managed to get inside the hangar—actually called Building 18A—and filmed some large freezing units that may at one time have contained the ultimate proof of UFO visitation. A Wright-Patterson spokesman claimed that the freezers were merely used to test airplane parts under subfreezing conditions and had nothing to do with keeping aliens on ice. Senator Barry Goldwater, a former air force pilot, tried to penetrate Hangar 18 and the "Blue Room" at Wright-Patterson Air Force Base. He was told that the information

Megadeth, the heavy metal group, went to extreme lengths to replicate a secret government facility housing the remains of space aliens in special capsules for their video "Rust in Peace."

he was seeking was "above top secret" and never to ask again.

Aloid himself was riding in a car on I-84 between Connecticut and New York in 1982 when he spotted a mysterious triangular formation of lights hovering silently only a few hundred feet above the roadway. ACM Records, a company run by Al Cohen and his wife, Eve, currently supplies music to top names in the music industry including Universal, Arista, and Motown. The company's music is heard on such television shows as *JAG, Ed, Malcolm in the Middle,* and on MTV.

The Pixies, one of David Bowie's favorite acts, paid tribute to Roswell—the Holy Grail of UFOlogy—on their song "Motorway to Roswell" from their 1991 album, *Trompe le Monde.* The Foo Fighters were so enamored with the landmark UFO case that they officially named their label Roswell Records. Megadeth, the heavy metal group, went to great lengths to re-create the so-called Roswell alien corpses lying in freezing chambers on the video for their *Rust in Peace* album. Filming was done in an abandoned power plant to give the feeling of a top secret military installation. The Powers-That-Be were gathered in the secret room. The Orb's album *U.F.Orb* contained the tune "Blue Room," the nickname for the place where the U.S. air force allegedly kept the ultimate proof of UFO visitation away from the public's prying eyes.

More recently, British rockabilly singer Graham Holly, a devotee of American rock 'n' roll legend Buddy Holly, recorded "Dangerous," a tune about Roswell, which he called "the daddy of all UFO cases." Graham decried the ongoing cover-up. American astronauts Gordon Cooper and Edgar Mitchell would agree with him. They are on record as saying that whatever crashed one summer night during a fierce lightning storm in Roswell was extraterrestrial in origin.

# JOHNNY ROTTEN CONFRONTS THE UFO COVER-UP

Ex–Sex Pistol Johnny Rotten, whose real name is John Lydon, was an unlikely visitor at a San Francisco UFO symposium titled "The Truth," aimed at uncovering evidence about the cover-up of the Roswell UFO crash. Joseph Firmage, the former chief executive officer of US Web Corp., a Silicon Valley computer company, organized the symposium, which featured UFO researchers Bob and Ryan Wood. Firmage is convinced that he was once contacted by a being from another world and has ever since led a public crusade to bring UFO information to the masses, taking full-page advertisements in daily newspapers in major American cities. He is on a one-man mission to learn the secrets of extraterrestrial technology. It is generally believed that whoever gains such knowledge could rule the world.

Lydon, who once terrorized England with his musical rants against the queen and the establishment, now lives in Venice, California, has recorded several albums with Public Image Ltd., and also produced a recent solo album. Mr. Rotten sat quietly in the audience listening to the Woods' claims that they are in possession of new MJ 12 documents proving that the U.S. military recovered the remains of alien astronauts in the New Mexico desert in 1947. The authenticity of the new MJ 12 documents has been challenged, but the original MJ 12 papers analyzed by veteran Roswell researcher and nuclear physicist Stanton Friedman offer keen insights into an apparent ultra-top-secret government program that kept the news of the crash away from the public's prying eyes. The MJ 12 group was set up during the days of President Harry Truman. Truman told the public that flying saucers, if they exist, certainly weren't manufactured on Earth.

Janus, a former protégé of the distinguished Greek composer Vangelis and Britain's foremost synthesizer pioneer, turned heads in England in 2002 with a series of high-voltage electronic concerts titled Roswell and Beyond, employing sound, light, and laser spectaculars. Mike Heggett, Pink Floyd's former lighting director, collaborated with Janus on the elaborate production. Representatives of Steven Spielberg's movie company, DreamWorks, and Paramount Pictures attended the showing. The main theme music from Janus's *Roswell: The Album* made the top ten in the International Underground Music Association charts on the Internet. *Roswell: The Album* is part of Janus's critically acclaimed trilogy, which also includes *Flying Saucers*, which is based on Kenneth Arnold's historic sighting of nine flying saucers over the Cascade Mountains in Washington State on June 24, 1947, and *S.E.T.I., the Search for Extraterrestrial Intelligence*.

Janus recently embarked on his next recording, *Rendlesham Forest*, based on England's own Roswell-type incident in 1980 outside a NATO air force base. A triangular-shaped object floated down and left deep impressions in the ground. Georgina Bruni, author of *You Can't Tell the People*, a book about the Rendlesham UFO incident, is assisting Janus with the album. Former British prime minister Margaret Thatcher told Georgina that the truth about the Rendlesham UFO had to be kept under wraps, presumably because most people couldn't handle the news. What planet is she living on?

A onetime child prodigy, Janus studied classical violin beginning at the age of five and was composing his own material by ten. His first venture into the live arena as a synthesizer soloist was the Vortex concert that took place at St. Georges Hall in London in January 1980. He collaborated with Mick Jagger's brother, Chris, on the show. Looking back on the event, Janus said, "It was important to me that for an hour and a half people could be transported to other worlds and privately ignite their own imaginations. The music I play, the visuals and special lighting, are purely the catalyst." The same thing applies to Janus's innovative Roswell and Beyond program.

Janus's musical involvement with UFOs came on the heels of a close encounter he had in Hampton, Middlesex, England, in 1984. The incident profoundly altered the skepticism he once had toward the subject. Janus said that the object hovered silently some two hundred feet above him and was "best described as the underside of the *Millennium Falcon* spacecraft in the *Star Wars* movie." Suddenly it "hurtled at an unimaginable speed upwards and upwards before disappearing completely." He couldn't account for some "missing time," a syndrome that has accompanied many UFO abductions.

Canadian singer Karen Linsley and her late songwriting partner, Lloyd Landa, created "The Road to Roswell," the title track on her latest CD. "The Road to Roswell" is a haunting fantasy about how two women—an alien and a human—meet at Roswell, New Mexico, in 1997, on the fiftieth anniversary of the crash landing of a flying saucer in the middle of the desert. The CD serves up a rocking satire of the entire science fiction industry with Karen and Lloyd's tongue-in-cheek "Nobody Knows That I'm Really an Alien." Their song, "Pioneers of Mars" was the winner of the Mars Society's Rouget de Lisle award for a national anthem celebrating the hoped-for human colonization of Mars.

Texas-born Rudy Martinez had his name changed legally to ? (Question Mark) as in ? and the Mysterians, after his garage band scored a number one hit in 1966 with the catchy song "96 Tears." ?, who makes it a point of never removing his sunglasses, said that he decided to re-form the Mysterians after he heard voices in his head—the same ones that had supplied him with song lyrics since he was a child—instructing him to reunite in 1996. Today the Mysterians consist of ? on lead vocals, Bobby Balderrama on rhythm guitar, Frank Lugo on bass, Frank Rodriguez on organ, and Robert Martinez on drums, and are based in Flint, Michigan. A believer in the paranormal, ? has explored every subject under the sun from extraterrestrials to life on Mars and the Shroud of Turin.

The chief field investigator for the U.S. Colorado Project, the largest government search for scientific evidence of UFOs ever undertaken, was a great fan of flying saucers until he passed away last March at the ripe old age of seventy-nine. "I love them," said Roy F. Craig, who wrote a song titled "The UFO" under the pseudonym John D'Arcey. What was surprising about Craig's music was his use of weird sounds played on the dulcimer. Craig called these sounds "whistlers from outer space," but never explained if they were real or imaginary. Craig took the riddle of the origin of the "whistlers" to his grave.

# MARILYN MANSON "AREA 51"

Mysterious Area 51, located in Groom Lake, Nevada, is second only to Roswell in achieving UFO pop-culture status. Catapulted overnight to international stardom when the film *Independence Day* was released, no place has captured the public's imagination quite like Area 51, yet precious little is known about what really goes on there behind locked gates.

Area 51's notoriety has spawned a popular arcade game featuring the voices of shock rocker Marilyn Manson as Edgar, the gray alien, and actor David Duchovny, star of *The X-Files*. Paramount Pictures is planning a movie called *Area 51* based on the home game. There are reports that Manson, who bills himself as the Antichrist, may play an extraterrestrial in the film. Manson certainly looks the part with his trademark glass eye and ghoulish white makeup. He previously portrayed an alien on the cover of 1998's *Mechanical Animals*. In what could well be the understatement of the century, Manson said, "I'm open to the idea of aliens." Manson explained, "I feel like I've landed on a planet that I'm not from." Naturally his choice for president of the United States is David Bowie.

Daniel O'Brien, a young Scottish student at Glasgow University, was so fixated on Area 51 that he produced a concept sound track for a new rock musical titled *Area 51*, which is dedicated to the top secret air force base whose very existence was denied by the U.S. government until recently.

Rumors have it that crashed saucers from Roswell and elsewhere may secretly have been transported to Area 51, where reverse-engineering projects led to the development of secret aircraft that appeared to defy conventional physics. UFO researchers staking out the Extraterrestrial Highway near Area 51 have long reported strange UFOs operating over the air base. Governor Bob Miller officially christened State Route 375, which runs through Rachel, Nevada, the Extraterrestrial Highway. Stars of the UFO-invasion movie *Independence Day* attended the highway dedication.

Actress Claudia Christian, who was one of the stars of the popular television sci-fi show *Babylon 5*, said that she is prepared to play the female lead in the stage production *Area 51*. The album and the planned theatrical send-up, which features a variety of musical styles including hip-hop and funk, "chart the exploits of scientist Rick Adams, who must halt the invasion of a malevolent extraterrestrial presence before all of humanity succumbs to the onslaught." Right about now the Pentagon must be tearing its hair out that a highly classified project could eventually turn into a hit show on Broadway!

Hollywood actor and esteemed "Blues Brother" Dan Aykroyd said that he personally paid a visit to Highway 371,

Shock rocker and all-around alien Marilyn Manson is one of the featured voices on a popular "Area 51" arcade game and may soon be tapped to play an extraterrestrial in a film titled *Area 51,* based on the same game. Area 51 is a top-secret air force base whose very existence was denied by the U.S. government until recently.

the Nevada route where an infamous black mailbox is located—the marker to the entrance of the Groom Lake complex better known as Area 51. "Many people go there and have a beer at the Little A'Le'Inn in Rachel," Aykroyd said. "They watch the mountains for activity and look for distant objects displaying unconventional flight characteristics." Pat Travis, owner of the Little A'Le'Inn, a bar, restaurant, and motel, said, "A beam of light came through my back door. It came about six feet into the room. It was twenty degrees below zero at the time."

A rave party called Abduction was held on August 24, 1996, in

Actress Claudia Christian, one of the stars of television's hot series *Babylon 5,* is poised to play the female lead in the stage production *Area 51.* Daniel O'Brien, a young Scottish student at Glasgow University, has already released an *Area 51* CD that blends a variety of musical styles including hip-hop and funk.

the tiny desert community outside Area 51, in an attempt to capitalize on the public's curiosity about the top secret base. Jason Suttle, the show's promoter, said that the event came about because "my father was interested in UFOs and I was interested in techno music. The rave scene is a lot cleaner here because everyone has to be twenty-one." The drinking of alcohol was prohibited. UFO abductees lent an air of authenticity to the proceedings. During the event petitions were signed urging the government to release more information about Area 51 and the cover-up of a crashed alien craft in Roswell, New Mexico, on July 4, 1947.

Area 51 is so well-known at this point that an Area 51 Lounge opened up in Lebanon of all places for a battle of the bands held in September 2002. Participating groups included Echoes, Solitaire, Everlasting Greed, Black Roses, and Utopians.

Third Stone Invasion, a heavy metal group from Connecticut in the tradition of Black Sabbath and Led Zeppelin, filmed the video for their self-titled CD on location outside Area 51. Signs warn trespassers that the use of deadly force is authorized, but that didn't deter Third Stone Invasion from completing the project. "The issues that we deal with are ones that strike a chord on a most basic level: fear, the unknown, danger, powerlessness, outrage about things that you have no control over," said guitarist Frank Moriarity. "It just seems that the strength of big amplifiers and loud guitars suits these topics more appropriately than keyboard drones."

Moriarity had an unusual sighting near Philadelphia in 1997. He spotted an object at night that looked "almost like a slow-moving fireball that seemed to have pieces coming off of it. What made it particularly strange was that it was misting and the cloud cover was very low, and this object was under the clouds." Similar "fireball" sightings were reported at the time across the entire northeastern United States.

In marked contrast to the majority of rock groups that deal

sympathetically with UFOs and space aliens, Third Stone Invasion views alien abductions and encounters as a potential threat. Moriarity has spoken out against "forced medical experiments, embryo harvesting, bio-device implanting." His last reference was to small implants that certain UFO abductees claim have been put there by aliens to track their everyday movements.

Frank Black mentioned the implants in a song, "Parry the Wind High, Low" on his self-titled solo album. *Implant* is also the title of Eat Static's second album. Quite a few of these so-called alien implants have surgically been removed. In every instance to date the implants that were tested appeared to be composed of materials manufactured here on Earth. However, more testing is planned. The retrieval of even one genuine extraterrestrial implant would constitute final proof of alien interaction with the human race.

Rock 'n' roll was well represented in a major television series devoted to alien abductions. Lisa Clarke, one of the main characters in Steven Spielberg's unprecedented twenty-hour miniseries, *Taken*, broadcast on the Sci Fi Channel, is the drummer in a punk rock band who gives birth to "the next stage of human evolution." Actress Emily Bergl, who played Lisa, said, "I was attracted to my character because she is someone who really has to defend herself. Because she is part alien, the aliens are keeping tabs on her—so is the government." *Taken* traces the development of three families through four generations and their various interrelationships. The Clarke family experiences a benign love affair between a woman and a mysterious alien visitor who looks human. Their son is half-alien and has special powers. His daughter Lisa eventually breeds with a member of the Keys family during a classic abduction experience inside a spaceship. Their offspring, a little girl named Allie Keys, is the central character of *Taken*, who narrates it and has incredible powers.

# ALIEN ABDUCTION POLL SHOCKER

The highly respected Roper Organization delved deeply into the views of Americans toward UFOs and alien abductions and drew some startling conclusions. Based on a sample of over a thousand adults, both male and female, the Roper Poll concluded in September 2002 that a shocking 2.9 million Americans have experienced at least four of five key events that indicate a probable encounter with alien kidnappers. Participants in the poll were asked a series of "indicator questions." The questions focused on waking up paralyzed with a sense of a strange person or presence in the room, finding puzzling scars on your body, experiencing a period of missing time, feeling that you were flying in the air, and seeing unusual lights or balls of light in a room.

Here are some of the Roper Poll's other highlights:

- 74 percent or three in four Americans claim that they are at least somewhat psychologically prepared for an official government announcement regarding the discovery of intelligent extraterrestrial life.
- 88 percent said that such an announcement would have no impact on their religious beliefs.
- 55 percent said that the government does not share enough information with the public.
- 56 percent think that UFOs are real and not just in people's imaginations.
- 48 percent believe that UFOs have visited Earth in some form.
- 14 percent or one in seven Americans said that they or someone they know has had an experience involving UFOs.

At least two features were repeated over and over throughout the Roper Poll. First, the younger the population, the more likely they were to believe in UFOs, and second, for some unknown reason a UFO gender gap exists: males are more inclined to believe in UFOs than females.

Public awareness of alien abductions was sparked in 1966 with the publication of the book, *The Interrupted Journey* by John Fuller, which explored the famous 1961 case of Betty and Barney Hill in New Hampshire. The case exhibited all of the classic traits of a UFO abduction, such as missing time and a medical examination performed by aliens on board a spaceship, and was especially noteworthy for the early use of hypnosis to get at the facts, a technique that would later become the hallmark of abduction research. The Betty and Barney Hill case was controversial for its time because the Hills were an interracial couple, something rare back in 1961.

Among the high-profile abduction cases during the next decades was the close encounter of two shipyard workers with strange beings in Pascagoula, Mississippi, in 1973 and the five-day disappearance of Travis Walton in Arizona in 1975. Six of Walton's fellow woodcutters saw him being hit on his chest by a strong light beam from a UFO. Initially local police investigated the incident as a missing-person case that possibly involved foul play. The police closed the case files when Walton was found five days later walking disoriented and dehydrated several miles away. The incident was dramatized in the film *Fire in the Sky*.

The abduction phenomenon reached a new peak in 1987 with the publication of Whitley Strieber's best-selling book *Communion*, which enabled hundreds of abductees to come out of the closet with their own incredible tales of alien encounters. Strieber claimed that aliens came for him at his cabin in upstate New York and inserted an implant in his brain.

Abduction research is currently divided into two distinct camps: those who think that extraterrestrials are basically benevolent and involved in a long-term project to help mankind achieve cosmic maturity, and those who believe that the long-range alien agenda is to harness human genetic material for the aliens' own sinister purposes.

Dr. Leo Sprinkle, a psychologist at the University of Wyoming at Laramie, pioneered the use of hypnosis to counsel abductees. He believes that the abduction experience is part of an evolutionary process to link mankind to the rest of the cosmos. Dr. John Mack, a Pulitzer Prize–winning Harvard professor of psychiatry, acknowledged that the abduction experience is usually traumatic, but compared it to a child being taken to the dentist. It may hurt a little, but it is for the child's own benefit. Dr. Mack believed that UFO abductees emerge from their experience with a heightened degree of spirituality, a renewed connection to the cosmos, and an urge to protect the Earth's environment.

Temple University historian Dr. David Jacobs charges that the aliens are embarked on an evil mission to slowly enhance their own species by mixing it with younger and more vital human genes. Dr. Jacobs thinks that all of the UFO sightings throughout the world over the last hundred years are connected to the alien abduction scenario.

Dr. Jacques Vallee, a French-American astrophysicist and UFO-research pioneer, considers abductions to be real, but not a product of extraterrestrial activity. Vallee believes that a link exists between the supernatural entities of traditional folklore and modern ufology. Paranormal researcher John Keel, author of *The Mothman Prophecies*—recently made into a movie starring Richard Gere—claims that all paranormal experiences, including so-called aliens and even religious experiences, are connected to very long frequencies in the electromagnetic spectrum in the human brain that make people think that they are seeing aliens, ghosts, or angels. The experiences are real to the witnesses, but not what they seem to be.

Finally, there is the strange disappearance of Philip Taylor Kramer, the onetime bassist for the rock group Iron Butterfly, on February 12, 1996. Kramer, who had an MX missile security clearance, had reportedly been working on a faster-than-light communications system when he vanished without a trace, never to be heard from again. Just days before his disappearance, Kramer and his father believed that they had come up with a mathematical formula that would allow the nearly instantaneous transmission of matter. "We're talking 'Beam me up, Scotty' time," said Ron Bushy, Iron Butterfly's cofounder. All sorts of theories have been put forth to explain Kramer's disappearance, from abduction by alien beings to kidnapping by shadowy government agents to suicide, but no one really knows what happened to the successful rock star who may have scored a supertechnological breakthrough that would have made it possible to build a *Star Trek* transporter to travel to distant stars. Kramer dared to go where no rock star had gone before, and he paid the ultimate price. He probably won't be returning home anytime soon.

# 7

# EXTRATERRESTRIAL
# RAVERS 'N' ROCKERS

Psychedelic poster from the UFO Club in London, which was a gathering place for spaced-out groups such as the Crazy World of Arthur Brown and other rock musicians on the way up. John Lennon and Paul McCartney were among the visitors to the UFO Club. Brian Jones and Keith Richards also dropped by.

ondon's legendary UFO Club was the grand-
daddy of today's rave movement, attaining mythic status in
early 1967 although it operated only once every two weeks
in an old dance hall located in a basement at Tottenham
Court Road and lasted less than a year. UFO Club posters
printed in expensive metallic inks and emblazoned with flying saucers beckoned thousands of members of the counterculture to come join the madcap psychedelic celebration.
UFOs were surely a sign of the times. Flying saucer waves
had been reported worldwide. News had leaked out that the
British Ministry of Defense had conducted official investigations into these alleged visitors from outer space. The U.S. government held congressional hearings into flying saucers, and
the U.S. air force was forced to open an official UFO investigation. The underground press covered UFOs in the same way
that they covered the Vietnam War, the sexual revolution, and
the street scene. Searching for UFOs became a part of the hippies' rites of passage. But the UFO Club's name had an alternative meaning that reflected the venue's freewheeling spirit:
Underground Freak Out.

The UFO Club was the place where rock musicians and their
friends and fans partied all night long in wild abandon into the
next day. John Lennon hung out with Yoko Ono at the UFO Club.
Paul McCartney cheerfully made the scene. Pete Townshend of
the Who and Brian Jones and Keith Richards dropped by every
now and again to hear emerging artists. Townshend met his first
wife, Karen, there. Pink Floyd was the club's supercharged house

band. Such rising young performers as Jimi Hendrix, Procol Harum, the Soft Machine, The Crazy World of Arthur Brown, and Tomorrow honed their acts at the UFO Club. Record producer and underground impresario Joe Boyd worked as the club's musical director. Jugglers, poets, and mimes mingled with the spaced-out crowd. Bizarre clothing was the official dress code.

McCartney said that parties at the UFO Club resembled "a trippy adventure playground, really. Chaplin films going there, Marx Brothers here, [Pink] Floyd up there, conjurer over here . . . just a circus-cum-adventure playground."

Steve Howe, then the guitarist for Tomorrow, called the UFO Club "a mass happening. . . . You were part of something: you felt like you belonged somewhere. The whole movement was about to change in attitude from aggression to peace. I re-member the power of what we got going there. . . . What happened was the group discovered a kind of release, a kind of meditation, a kind of higher state of mind, and we were all right there together."

One of the greatest heavy metal rock acts of all time, UFO, chose their name based on the UFO Club.

Slides and strobes transformed the club's basement site into a veritable Aladdin's cave. Experimental light shows had never been seen in London before. "We had a light show which changed color with the mood of the music," said Arthur Brown. "I also had all these costumes on. The interior world of one person was mirrored in the costumes, because I wore different layers under each other and took them off as I performed. There was, first, a guy with this huge Ti-betan monk's robe and silver mask. That came off; under-neath was a black cape, and it'd be 'I Put a Spell on You,' the magician. [For] 'Come and Buy,' we had lights and a Sun god's outfit, a sort of huge Sun with flames, rays of light coming out of it. There were huge costumes with these geometric patterns—orange, red, blue, not hellfire, but pure radiant fire. There was also the fire helmet. We would end the stage act with 'I've Got Money,' it'd be just shirt and trousers, I'd be a normal guy."

The club's grand opening party, "UFO Presents Night Tripper," was held on December 23, 1966. Pink Floyd, the Giant Sun Trolley, Dave Tomlin, Fanta, and Odd provided the music. The flying saucer icon was used extensively on club posters. A poster headlined "UFO COMING" showed several flying saucers hovering above beautiful naked damsels partially covered by butterfly wings. Another designed by Hapshash and the Coloured Coat especially for Pink Floyd showed a flying medieval castle from which a squadron of flying saucers emerged.

A benefit for the underground newspaper *International Times* held on October 15, 1966, at The Roundhouse proved to be the kickoff event for the UFO Club. Joe Boyd, the American who ran the UFO Club with his partner, John "Hoppy" Hopkins, said that it was started to provide an outlet for experimental pop music and also for the mixing of media, light shows, and theatrical happenings. The club showed New York avant-garde films. It was an almost instant hit, said Boyd, because "no attempt was made to make people fit into a format, and that attracts the farther-out kids in London. If they want to lie on the floor, they can, or if they want to jump onstage, they can—as long as they don't interfere with the groups."

Hopkins said, "UFO was done from the heart with a purpose, which was to have a good time. We decided to run UFO all night, and it was a piece of all-night culture suddenly flashing into being that really made it popular. People would stay till it was light outside." Far more than just a venue for rock bands, the UFO Club "was primarily a cultural event, the springboard of the new psychedelic and underground cultures in all their ramifications," said Hopkins. "Records would be played from time to time, but then someone might decide to do a little poetry. . . . people didn't listen to just one sort of music. You'd find people listening to avant-garde jazz, blues, and serious music like John Cage."

On July 28 the program included a band called CIA vs. UFO, opening for Pink Floyd and Fairport Convention. A story in Britain's largest tabloid lambasted the club for being unruly, and word spread that the police were preparing to raid the anti-establishment. The club permanently closed its doors in August and reopened at The Roundhouse, a larger venue in London's Chalk Farm area. On some nights as many as twelve hundred people were partying. But skinheads and local protection-racket thugs started to prey on the crowd. "We were just a bunch of hippies and we really didn't know how to deal with that," said Mick Farren of The Deviants. The UFO Club at The Roundhouse shut down for good on October 20, 1967. Vanilla Fudge played the last show. "After UFO closed, the scene moved to the Middle Earth in Convent Garden, but it was never quite the same," recalled club stalwart Jeff Dexter. "UFO had been the spearhead for the underground in England." It was now gone, but not forgotten.

Technicolor Dream, a fourteen-hour extravaganza bene-fit for the *International Times,* took place on April 29, 1967, at the Alexandra Palace in London and attracted seven thou-sand kids. William Burroughs and Bertrand Russell were writers for the underground newspaper. British journalist Ronald Maxwell tried to dismiss Technicolor Dream as a nightmare. "The whole thing was rather like the last strug-gle of a doomed tribe trying to save itself from destruc-tion," Maxwell wrote. But music journalist Nick Jones disagreed: "Could this be explained by the fact that most people were not at the Dream to hear the music, but be-cause this was the first all-night rave in aid of Freedom? Didn't the majority of the audience go up there . . . be-cause they were being presented with not just an ordi-nary dance-rave, but also the chance to be part of something?" Rather than being the "the last struggle of a doomed tribe," Jones said that Technicolor Dream "was the beginning of a healthy young attitude towards total freedom for the individual."

# RAVING WITH ALIENS

Aliens and outer space are presently a recurring theme of rave parties that have attracted hundreds of thousands of young people who have danced through the night over the last fifteen or more years at unmarked warehouses and underground clubs in the United States, England, Germany, and other parts of the world. Images of extraterrestrial flying machines and planets are routinely used on provocative invitations to rave parties. An outdoor rave held in the woods on Long Island, New York, displayed alien banners and broadcast music from *Close Encounters of the Third Kind*. T-shirts sporting alien motifs are a growing fashion trend among ravers. When they're not dancing, many ravers discuss the latest reports of alien abductions.

Brian Behlendorf, a student of rave culture, said, "At a rave, the DJ is a shaman, a priest, a channeler of energy—they control the psychic voyages of the dancers through his choice in hard-to-find music and their skill in manipulating that music, sometimes working with just a set of beats and samples, into a tapestry of mind-bending music. A large part of raves is built upon sensory overload—a barrage of audio and often visual stimuli are brought together to elevate people into an altered state of psychical or psychological existence."

Rave music borrows from the music played by tribal cultures

Flying saucer imagery is extremely popular on posters promoting all-night rave parties that have proliferated in cities in the United States and Europe.

Stereotypical gray alien with huge wraparound eyes is featured on this futuristic invitation to an underground rave party held in 1995.

in Africa and the Amazon and the North American Indians. This music relies on continuous hypnotic drumming to achieve communion with universal forces.

"The music [at raves] has to take people to another place," states a rave manifesto posted on the Internet. "It has to lull the conscious mind while at the same time stimulating the subconscious as well as the body. Most, but not all, music played at raves is intended to lose yourself in. Techno played at raves is a faceless, nameless organism, free of the chains of pop-song structure and major-label hype. It may have a hook, but no chorus. It may have a voice, but no lyric. Time stops when the mind's clock of frequent distractions is disconnected by the surreal, hypnotic syncopated rhythms being woven around your head by the DJ on the decks. Time stops and The Vibe begins."

The rave scene is about culture as much as it is about music and dancing. "It's like someone created a sound track for the next millennium," observes one DJ who goes by the name Visitor. "Part of what attracts me to this whole scene is the facelessness of it. So much emphasis is being placed on pride of cultural heritage, and I think it's dividing us. The music is really beautiful and it transcends race, religion, and nationality and political correctness." Lonnie Fisher, a Baltimore, Maryland, DJ and rave promoter who uses the name Entity adds, "I see the scene as an important movement towards enlightenment."

Unlike rock clubs, which sometimes can last for years or even decades, rave venues are strictly temporary, often just a single one-night event. The venue can be a warehouse, dance club, or open field, any place that provides a good-sized floor for continuous dancing. Size of raves vary from city to city. Some can be as small as fifty people, while some in European cities routinely attract well over ten thousand people. The music moves fast, 115 to 300 beats per minute. DJs practice the art of spinning, using different pitches, different speeds, and an equalizer to create an ever-changing wall of sound.

There are both obvious parallels and important differences between the rock and hippie underground of the late sixties—as it developed in London's Technicolor Dream and the UFO Club—

and today's scene. A seasoned rave observer pointed out, "Many people attracted to raves spout philosophies that sound like they were plucked straight from the 1960s. They talk of harmony, unity, acceptance, and community. They speak of transformation and spirituality through dance. The core ravers will tell you this is their religion, their life." Something else both scenes share is a general acceptance of the existence of extraterrestrials and UFOs in our midst.

Outer space is a prevalent theme of rave culture. Ravers seek to escape their humdrum lives on Earth. They routinely trade information about alien abductions and discuss the latest news about ETs and Mars.

Spaceships and alien beings pop up all the time on rave flyers the same way that they appeared in psychedelic posters advertising concerts at London's UFO Club. They are the main deities in the rave universe. A card produced for a rave in Madison, Wisconsin, in 1995 shows three metallic saucers flying at great speed over a psychedelic rendering of a Southwestern desert landscape. A rave invitation for 1994's "muzik new york" goes to the heart of the UFO abduction phenomenon. It shows a classic alien sitting atop a flying saucer and a beam of light abducting a kid. The text reads, "ALL Natural—Where Society fades into a laughable memory . . . Shocking but true!!! You have to see it to believe it!!!" A 1991 rave invitation promoting 'nasa seltzer new york" is a fictional takeoff on a nonexistent supermarket tabloid called "NASA PUBLICATION UFO WEEKLY." It features a full-page photograph of the famous scene of robot Gort descending from a flying saucer in the science fiction film *The Day the Earth Stood Still.* The text states, "NASA CHILDREN, Science can't explain their existence! Where do they come from? What do they want? Inside exclusive answers." A weird alien monster with multiple tentacles frightens a scantily clad maiden in the invitation for 1992's "NASA's Midnight-

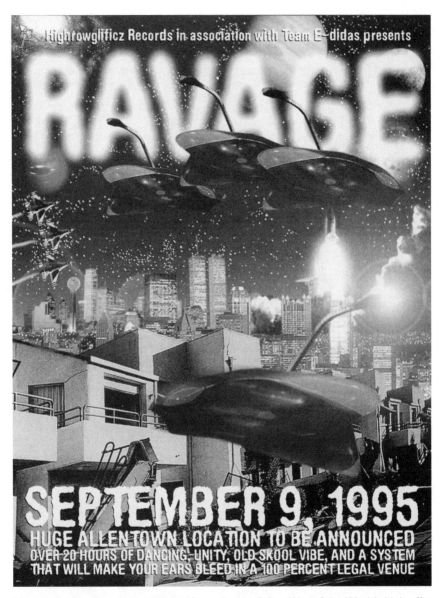

Marauding Martian war machines from the sci-fi film *War of the Worlds* kick off a twenty-hour rave megaparty called Ravage held at a secret location in Allentown, Pennsylvania. Promoters of rave events count on invitations like this plus word of mouth to attract thousands of young attendees.

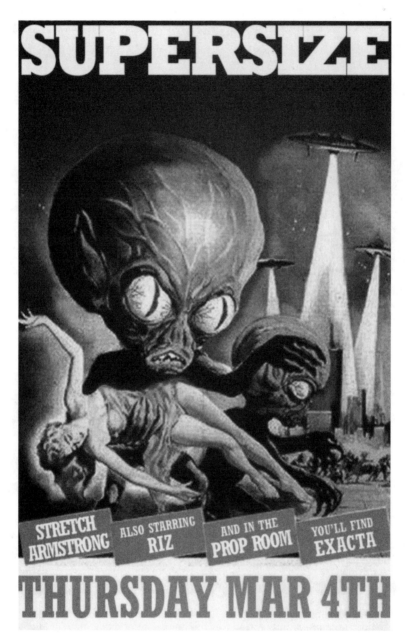

Giant, bug-eyed aliens from the film *Invasion of the Saucer Men* run amok in an invitation to a Supersize rave event held in 2004 at Crowbar in New York City.

Mask-A-Rave." The message reads, "We cannot change unless we survive—but we cannot survive unless we change." Rave invitations have been compared to a spreading communications virus. The Levi's jean company borrowed the concept of "viral communications" in an attempt to reach the hip youth market.

Unlike the previous counterculture, though, ravers believe that rock 'n' roll is the music of the past, much the same way rockers once felt about jazz or classical music.

Despite harassment from the police, the rave movement shows no sign of slowing down. A whopping twenty-two thousand people attended the Metropolis rave held at the Santa Clara Fairgrounds in California. The typical raver is between seventeen and twenty-five years old. Males usually wear baggy pants. Women typically have short hair or their hair in pigtails. Pacifiers, stuffed animals, and lollipops are common rave adornments.

The rave movement started in 1970 in Detroit and Chicago when deejays like Frankie Knuckles programmed drum rhythms and played disco records over the top of their beats. The first rave club, The Warehouse, opened in Chicago in 1977. This is where the term *house music* came from. From there the rave scene caught on big in England and took various forms in both the United States and England such as Techno, Trance, Jungle, and Drum-n-Bass. Since then rave has exploded internationally.

Since 1990, Stephanos Gouvianakis, better known as Sigmatron, has organized extraterrestrial rave parties in Greece, Holland, England, and other parts of Europe. "I like to organize most of my events in fields, warehouses, and factories," he said. Sigmatron takes empty spaces and transforms them into galaxies and planets, suspends alien bodies in giant glass tanks full of liquids, positions a mother ship on the ceiling with smaller scout ships nearby, and constructs tunnels with glow-in-the-dark aliens and spaceships big enough for guests to climb into. Sigmatron has seen UFOs several times in Glasgow, Scotland, and Athens, Greece, and has done research on paranormal phenomenon for fifteen years.

Not to be outdone, heavy metal rockers have quickly hopped aboard the extraterrestrial spaceship. The famous British group UFO, which adopted its name from London's UFO Club, is currently trying to stage a comeback. Heavy metal groups like Led Zeppelin, Megadeth, and Deep Purple have all plugged into the UFO mystique. Incubus is seeking to cash in on the UFO fad with a song having these lyrics: "I lay my head onto the sand . . . the sky resembles a backlit canopy, with holes punched in it, I'm counting UFOs, I signal them with my lighter, and in this moment I am happy . . . happy, I wish you were here."

Gamma Ray's 1998 album, *Somewhere Out in Space*, contained the tracks "Men, Martians and Machines," "The Guardians of Mankind," and "The Landing." An artist who goes by the name Ayreon has invented a style he calls space metal. His album, *Star One*, includes the cuts "Lift-Off," "Set Your Controls," "High Moon," "Intergalactic Space Crusader," and "Starchild."

Meanwhile, a progressive metal trio from Texas called Little Green Men entertained thousands of people at the Roswell Festival in New Mexico, honoring the aliens who fell to Earth over fifty years ago. The group consists of Andrew Williams on guitar; Steele Lane, lead vocals, bass, and keyboards; and Crit Fowler on drums. Their 1996 CD, *Encounters*, incorporates elements of early Rush, Van Halen, Metallica, and Iron Maiden.

Punk rockers have also managed to get in on the act. Frank Abel of Hide the Crown produced a double CD titled *Area 51* to coincide with Roswell's fiftieth anniversary. Over fifty punk rock groups can be heard on the *Project Dreamland* CD, including Earth Crisis, Fahrenheit 451, Celestial Season, By the Grace of God, Down But Not Out, and Warzone.

A flying saucer operated by a little green man swoops down to abduct a raver at an All Natural party held in November, 1994, which lasted twelve full hours. Ravers frequently share their views about UFOs and space aliens and the latest discoveries in the universe.

Among the pioneers of electronic space music are Tonto's Expanding Headband, Klaus Schulze, Jean Michel Jarre, and Tangerine Dream. Hawkwind, a British group, has been the leader of the space rock movement since the early 1970s. Hawkwind's albums include *Space Bandits, In Search of Space,* and *Space Ritual.* Hawkwind performed in 1997 at Strange Daze, America's first space rock festival held in Sherman, New York. They were joined by Quarkspace, Melting Euphoria, Alien Planetscapes, Nucleon, and Architectural Metaphor. The space rock genre keeps on growing. A split exists between space rock groups such as Hawkwind who look to the skies for some of their inspiration, and others who are content to thematically explore the inner reaches of the mind.

# 8

# THE MARTIAN MYSTERY TOUR AND THE DARK SIDE OF THE MOON

hirty years after the Grateful Dead fantasized about living in the Mars Hotel, rock 'n' roll has officially invaded Mars. The Beatles' songs "Good Morning, Good Morning" and "We Can Work It Out" were among scores of wake-up songs played by NASA officials to spur on exhausted engineers and scientists working on the Mars *Spirit* rover mission, which along with its twin, *Opportunity*, discovered extraordinary evidence of an ancient ocean bed on the Red Planet. The eclectic playlist, selected by *Spirit* mission manager Mark Adler, included "Satisfaction" and "Start Me Up" by the Rolling Stones, "Get Up, Stand Up" by Bob Marley, "I Get Around" by the Beach Boys, "Born to Be Wild" by Steppenwolf, "We Will Rock You" by Queen, "Livin' on a Prayer" by Bon Jovi, "Way Over Yonder" by Carole King, and "Working in a Coal Mine" by Devo.

The *Opportunity* rover's own playlist included "Happy Together" by the Turtles, "Stand" by R.E.M., "I'm Still Standing" by Elton John, "I'm Free" by The Who, "Wake Me Up" by Wham!, "Spinning Wheel" by Blood, Sweat and Tears, "I Am a Rock" by Simon and Garfunkel, "Riders on the Storm" by the Doors, "Rock Around the Clock" by Bill Haley and His Comets, and "Let It Be" by the Beatles.

European scientists had planned to herald the arrival of the *Beagle 2* lander on Mars with specially recorded music by the sensational British pop band Blur that was supposed to be transmitted as a call sign from Mars back to Earth, but the lander mysteriously disappeared on Christmas Day 2003. *Beagle 2* mission manager Dr. Mark Sims from the University of Leicester's Space Research Center said that the European Space Agency had photographed a small UFO moments after the *Beagle 2* made its descent. Baffled scientists were trying to analyze whether the object seen in the photograph was a feature of the optics of the camera or bits of spacecraft. "It could be nothing, but it could be everything," said Dr. Sims. "It's a case of wait and see." Ultimately a government panel sidestepped the UFO issue and blamed *Beagle 2*'s failure on a lack of sufficient funding. Of thirty-four unmanned missions to Mars since 1960, two-thirds have ended with the craft lost.

Vangelis (full name Vangelis Papathanassiou), the Greek musical genius who was a formidable space music pioneer, was chosen to write and perform "Mythodea," the heroic theme music for NASA's *Mass Odyssey* mission in 2001. A progressive-rock keyboard god in the 1970s, Vangelis worked with Jon Anderson and Yes. His career originally took off in the 1960s when he was a well-known pop star in Europe performing with Aphrodite's Child. Years later he composed the complete soundtracks for the hit films *Chariots of Fire* and *Blade Runner*. In 2001 Vangelis pulled out all of the stops for an unprecedented PBS special space spectacular that was set amid the ruins of the Temple of Zeus in Athens. Picture twenty-four timpani drummers, a hundred-voice choir, a seventy-piece orchestra, and a projection screen nearly one thousand feet long and five stories high, and you'll get an idea of the grand scale Vangelis relishes. "I don't try to describe space," said Vangelis. "I'm just working with space. If you describe space, then it's a different thing. It's like science fiction, but space itself is enough to impress us."

# MARS AND MUSIC

Wind Crest Productions, a company in St. Paul, Minnesota, deserves credit for producing "Winds of Mars," a musical journey that fuses wind data from Mars from NASA's *Mars Pathfinder*, which landed on the Red Planet on July 4, 1997, with the music of Johann Sebastian Bach, performed on a single piano. "Winds of Mars" is a welcome opportunity for music lovers to explore another planet with their ears. In the spring of 2002, a group of scientists who have nicknamed themselves The Extremophiles and work in the Mars Desert Research Station—a simulated Mars base in Utah—conducted a unique experiment to test how music could play a role in entertaining crew members on a future Mars mission. Among the instruments they played were guitars, percussion, harmonica, and piano. Getting way ahead of the game, the Australian rock electronica group B(if)tek has produced a song titled "2020" that Kate Crawford and Nicole Skeltys conceived to be the soundtrack for the first manned mission to Mars. Crawford and Skeltys have asked NASA to play their music during astronaut training and on the Mars flight itself. No word yet from NASA if they're considering the offer.

Today the mere mention of the planet Mars is a surefire way to command public attention, and nobody knows that better than Shannon and Jared Leto, who formed the progressive metal rock group 30 Seconds to Mars. Jared was struck by the image summoned up by David Bowie's song "Life on Mars," but added his own twist. The lyrics have a distinct otherworldly sensibility. The band calls their fans Mars Army. And aided by the Internet, the army appears to be acquiring more troops all the time.

Other postpunk bands such as the heavily hyped The Mars Volta and The Men From Mars, a lesser-known trio

ALIEN ROCK

that hails from Milwaukee, Wisconsin, have sought to capitalize on the Martian mystique simply by invoking the name Mars. The Mars Volta's shock-provoking album, *Deloused in the Crematorium,* was produced by Rick Rubin from Slayer and has bass instrumentation by Flea of the Red Hot Chili Peppers.

Veteran rocker Sammy Hagar fell head over heels into the Martian spirit with his prophetic anthem "Marching to Mars," with the optimistic lyrics, "Everybody's marching to Mars, / Gonna settle down there, / Get me a house and a car."

Wild man Alice Cooper belted out the musical lament "Might as Well Be on Mars," singing, "You've turned my world into a dark and lonely place, / Like a planet lost in space, . . . I might as well be on Mars." A group called Monster Magnet penned the punk song "King of Mars."

Deep Purple set the tone for space exploration early on with their seminal hit "Space Truckin'." Deep Purple crooned, "We had a lot of luck on Venus, / We always had a ball on Mars, / . . . We're space truckin' round the stars." Recently reunited, Deep Purple's new album, *Bananas,* contains a poignant instrumental tribute to the space shuttle *Columbia*'s astronauts titled "Contact Lost." NASA astronaut Kalpana Chawla was a big fan of Deep Purple and took along three of their CDs on the ill-fated mission. She even exchanged emails during the tragic flight with members of the band. Deep Purple guitarist Steve Morse said that he has donated his "Contact Lost" songwriting royalties to the hero astronauts' families.

Some years ago Roger McGuinn of the legendary sixties group The Byrds recorded a compilation album, *Live from Mars,* featuring lively folk renditions of "Mr. Tambourine Man," "Hey Mr. Spaceman," "Eight Miles High," "King of the Road," and "Heartbreak Hotel." Nils Lofgren performed "Trip to Mars," Laura Nyro and Television both had tunes simply named "Mars," and Matthew Sweet served up *Blue Sky on Mars.* Hundred Million

Martians, a Scandinavian rock 'n' roll band, has issued CDs titled *Martian Arts* and *Mars Bars*. Mars Electric has also plugged into the Mars fever with a new album titled *Beautiful Something*.

The beloved Flaming Lips star in a new movie, *Christmas on Mars*. Wayne Coyne, the Lips' lead singer, plays a Martian Santa Claus. Set deep in the future, *Christmas on Mars* is the story of the first human birth on Mars, which occurs at the stroke of midnight on Christmas Eve. The outrageous film will be shown in concert venues, not traditional movie theaters. Snow machines will be used to enhance the overall viewing experience. The Lips' repertory includes "Take Me Ta Mars."

Elaine Walker, a member of the Space Frontier Foundation, has earned herself a permanent spot in the Mars musical vanguard. A percentage of the proceeds from her CD *Mars* will be donated to the NASA/SETI Haughton Mars Project, studying the Martian-type terrain on Devon Island in the Canadian Arctic. Elaine, who once was a member of the group Zia, performs such songs as "Red Dreams," "Devon Island," "Martian Nation," and "Humans and Martian Machines." She made a pop music video on Devon Island to help promote to young audiences the idea of humans traveling to Mars. A second album by Walker, titled *Frontier Creatures*, contains an instrumental tune for "The Tenth Planet." She also manages to keep ahead of the space curve with a brilliantly titled instrumental album supplying "space elevator music."

Mark Dwane's New Age electronic keyboard masterpiece, *The Monuments of Mars*, is a heartfelt musical tribute to discoveries by independent researchers and scientists of humanlike faces, pyramids, and other artificial structures on the Red Planet. Zeroing in on the Cydonia region of Mars, where all the action is (the Sphinx-like face and the giant D&M Pyramid are located in Cydonia), Richard Hoagland, author of *The Monuments of Mars*, said in the liner notes "The intimation of looking down on something that had once had people on

New humanlike face on Mars announced by the author of this book is a real head turner. Researchers are divided whether the person seen in the official NASA photograph snapped in Syrtis Major is a man or a woman, but most agree it is the most stunning evidence to date of a past intelligent civilization on the Red Planet.

it, had been the center for commerce, art, communication, all things that people do in pursuing their own lives, was overwhelming. I could trace the broken edges of the pyramids, feel as though I was floating down half-mile-wide avenues which once might have bustled with activity. . . . I was gazing at the remains of something

269

Roger McGuinn, formerly of The Byrds, issued his CD *Live From Mars* as a belated follow-up to his hit 1960s novelty song, "Hey Mr. Spaceman."

that had once been grand and beautiful, whose grandeur, across countless millennia and the vast emptiness between worlds, still clung to the crumbling shapes casting their long shadows out across the sands of this strange world." Dwane has dedicated other instrumental masterpieces to the Nefilm, the biblical name for the people who came down in prehistory to Earth from Planet X and may have created humans in a test tube; and his "Paradigm Shift" symbolizes the coming massive changes in world consciousness.

"The Pioneers of Mars" is among a galaxy of space songs on the cutting-edge album *To Touch the Stars—a Musical Celebration of Space Exploration*, produced in association with the Mars Society and the National Space Society. The concept album has won the endorsement of NASA astronaut Buzz Aldrin, the second man to walk on the Moon. Aldrin said, "As someone who has actually set foot on the threshold of space and experienced firsthand its majesty, I am thrilled at this new collection of original songs celebrating the beginnings of our great endeavor to reach for the stars." Aldrin was particularly moved by a song titled "Fire in the Sky," written in honor of the astronauts who lost their lives in the space shuttle *Columbia* when it broke up over Texas in February 2003. He was overcome with emotion when he heard the line "As they passed to us in glory, riding fire in the sky." Mars advocate Robert Zubrin said, "If we are to win the hearts and souls of humanity to the vision of a space-faring future, the space exploration movement must also develop its songs."

New York City rock musician and visual artist Emil Sotnyk views Mars in an entirely different light. His band follows in the footsteps of Jim Morrison and the Doors. "For years researchers have been trying desperately to unlock the secret of this mysterious planet by searching for artifacts at ground level," said Emil, who is now convinced that some of the biggest secrets of Mars can only be found by examining the entire planet from a distance—much like the Nazca lines of Peru.

Emil has discovered strikingly colossal terra art forms on Mars that are often the size of continents, such as a Martian lion and a couple locked in a passionate embrace and a kiss that he has dubbed A Starry Martian Night. Emil believes that the images may have been used as navigational icons by an ancient Martian civilization. His study has included official NASA photographs

Electronic musician Mark Dwane dedicated an entire CD, *The Monuments of Mars,* to the planet. Many of the monuments are located in Mars's Cydonia region, including a Sphinx-like face, a giant five-sided pyramid, and other unusual surface features that do not appear to be natural.

taken by *Mariner 4* in 1965, the *Viking* orbital mission of 1976, and the current *Mars Global Surveyor.*

The Orb's record *Cydonia* is an electronic ode to the Cydonia region of Mars, the epicenter for the discovery of artifacts most likely constructed by Martians millions of years ago. Upon close-up examination, scientists have determined that various structures located in Cydonia, including the famous Sphinx-like face, the D&M Pyramid, a fortresslike structure, and other intriguing shapes, appear not to have been put there randomly, but rather seem to be part of a complex urban geometric plan.

The Martian pyramids, which resemble the treasured pyramids of Egypt, moved New York's Aloid and the Interplanetary Invasion to record their enchanting song, "Pyramids on Mars." The latest mind-boggling discoveries about Cydonia, made by Tom Van Flandern, a former chief astronomer for the United States Naval Observatory in Washington, D.C., are signs of huge glasslike tubes, also located elsewhere on Mars. The tubes run in and out of the surface of the entire planet and may have been used for underground transportation or water. The tubes have equally spaced ribbing and measure about sixty feet in diameter and up to thousands of feet long. Ironically, there are also "spiders," as in Ziggy Stardust and the Spiders from Mars. These spider shapes seem to be composed of vegetation that has sprouted on what was long thought to be the cold, desolate planet described by Elton John on his best-selling song, "Rocket Man." After examining pictures from NASA's *Mars Observer*, Arthur C. Clarke made the astounding statement that giant banyan trees also appear to be growing on Mars.

New revelations of evidence of methane gas on Mars by scientists at both the European Space Agency and NASA indicate that the Red Planet is likely teeming with everyday life. The presence of methane—a waste product of living organisms on Earth—has long been considered by scientists to be Mars's Holy Grail. Vittorio Formisano of the Institute for Physics and Interplanetary Science in Rome called the presence of methane "significant." Michael Mumma of NASA's Goddard Space Flight Center in Maryland said that the apparent detection of newly produced methane pointed to biological origins of the gas. No formal announcements about methane have yet been made to the public.

The rapidly accelerating search for signs of both past and current life on Mars received a huge boost as the result of announcements by both European and American scientists that at least part of Mars was drenched in water and covered by a saltwater ocean. Water is a key prerequisite for life.

The question of Martian biology was first addressed by NASA in an earthshaking announcement in 1997 that a Martian meteorite known as ALH-84001, which was found in Antarctica, probably contained the remains of fossilized life. Since then NASA has spoken in terms of "life on Mars," but not a word has ever been spoken about even the remote possibility that extraterrestrials may be operating today in the vicinity of Mars—that is not until March 11, 2004, when NASA officially announced that the *Spirit* rover had caught a picture of an unidentified flying object streaking across the Martian sky.

In the unprecedented statement, Dr. Mark Lemmon, a rover team member from Texas A&M University, asked, "Is this the first image of a meteor on Mars or an image of a spacecraft sent from another world at the dawn of our robotic space exploration program? We may never know, but we are still looking for clues." NASA posted the statement on its official website under the headline "Is It a Bird, Is It a Plane . . . ?" Later the Jet Propulsion Laboratory claimed at a press briefing that the UFO was actually the out-of-commission *Viking 2* probe. But that didn't put an end to the Mars UFO controversy, not by a long shot.

Mars is the fourth planet from the Sun and the second-closest planet (after Venus) to Earth. Its name derives from the Roman god of war. About half the size of Earth, Mars is marked by polar ice caps, atmospheric clouds, canyons, ancient waterways, mountains—including Olympus Mons, the largest mountain in the solar system—deserts, and craters. It has two moons, Phobos and Deimos. A Martian year has 687 days, the time required for it to complete a full orbit

The Grateful Dead were way ahead of their time with their *Grateful Dead from the Mars Hotel* album, released thirty years ago. A manned mission to Mars is on NASA's drawing boards, and terraforming could make it possible to establish human colonies on the Red Planet.

around the Sun. The discovery of life in a Martian meteorite sent shock waves around the world in 1997. NASA scientists revealed that a piece of Martian rock that had been hurled into space by a meteor impact and wound up in Antarctica exhibited evidence of early life in the form of fossilized nannobacteria.

Mars apparently served as a way station for the gods of Planet X on their way to Earth in ancient times, according to scholar Zecharia Sitchin. Sitchin said, "In their descriptions of our

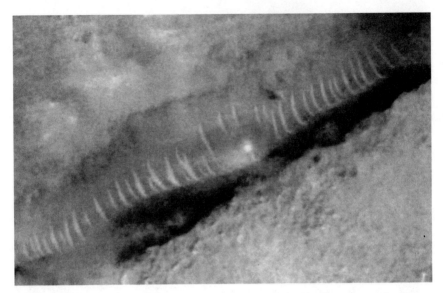

Strange ribbed, transparent tunnels measuring sixty feet in diameter and with exposed sections thousands of feet long dart in and out of the Martian surface. Some scientists believe that these tunnels were artificially constructed and may have been used for transportation or water. Note the round object.

planetary system, in their discussion of travel between Nibiru [Planet X]—the planet of the Anunnaki—the Sumerians said that there was a change of course as their spacecraft neared Mars. Mars is referred to as the way station and the Sumerians even have a route map in the British Museum that shows how there is a turn made at Mars to pass between Mars and Jupiter; so all of this led me to the conclusion that the Anunnaki had a space base on Mars."

Rock 'n' roll had not yet been invented way back in 1938 when Orson Welles panicked many with his all-too-realistic radio version of H. G. Wells's *The War of the Worlds*, which terrorized more than a million people and had them believing that Martians had invaded Earth. An updated rock 'n' roll version of *The War of the Worlds* broadcast by WKBW radio in Buffalo, New York, on October 31, 1968, drove four thousand people nearly mad. They frantically called Buffalo police stations and media outlets to find out if the Martian attack was real. The station deliberately used real DJs such as Sandy Beach, who spun records like Cream's "White Room" and the Beatles' "Hey Jude," interrupting the songs with periodic news updates about an unfolding Martian invasion. The broadcast seemed so real that the Canadian National Guard sent units to the Peace Bridge, Rainbow Bridge, and Queenston Bridge to repel alien invaders, a county civil defense unit went on alert, and a local newspaper sent a team of reporters and photographers to Grand Island to cover the alleged Martian landing.

An even more frightening version of *The War of the Worlds* was staged by Jeff Wayne as a rock opera in London in 1978. Justin Hayward of the Moody Blues, Phil Lynott of Thin Lizzy, and David Essex performed songs, and Richard Burton provided the narration. The music was written by Wayne along with Gary Osborne. A double album released by Wayne has sold a whopping 6 million copies to date. Hawkwind performed outdoors at a Jeff Wayne "War of the Worlds" concert held in Manchester, England, in 2002, featuring a sixty-foot-tall Martian war machine marauding across the stage. Martian mania had scaled new heights.

# DARK SIDE OF THE MOON

Ever since songwriting began, hundreds of songs have been composed about the Moon, which is Earth's closest celestial neighbor. At times the Moon can come to within 218,000 miles of Earth, a mere blip on the cosmic radar screen. The Moon is less than one-

A classic flying disc appears in this still frame from film footage shot by Apollo 16 astronauts on a journey to the Moon. The Moon has always been a favorite subject for songwriters. Pink Floyd's "Dark Side of the Moon" is the most popular lunar song of all time.

third the diameter of the Earth and 2,160 miles across. A full orbit around the Earth takes 27.3 days to complete, but because the Moon also rotates on its axis in the same amount of days, it always keeps the same face toward Earth.

Pink Floyd's album *Dark Side of the Moon*, released in 1973, contained the climax cut "Eclipse," which is symbolically based on the image of a small, dead, barren Moon blocking out the huge life-force of the Sun. The juxtaposed twin images are used to portray good and evil, success and failure, and sanity and insanity. The album immediately struck a nerve with the public. To date nearly 30 million copies of *Dark Side of the Moon* have been sold worldwide, and it is estimated that one in every fourteen people in America under the age of fifty owns a copy.

Something about the Moon is both romantic and haunting. In 1983, British rock musician Brian Eno released the instrumental album *Atmospheres and Soundtracks*, which was entirely devoted to the U.S. Moon landing. David Bowie introduced us to "Moonage Daydream." Michael Jackson's *Bad* album carried the song "Moonwalker." Van Morrison sang "Moondance," Ozzy Osborne performed "Bark at the Moon," Duran Duran recorded "New Moon on Monday," Carlos Santana performed "Moonflower," the Police gave us "Walking on the Moon," R.E.M. presented "Man on the Moon," Creedence Clearwater Revival warned us in "Bad Moon Rising," Jim Morrison and the Doors took fans on a "Moonlight Drive," Emerson, Lake, and Palmer unveiled a "Black Moon," and the Grateful Dead scaled "Mountains on the Moon." That unforgettable chestnut "Blue Moon," was turned into a runaway rock hit by the Marcels in the 1950s.

The Byrds, on their 1969 album, *Ballad of Easy Rider*, sang this hymn to the Apollo 11 astronauts, the first humans ever to set foot on the Moon: "Armstrong, Aldrin and Collins, / Were launched away in space, / Millions of hearts were lifted, / Proud of the human race . . ." Not to be outdone, the Leningrad Cowboys, who hail from Russia, released their song "Where's the Moon?" on their *Go Space* album in 1996. The lyrics go, "Where's the moon now, / We're lost in space, / Where's the moon now, / We've been lost for days, / We're on a trip around the sun, / With vodka, tractors and rock 'n' roll."

David Bowie said that the recent scientific discovery of water on the Moon was a sure sign of extraterrestrial life. "Rather than life on Mars, I think water on the back of the Moon is more interesting. I think that was an extraordinary finding. Water on the dark side of the Moon, that's really scary. 'Cause you know that contains life without a doubt. If there's water on it, my God! Don't bring it back here! That's what I say."

Bijou Phillips, the daughter of Michelle Phillips of the sixties group the Mamas and the Papas, is convinced that extraterrestrials have set up housekeeping on the dark side of the Moon. She believes, "We are already in touch with aliens. They are already here. . . . And they're just watching us. I've seen spaceships. It was unbelievable." Bijou may not be that far off the mark. UFOs have been photographed near the Moon, and NASA's *Clementine* probe, sent up to map the entire lunar surface, disappeared without warning. Moreover, NASA photographs captured images of pyramids, monoliths, and other strange structures on the Moon that appear to many experts to be artificial.

Officially astronauts have been instructed to remain quiet about UFOs. NASA's code word for UFOs is *bogey*, and certainly plenty of bogeys have been reported by astronauts from the space shuttle and the International Space Station. Engineers for the space agency coined the phrase *moon pigeons* to describe "unexpected objects seen in operational photography that defy positive identification." *Santa Claus* was the code word used by astronauts during the Apollo 11 mission to indicate that they had unexpected company. A 16mm film taken during the 1972 Apollo 16 mission clearly shows a metallic, disc-shaped object right above the corner of the Moon. Operating Apollo 16 were crew members John Young, Thomas Mattingly, and Charles Duke. While backstage at television's *Geraldo* show, this writer handed Apollo 14 astronaut Edgar Mitchell a copy of an official NASA photograph filmed by Apollo 16 of a cigar-shaped object above the craters of the Moon. He examined it and exclaimed, "I don't know *what* that is!"

A large, semitranslucent, cylindrical-shaped object was photographed by NASA astronauts on the Apollo 16 mission to the Moon. The object casts a shadow on the lunar surface, indicating that it is solid. Giant craters can be seen below.

The full history of lunar anomalies goes back to at least the invention of the telescope and the rise of modern astronomy some four centuries ago. A report issued by NASA in the 1960s, during the hectic days of the Apollo program, listed a staggering 579 observations of unexplainable lights and other phenomena in or around the moon logged by astronomers between 1540 and 1967. These are officially labeled Lunar Transient Phenomena or LTP.

# THE MUSIC OF THE SPHERES

Undeniably, space is the place to find music as well as UFOs and extraterrestrials. Just ask astronaut Dr. Story Musgrave, who retired from NASA in 1997 after a thirty-year career that included salvaging the Hubble Space Telescope in 1993. Dr. Musgrave said that he heard "noble, magnificent music" in space on his last flight in 1996 at the age of sixty-one, but he didn't know where the stirring music came from. His crewmates didn't hear a single note. "I wasn't hearing things," insisted Dr. Musgrave, whose claims freaked out NASA. "I was a little on the margin . . . I was walking on the edge," he said. Dr. Musgrave said that he regretted that the U.S. government is no longer funding any search for extraterrestrial life. "Any form of contact or the detection of any signal . . . would be the most momentous thing that could happen to us," he said.

Perhaps the music Dr. Musgrave heard in space was connected in some way to the Music of the Spheres, the natural harmonies produced by each of the planets in Earth's solar system. Johannes Kepler, the great Bavarian astronomer, published his landmark book, *Hamonices Mundi* (Harmonies of the World), in 1619. Kepler said, "The heavenly motions are nothing but a continuous song for several voices, to be perceived by the intellect, not by the ear; a music which through discordant tensions, through syncopations and cadenzas as it were, progresses toward certain predesigned six-voice cadences, and thereby sets landmarks in the immeasurable flow of time."

The Greek philosopher and mathematician Pythagoras speculated that as planets move through space, the distances between them—like the divisions of strings of a lyre—produce spatial harmonies. Pythagoras realized that each planet had its own distinct tone. By applying Johannes Kepler's theories to modern computer technology, two Yale University professors, geologist John Rodgers and music professor Willie Ruff, produced forty minutes of ce- · lestial music on a stereo LP titled *The Harmony of the Worlds.*

Dr. Fiorella Terenzi, an astrophysicist trained at the University of Milan in Italy, who was once described by comedian Dennis Miller as "a cross between Carl Sagan and Madonna," won critical acclaim in 1991 when she issued *Music from the Galaxies,* an album that translated radio-telescope data into musical compositions. Dr. Terenzi invented "acoustic astronomy" at the Computer Audio Research Laboratory at the University of California in San Diego. She tuned in to radio emissions from a galaxy in Coma Berenices, between Virgo and Leo—180 million light-years away—and then set them to music, thrilling fans the world over.

"I realized that radio waves coming from a celestial object were very similar to musical notes," said Fiorella. "Both have an intensity that gives you loud or soft sound. They also both have a frequency that give you high or low pitch." She performed her music live at the Greenpeace Music Nature Festival in Milan with Paul Winter and at Montreux. "I performed the galaxy using a synthesizer, a sampler, and an oscilloscope to show the wave form of the vibrations. . . . On the second part I had a musician playing shells, stones, coconuts, and flute. I associated the galaxy with primitive instruments because the sounds are one hundred and eighty million years old. And then I got to the future. The galaxy was performed with harp, bass, saxophone, drummer, congas, and piano—with everyone following the score."

Dr. Terenzi collaborated with Thomas Dolby by supplying vocals on Dolby's 1994 *Billboard* Top 20 Music Video, "The Gate to the Mind's Eye." In 1997 she worked with Timothy Leary on a musical tract titled "Star Light." Fiorella studied opera and composition at the Conservatory G. Verdi in Italy and in 1998 joined jazz great Ornette Coleman on his European tour. She has also appeared with Herbie Hancock.

Fiorella would be excited to learn that an international team of cosmologists has begun to hear the "music of creation" in its discovery of acoustic "notes" in the sound waves that rippled through the universe split seconds after the Big Bang. "The early universe is full of sound waves compressing and rarefying matter and light, much like sound waves compress and rarefy air inside a flute or trumpet," said Paola deBernardis, the Italian team leader for a group of cosmologists belonging to the BOOMERANG (Balloon Observation Millimetric Extragalactic Radiation and Geophysics) experiment.

U.S. team leader Andrew Lange of the California Institute of Technology in Pasadena, California, said, to use a musical analogy, "Last year we could tell [by examining the data] what note we were seeing was C-sharp or F-flat. Now, we see not just one, but three of these peaks, and can tell not only which note is being played but also what instrument is playing it; we can begin to detail the music of creation." BOOMERANG is an extremely sensitive microwave telescope suspended from a balloon that circumnavigated the Antarctic in late 1998. The balloon carried a telescope at an altitude of 120,000 feet. Thirty-six team members came from sixteen universities and organizations in Canada, Italy, Britain, and the United States.

Don Gurnett, a physicist at the University of Iowa, has devoted over forty years to collecting sounds in space by using scientific instruments from NASA's *Voyager*, *Galileo*, *Cassini*, and more than two dozen other spacecraft. Dr. Gurnett has taken plasma waves, converted them to sound, and has put together a ten-movement musical composition called *Sun Rings*. The Grammy-nominated

Kronos Quartet premiered *Rings* at the University of Iowa's Hancher Auditorium in October 2002. Willie Williams, who has created multimedia shows for Rolling Stones concerts, was brought in to supply the visuals. Some of the images came from the twin *Voyager* spacecraft flybys to the outer planets, including a video clip of Jupiter rotating. One of the most remarkable sounds Dr. Gurnett has detected is lightning on Jupiter in the form of radio waves.

William Kurth, a physics professor who has worked closely with Gurnett, said that solar winds appear to oscillate like the guitar strings played by rock stars. "If you think about what happens when you pluck a guitar string," he said, "you don't really hear the strings vibrating. What you actually hear are sound waves that propagate through the air to your ear. It's more or less the same in this boundary area known as the inner heliospheric shock. The electron plasmas oscillations are the vibrating strings, and the radio waves we detect are the sound waves."

Surprisingly, the lowest note in the universe appears to come out of the mouth of a black hole. Dr. Andrew Fabian, an X-ray astronomer at the Institute for Astronomy at Cambridge University in England, said that the black hole is singing "notes" in B-flat—a B-flat fifty-seven octaves lower than middle C. Moreover, the black hole that was studied may have been singing for more than 2 billion years. Dr. Bruce Margon, an astronomer at the Hubble Space Telescope Institute, said, "It's the longest-lasting symphony we know of." An international team of scientists used NASA's Chandra X-Ray Observatory to detect the black hole's notes as ripples of luminosity in the X-ray glow of the Perseus cluster of galaxies, 250 million light-years away.

The universe is a never-ending symphony of sound. Rock 'n' roll music is part of that symphony. A group of NASA astronauts has already formed a rock group, called Q Max, which so far has only performed on the ground. A rock concert on the Moon or Mars with superstars from Earth may sound like a dream, but it's destined to take place in the near future as mankind charts an accelerated course to the cosmos. The musical adventure in space is just beginning.

# 9

# UFOS OVER WOODSTOCK, ALTAMONT, AND THE ISLE OF WIGHT

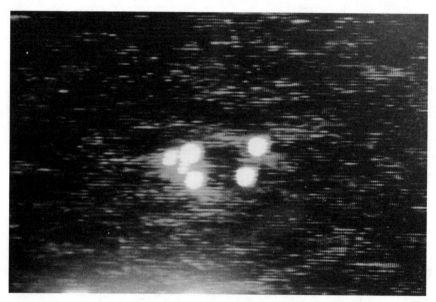

A strange aerial object equipped with lights is captured on video in Pine Bush, New York, the Grand Central Station for UFO activity on the East Coast. Nearby Bethel, NY, where the Woodstock Festival was held as well as surrounding areas have long been a magnet for exotic spacecraft that appear to defy the normal laws of physics. Rock concerts at Altamont, the Isle of Wight, and Hawaii have been marked by UFO visitations.

"Rock 'n' roll and UFOs" is the mantra of the new millennium. The Signal to Space, one of the largest concert tours in history, which will beam a live musical message of peace to the solar system from three different continents, is planned to take place in 2006. The hope is that extraterrestrials will send a signal back—the first huge step in joining the civilizations. Flying saucers from other worlds dropped in unexpectedly at the original Woodstock Festival in New York; at the Jimi Hendrix Rainbow Bridge concert in Hawaii; at the Rolling Stones' infamous concert at California's Altamont Speedway; at a Michael Jackson concert in London's Wembley Stadium; at the Isle of Wight Festival in England; and at rock and pop concerts held in Japan, Russia, and Switzerland.

Folksinger Richie Havens, the symbol of the Woodstock Festival, reported UFOs flying overhead during three days of peace, love, and music on Max Yasgur's farm in Bethel, New York, the weekend of August 15, 16, and 17, 1969. Havens said that they appeared like stars in the night sky, but moved around silently and swiftly. Many members of the Woodstock Generation camped out under the stars and witnessed brightly lit objects dancing in the sky.

Richie was not at all alarmed about seeing flying saucers over Woodstock. He had long been a UFO advocate and a firm believer in the paranormal, and upstate New York was a virtual beehive of UFO activity. "People came to Woodstock because they had to be there," explained Richie. "It was like *Close Encounters of the Third Kind,* know what I'm saying? It was their constituency and they were going to be there. They had been called a counterculture long enough; now they were going to show how much of a counterculture there really was."

In the film *Close Encounters,* actor Richard Dreyfuss plays a character who is compulsively drawn to Devils Tower in Wyoming, where the government has secretly constructed a high-tech landing strip to accommodate the landing of a giant mother ship and serve as a meeting place for representatives of human and galactic civilizations. Music is the medium of communication. Giant speakers broadcast musical tones directed at the mother ship. Instantly the mother ship repeats and amplifies the tones. Contact has begun.

On a trip to Israel, where he performed his final concert of the tour in Jerusalem, Havens spotted the mountain that King Herod used as a summer palace when Jesus was alive. "Herod's mountain happened to be shaped almost exactly like Devils Tower," said Richie. "Here I had been thinking and talking about this remarkable movie that had not yet come to Israel, and suddenly I was in the middle of the desert, looking right at a mirror image of the land site that was nearly a living character in the film. . . . It dawned on me that if visitors from another planet were ever going to land anywhere on this planet to make contact, it would of course be right here in the Holy Land, where it all started."

The story of how Richie came to play a pivotal role at the Woodstock Festival is a cornerstone of rock 'n' roll history. The Greenwich Village folksinger was scheduled to play fifth on the bill, but the show was late in opening. Producer Michael Lang wanted to get it under way due to heavy rains. He needed an acoustic act and Richie filled the bill. The problem was that the other acts weren't ready. Richie was forced to sing nonstop for two hours and forty-five minutes in what proved to be one of the festival's

Folksinger Richie Havens, the symbol of the original Woodstock Festival, kept his eyes on the sky during three days of peace, love, and music in upstate New York. Richie's persistence paid off. He spotted UFOs dancing among the stars. UFOs have dropped in unexpectedly at some major rock concerts, to the delight of the fans.

highlights. "Each time I didn't know what I was going to sing; I started tuning my guitar, stalling, trying to come up with something, and eventually, 'Freedom' just came out," said Richie. "It was just one of those magical moments." Among the star-studded lineup for the Woodstock Festival were Sly and the Family Stone; the Jefferson Airplane; The Who; Blood, Sweat and Tears; Crosby, Stills and Nash; and Jimi Hendrix.

In a surprise appearance at the first ever UFO Festival at the Village Gate in New York City, Havens made it clear that he took

UFOs seriously and was opposed to any attempt by the powers-that-be to maintain a cover-up. The festival had something for everyone: lectures; films; a concert; a groundbreaking UFO play by Dr. Jean Mundy, a psychotherapist and professor emeritus of psychology at Long Island University; and an unprecedented exhibition of UFO paintings and alien sculptures, many based on real-life experiences. Dr. Mundy's play, *Believe Me!*, dealt with a family's stunned reaction to their son's close encounter. "I want the audience to realize that it's not only okay to acknowledge UFO sightings, but essential to your mental health and the health of our society," said Dr. Mundy.

New York psychic and performance artist Joan Carra wowed the UFO Festival with her satirical song about comedian Jackie Gleason and the dead space aliens. Gleason's first wife, Beverly McClintick, claimed that President Richard Nixon, a close friend of Jackie's, took him to Homestead Air Force Base in Florida and showed him the bodies of extraterrestrials. New York radio legend Art Ford has confirmed that Jackie was a UFO believer and kept an impressive library of books on the subject in the basement of his home in Peekskill, New York. The house, which Jackie fondly called the Mothership, looked like a flying saucer, and the first thing that struck visitors was that all of the rooms were round, too. The garage was also round. Jackie called it the Scout Ship. Gleason did see UFOs in Palm Beach, Florida, but the story of President Nixon and the alien bodies has never been confirmed.

Craig Silver, the Space Troubadour, performed the UFO Festival's theme song, "UFOs Are Here to Stay," before television cameras outside the Village Gate. Silver's first release was titled, "Greetings from Saucer City." Silver's songs include "We Are Not Alone," written after the earthshaking discovery of signs of life in a Martian meteorite; "I Saw Elvis in a Flying Saucer"; "I Wanna Be an Alien from Outer

Space"; and a Bob Dylan send-up called "Everyone Must Get Cloned." *Billboard* magazine has likened Silver's music to that of the great folk artist Phil Ochs. The singer is a direct descendent of Guillame IX of France, known as the First Troubadour. Among Silver's critically acclaimed CDs are *Infinity River* and *Planet Dancer.*

Chic UFO fashions by designer Andre Van Pier capped the alien celebration. Models clad in silver clothing sported giant mothership hats three and a half feet in diameter that were adorned with blinking lights. Van Pier's imposing space robot greeted UFO Festival visitors. The futuristic couture was filmed for Carl Sagan's program, *Space,* on the Sci Fi Channel and also shared the spotlight at the Roswell Festival East held on the fiftieth anniversary of the Roswell incident at the Hudson Grill in New York City. Among the rock stars who have worn Van Pier's creations are Mick Jagger, Madonna, David Bowie, John Lennon, and Sting.

The 1969 Rolling Stones concert at Altamont Speedway in California will long live in rock 'n' roll infamy for the violence produced by the Hells Angels, who were mistakenly put in charge of security. The concert cost a young black man his life. Two people died while sleeping when they got run over in their sleeping bags. One person drowned. But amid all the chaos and Mick Jagger pleading from the stage for everyone to cool it, was the UFO that showed up and was captured on film by the Maysles brothers in the film documentary *Gimme Shelter.* All of a sudden hundreds of heads in the crowd turned away from the stage to get a look at a mysterious object maneuvering overhead. To this day no one has furnished a satisfactory explanation of what the object was and from where it came.

The Altamont concert was the last stop on the Stones' triumphant tour of America. Sharing the bill were the Grateful Dead, Santana, Jefferson Airplane, and the Flying Burrito Brothers. Admission was free. The concert was originally planned to take place in San Francisco, but the show was abruptly moved to the Altamont Speedway twenty hours before the event once it was realized that too many people were going to show up. The arrival of a UFO at the raceway offered a temporary diversion from myriad problems that were unfolding at ground level.

An exotic jellyfish-shaped UFO made an unscheduled appearance at a Michael Jackson concert at Wembley Stadium in England on July 31, 1992. John L. Clarke, a retired flying officer and police officer confirmed that he spoke to witnesses in the crowd who saw the luminous UFO, which eventually drifted out of sight. Clarke said that a number of startled spectators turned their back on the stage and stared up into the sky to see the object, which was hovering above the stadium roof. Security men and other police officers also viewed the flying jellyfish. UFOs are reported in all colors, sizes, and shapes, but a jellyfish-shaped UFO is practically unheard of. Author and researcher Trevor James Constable claimed that some UFOs are living beings themselves. This jellyfish-shaped UFO may well be one such example.

England's Isle of Wight Festival, where Jimi Hendrix made his last appearance, in 1970, was rife with speculation that aliens were going to land right in the middle of the concert. Tina Curran, a former girlfriend of musician Robert Fripp, attended the Isle of Wight concert. She said that the crowd's excitement mounted when clouds above the concert site started to take on a luminous glow and changed colors exactly as they had done in the Steven Spielberg movie *Close Encounters of the Third Kind.* A landing seemed imminent when all of a sudden other lights were seen piercing the night fog and approaching the stage. These lights turned out to be from a helicopter that was carrying the fourteen-year-old Guru Maharaji to the festival. The riddle of the strange luminous clouds has never been solved.

Singer David Johansen, formerly of the New York Dolls,

said that fifty thousand Japanese fans nearly went ballistic when three pearl-colored flying saucers appeared over an outdoor concert arena where he was performing his final number. David said the crowd shouted, "Take us away! Take us away!" and ran for the exits after them. The UFOs hovered over a hill in the distance and then disappeared. "If a UFO is going to land, it'll probably happen in Japan," quipped Johansen. "If the aliens need a small part or something, they can get it there."

A small UFO managed to steal the show from Maja Dschawa, a well-known pop singer from Georgia, the then Soviet republic, in 1989. A videotape taken by Beso Ormoschadse for Georgian TV shows Maja, an attractive young brunette, slowly descending a staircase from an old palace into a garden in Tbilisi, the capital of Georgia, performing a romantic tune. Then the camera captures something unusual: the large crowd suddenly turns away from the stage and points toward the sky. A small, whitish object, somewhat oval in shape, can be seen crossing some electrical cables. Even the star stops singing for a moment to try to figure out what on Earth is happening. The UFO approaches a church tower, only to bounce back to the electrical power cables. That the UFO can be seen behind the cables indicates it is a real physical object in the sky and not a camera effect. This UFO sighting coincided with a huge Soviet UFO wave marked by the daytime landing of a strange spacecraft at a park in the Russian city of Voronezh. Tass, the official Soviet news agency, reported that a group of schoolchildren witnessed a tall alien and a robot disembark from the craft and walk around the park before returning to the ship and disappearing. The story made front-page news not only in the USSR, but in the Western media as well.

The future of rock festivals could well be thematically linked to extraterrestrials. Space is poised to become music's next brave new frontier. Appearing at the Woodstock 1994 Festival in Saugerties, New York, Perry Farrell, former lead singer of Jane's Addiction and Porno for Pyros, talked enthusiastically about his fascination with crop circles. The cofounder of the Lollapalooza franchise, Perry announced plans in 1996 for the ENIT Festival, originally conceived as an ambitious fourteen-city concert tour that offered experimental music, tree planting, sharing food, and contact with extraterrestrials. The size of the tour had to be scaled way back due to astronomical costs, but ENIT went ahead anyway, breaking new ground in the extraterrestrial entertainment arena.

"Alternative is dead," said Adam Schneider, manager of Porno for Pyros. "The [ENIT] concert supposedly is based on a rare text about interaction with aliens, *UFO Contact from Itibi-RA: The Cancer Planet Mission* by [German author] Ludwig Pallmann. The book says that an intergalactic ENIT festival takes place on every planet except Earth. Perry thought it would be nice if Earth took part in this intergalactic festival. ENIT is about everyone having a communal experience." Pallmann's philosophy is that by understanding our evolutionary destiny it will be possible to "stop this race of hatred and turn it to love." Among the performers on Farrell's bill for the ENIT Festival were Orb, Black Grape, Meat Beat Manifesto, Lady Miss Kier, Pharcyde, the Sun Ra Arkestra, the Flying Nutrinos, and the Rebirth Blues Band. Deejays spun house and ambient music between sets. "I haven't personally seen them [flying saucers and aliens], but I believe in them," said Farrell in an online interview.

Writer Ken Kesey and the Merry Pranksters frolicked at the ENIT concert held on November 22, 1997, at Bill Graham's Civic Auditorium in San Francisco in a special fourth-floor room set aside for the occasion. Psychedelic art created a Day-Glo paradise, including orange and green, melting Salvador Dalí clocks. Upstairs also were the

Jam Room, the Beach Room, and the Genie Room. A black-and-silver flyer described ENIT as "an interplanetary festival celebrating cosmic peace and sexuality." Farrell entered the hall wearing a dress with peacock feathers in his hair. Giant tropical flowers, parasols, and topless erotic dancers adorned the stage.

John Brower, a scrappy Canadian promoter, attempted to stage a giant outdoor UFO concert for the Alien Nation in July 1997 tied in with the fiftieth anniversary of the Roswell, New Mexico, UFO crash. Sheryl Crow and the Foo Fighters were to be the headline acts. Sadly the event fizzled and Brower became persona non grata. Town officials felt that he had oversold the event. Pepsi-Cola, the main sponsor, withdrew its support in the wake of the tragic deaths of members of the Heaven's Gate UFO cult. Brower decided nonetheless to set up a tent city on Herb Corn's fifteen-thousand-acre sheep and cattle ranch twenty miles north of Roswell, where a flying saucer supposedly came down carrying four alien pilots, and to charge $90 per pair of campers, but only five people took him up on his offer, and by the next afternoon only a single tent remained. Brower's plans took another hit when Corn decided not to allow an all-night rave dance party on his property. Corn said that he was concerned about the safety of the partygoers and wanted to prevent damage to the land.

By then Corn's farm had taken on the appearance of some sort of out-of-this-world religious shrine. Sandstone pillars resembling Stonehenge were donated anonymously and erected near the crash site. Seven meditation seats were installed to complete the alien memorial. A single stone was inscribed with these cryptic words: "We don't know who they were. We don't know why they came. We only know that they changed our view of the universe." There were no shortage of tourists willing to take a three-mile ride to see what could be the most important site in human history. Hundreds of people lined up for the tour and gladly paid $15 a head for the privilege.

Moby successfully produced the Area2 Festival that made a stop at the Jones Beach Theater in Wantagh, New York, on August 2, 2002. Asked what the Area2 Festival was all about, Moby said, "Space aliens. Bowie, Busta, Blue Man Group, myself, we're all space aliens." "General Bowie!" shouted Busta Rhymes upon seeing him onstage. Bowie introduced Busta to his supermodel wife, Iman, who said she was a huge fan. "My favorite moment," said Moby, "is when Bowie walks out and does 'Life on Mars'—just him and his piano." Blue Man Group, three blue-faced actors with bald heads who have starred off Broadway in their own show and appeared in television commercials, did a set with four drummers and a five-piece band playing homemade space-age instruments. A giant dance tent was packed wall-to-wall with Area2 concertgoers.

But there was more to come. . . .

# Epilogue

## THE SIGNAL TO SPACE CONCERTS

he cosmic curtain is soon set to rise on three Signal to Space superconcerts that are planned to begin during the summer of 2006 in Berlin, New York, and Tokyo. The history-making concert tour is a celebration of the future of all mankind and is based on this author's concept of beaming live music into space to make peaceful contact with an extraterrestrial civilization. The concerts will star a galaxy of Earth's leading rock, pop, and rap superstars whose names will soon be announced and will be televised around the world to tens of millions of viewers. Frank Yandolino, who has produced major music festivals in the United States, and Peter Saile, an entertainment entrepreneur who is based in Miami, Florida, are the concert's coproducers along with the author.

Sophisticated satellite technology and state-of-the-art lasers will be employed to send a signal to Mars and other planets in the solar system and beyond in the hope of getting a signal back. A return signal would have a profound effect on the human race, uniting us as a species and letting us know once and for all that we are not alone in the universe. Beaming a musical message to Mars will only take about ten minutes, and another ten minutes to get any response. Reaching the Moon with a musical message will take less than one and a quarter seconds and the same amount of time to receive a return signal. This contrasts greatly with the SETI program, which listens for incoming signals that take hundreds of years to reach Earth. While broadcast signals from television and radio filter into space, they are widely scattered random noise, not live music focused on specific targets.

Much more than an outdoor concert, Signal to Space will be a full-blown music and cultural festival representing the diversity of the entire planet. There will be music from independent groups from all three continents where Signal to Space will touch down, plus extraterrestrial exhibitions and displays focusing on the future of Earth from the very latest scientific and technological breakthroughs to alternative energy, health, and the environment. The centerpiece of Signal to Space will be a stirring "We Are the World"–type theme song performed by concert headliners. The audience will be invited to sing along with the song's lyrics, projected on giant screens throughout the concert site, and will hold up special flashlights to signal their desire to achieve contact.

Powerful pulsed lasers will sweep the sky throughout the concert to attract possible space visitors. Dr. Richard Haines, a former NASA research scientist, has reported in his book *CE-5: Close Encounters of the Fifth Kind* an astounding five thousand cases where signaling—the deliberate use of lasers and even flashlights directed toward UFOs—has resulted in apparent intelligent responses. Scientists at Harvard University, Princeton University, and the University of California are now developing Optical SETI, in which specially equipped ground-based telescopes look for laser signals that may be hitting Earth from advanced alien civilizations.

Psychic communication with ETs will be stimulated at the three Signal to Space concerts by harnessing an extraordinary brain-wave device invented by Japanese-American designer Masahiro Kahata that enhances psychic energy. The brain-wave device, which is similar to biofeedback equipment currently used by astronauts aboard NASA space shuttle missions, will actually be hooked up to some of the show's headliners onstage while they are performing. The brain-wave patterns will be beamed to outer space and simultaneously projected onto giant screens and connected to laser equipment that will produce spectacular lighting displays overhead.

The most dramatic point in the show will be when the audience observes a moment of silence and awaits a possible signal from outer space monitored by scientists. A Signal to Space blimp will fly above the crowd, supplying live shots of the entire area, and television cameras will be strategically placed to film any unexplained lights or aerial objects that may show up during the event.

Among special effects is a complete solar system consisting of individual planets suspended high above the concert stage, a time tunnel, animatronic robots, and a landing pad for any alien spacecraft that choose to join the celebration. Crop circles will be projected on to the landing pad to welcome extraterrestrials to Earth. The landing pad will be lined with beacon lights, and the area will be cordoned off with extra security.

Astronomers currently believe that there could well be 30 billion Earth-like worlds in the Milky Way alone and have pinpointed one hundred planets outside our solar system where there could be life. Using 4 million computers worldwide, scientists at the University of California at Berkeley recently identified 150 sources of possible intelligent civilizations. "Perhaps the notion that 'there's something out there' is closer to reality than we have imagined," said President George W. Bush in his 2004 budget.

Some astronomers calculate that the numbers are much higher. A new scientific study by Dr. Charles Lineweaver and Daniel Grether at the University of New South Wales and published in the *Astrophysical Journal* estimated that there are probably 10 *trillion* planetary systems—100 *billion* in our galaxy alone!

The number of celebrities, statesmen, and scientists

who believe in ETs is constantly expanding. Among the show business personalities who have experienced close encounters with extraterrestrial spacecraft are Academy Award winner Anthony Hopkins, *Star Trek*'s William Shatner, and veteran television news anchorman Walter Cronkite. Filmmaker Steven Spielberg donated $100,000 to support the Search for Extraterrestrial Intelligence Project (SETI). Best-selling author Anne Rice and television talk show host Rosie O'Donnell both believe that alien abductions really happen. Former world heavyweight champion Muhammad Ali has reported at least twenty-two UFO sightings, including one in New York City's Central Park witnessed by his trainer and a newspaper reporter when he was in training for a fight.

Two former U.S. presidents, Ronald Reagan and Jimmy Carter, sighted UFOs when each was governor of his respective state and vigorously spoke out in public on the issue. In 1974, Reagan ordered the pilot of his private campaign plane to chase a UFO. Reagan said, "I was in a plane last week when I looked out the window and saw this white light. It was zigzagging around. I went up to the pilot and said, 'Have you seen anything like that before?' He was shocked and said, 'Nope.' And I said to him, 'Let's follow it!' We followed it for several minutes. It was a bright white light. We followed it to Bakersfield [California] and all of a sudden to our utter amazement, it went straight up into the heavens. When we got off the plane, I told Nancy [Reagan's wife] about it." The Reagans later went to the library and found references to UFOs in ancient Egyptian hieroglyphics.

As reported in an earlier chapter, former president Bill Clinton attached a high priority to learning the truth about extraterrestrial life-forms. Other world leaders who have embraced the UFO theme are the late United Nations secretary-general U Thant, former Japanese prime minister Toshiki Kaifu, and Prince Philip of Great

Britain. U Thant believed that UFOs were the most important issue facing the world after the Vietnam War. Kaifu thought that "from the point of view of 'people' in outer space, all human beings on Earth are the same people, regardless of whether they're American, Russian, or whoever." Prince Philip pointed out that "there is so much evidence from reliable witnesses" that UFOs exist.

Monsignor Corado Balducci, a Vatican theologian insider close to the late pope John Paul II, proclaimed that UFOs are a phenomenon that "cannot be doubted." Monsignor Balducci announced that the Vatican has received a substantial amount of information about extraterrestrials and their contact with humans from its embassies in Mexico, Chile, Venezuela, and other countries. The late German professor Hermann Oberth, the father of rocketry, said, "It is my conclusion that UFOs do exist, are very real, and are spaceships from another or more than one solar system. They are probably manned by intelligent observers who are members of a race carrying out long-range scientific investigations of our Earth for centuries."

Musical communication with aliens represents totally unchartered territory for scientists. UFO-themed rock concerts notwithstanding, scientists don't really know exactly what type of sounds will bring extraterrestrials down here for a visit. A single chord based on universally shared mathematics might do it, or maybe a more elaborate musical composition is needed. But judging from UFOs that have been observed at quite a few major concerts, good old hard-driving rock 'n' roll might well do the trick.

Flying aboard NASA's *Voyager 1* and *Voyager 2* spacecraft are two identical gold records that are carrying Earth sounds into space. The twelve-inch, gold-plated copper discs contain greetings in 55 languages and samples of music from different cultures, including American rock 'n' roll. They also contain electronic information that an advanced technological civilization could convert into diagrams and photographs.

Gold disc containing earth's greatest hits was launched by NASA in 1977 on the *Voyager 1* and *2* missions to Jupiter, Saturn, and beyond. Rock music is playing an ever greater role in America's space exploration efforts.

The so-called *Earth's Greatest Hits* album contains a wide range of music from Beethoven to Chuck Berry. A standing joke in NASA and SETI circles is that the extraterrestrials will land and demand "send more Chuck Berry." Berry himself entertained a thousand people in 1987 who had gathered on the mall at the Jet Propulsion Laboratory in Pasadena, California, to celebrate the tenth anniversary of the launching of the *Voyager* spacecraft. Beethoven would likely have rolled over and smiled.

Sending an interstellar musical record barreling into the

Mixlife presents

# MISSION 2 MARS 2
## JUNE 5TH 2004

*<Start Transmission>* Date: 06/05/04.....Location: Sector 1 of M2M2.....Location Confirmed.....*<Over>* Fully Secured & Permitted....100% Dj Confirmation....2 Rooms.... Lots of visu.....*<Transmission Lost>*

Mars will be one of the principal targets of the Signal to Space Concert, which will beam live music to the Red Planet in the hope of making contact with any extraterrestrials in the immediate neighborhood. Possible current life on Mars includes bacteria, giant banyan trees, and perhaps small aquatic and animal life. Mars once supported an intelligent civilization.

cosmos was the brainchild of Dr. Carl Sagan, the late Cornell University astronomer who was best known for speaking on the *Tonight Show* about "billions and billions" of galaxies existing beyond Earth. Sagan designed the famous *Pioneer 10* and *11* plaque showing a naked human couple and the relative position of the Earth in the solar system.

Previous messages from Earth, including the *Pioneer* plaque and radio messages beamed from the Arecibo Radio Observatory in Puerto Rico, "had contained information about what we perceive and how we think," said Sagan. "But there is much more to human beings than perceiving and thinking. We are feeling creatures. . . . Music, it seemed to me, was at least a creditable attempt to convey human emotions." Sagan wanted to include the

Beatles' song, "Here Comes the Sun" on the "Earth's Greatest Hits" album. John, Paul, George, and Ringo all agreed, but the Beatles didn't own the copyright to the song and the legal status of the piece seemed in doubt. Chuck Berry's "Johnny B. Goode" was chosen instead to represent rock 'n' roll.

The Jet Propulsion Laboratory reported that Sagan and his associates assembled 115 pictures portraying the diversity of life and culture on Earth, and a variety of natural sounds such as those made by the surf, wind, thunder, birds, whales, and other animals. To this they added musical selection from different cultures and eras, and spoken greetings from Earth—people in fifty-five languages, and printed messages from then President Jimmy Carter and then United Nations Secretary General Kurt Waldheim. Among the music is Mexican mariachi, Senegalese percussion, Javanese gamelan, Pygmy girls' initiation song, Georgian chorus, Bulgarian shepherdess's song, Indian raga, Navajo night chant, and Peruvian and Melanesian panpipes. A special piece was titled "Music of the Spheres" in honor of Johannes Kepler's landmark literarary masterpiece, *Harmonices Mundi*.

The "Earth's Greatest Hits" record is encased in a protective aluminum jacket, together with a cartridge and needle. Instructions, in symbolic language, explain the origin of the spacecraft and indicate how the record is to be played. The 115 images are encoded in analog form. The remainder of the record is in audio, designed to be played at 16-$\frac{2}{3}$ revolutions per minute. It contains the spoken greetings, beginning with Sumerian, which was spoken in Sumer about six thousand years ago, and ending with Wu, a modern Chinese dialect. The record's first greeting is "May all be well." That greeting might just be the right calling card for the human race if scholar Zecharia Sitchin is correct that the extraterrestrials mentioned in the Bible and ancient Sumerican texts created civilization on Earth.

Following the section of the sounds of Earth, there is an eclectic 90-minute selection of music, including both Eastern and Western classics, and a variety of ethnic music. "The space-craft will be encountered and the record played only if there are advanced spacefaring civilizations in interstellar space," said Sagan. "But the launching of this bottle into the cosmic ocean says something very hopeful about life on this planet."

The record consists of two one-sided copper mothers each 0.02 inches thick, bound back-to-back. Instructions on how to play the record are permanently etched on the record cover. "In the upper-left-hand corner is an easily recognized drawing of the phonograph record and the stylus carried with it," said Sagan. "The stylus is in the correct position to play the record from the beginning."

On February 14, 1976, a radio telescope system known as Cyclops, based in Arizona, picked up a complex blend of fluc-tuating tones with a rhythmic structure that included many sounds beyond the threshold of human hearing. The signal came from the star Ophiuchi, some seventeen light-years away from Earth. Dr. John Oliver, the project director of Cy-clops, said that the signal couldn't be translated into anything even vaguely resembling human speech.

Hermann Bernard, a musicology professor at the Massa-chusetts Institute of Technology, had the signal translated into musical notation. The "notes," said Bernard, "looked more like an expressionistic drawing than a piece of music. At times over five hundred notes are sounded simultane-ously, and the range of pitch seems infinite." Were aliens trying to make contact with Earth by broadcasting some form of complicated music? And were the UFOs that stole the show at some major rock 'n' pop concerts also looking to make contact with humans? Music is the message. The

Janus, England's electronic musical wizard, produced an entire record dedicated to the Search for Extraterrestrial Intelligence or SETI Project. Huge radio telescopes search the skies for intelligent signals from outer space. The same satellite dishes can be used to beam messages to distant extraterrestrial civilizations.

best advice is to keep watching the skies, especially around rock concerts. A return signal is all the proof that is needed to permanently lift the spirits of the human race. Earth would never be the same again.

Now for a quick look back in musical history. A song called "It Was a Little Man, a Very Little Man," performed in 1955 at the San Remo Song Festival—one of Europe's largest pop music festivals—set a wonderfully positive tone for human-alien contact envi-

West Coast surf guitarist Merrell Fankhauser sends a rock 'n' roll greeting to the universe in a concert that was broadcast live on hundreds of radio stations in the United States.

sioned by extraterrestrial concerts. The song, which followed hot on the heels of a flying saucer wave that hit Italy, France, and Spain in 1954, was about the landing of a spacecraft piloted by a group of little Martians who bring a message of peace and love. The lyrics described a disc that flies and turns fast as a thunderbolt and a humanoid who is sensible, clean, and tender. The humanoid is depicted on a San Remo Song Festival poster with an insignia

on his chest showing a kind of dove of peace. He is holding a flower in his right hand and extending an olive
branch with his left hand. It is the same type of
"starpeace" that Yoko Ono envisioned when she created her
*Starpeace* album—a bright omen for the future of humanity. Never could our planet use outside help more than
now.

# BIBLIOGRAPHY

# BOOKS

Andersen, Christopher. *Jagger—Unauthorized.* Delacorte Press, 1993.

——. *Michael Jackson—Unauthorized.* Simon & Schuster, 1994.

Beckley, Timothy Green. *UFOs Among the Stars—Close Encounters of the Famous.* Global Communications, 1992.

Bennahum, David. *The Beatles . . . After the Break-up—in Their Own Words.* Omnibus Press, 1991.

Berliner, Don, with Marie Galbraith and Antonio Huneeus. *UFO Briefing Document—the Best Available Evidence.* Dell, 2000.

Bernardin, Claude, and Tom Stanton. *Rocket Man—Elton John From A–Z.* Praeger, 1996.

Bishop, Nick. *Freak!—Inside the Twisted World of Michael Jackson.* American Media Inc., 2003.

Black, Johnny, *Jimi Hendrix—the Ultimate Experience.* Thunder's Mouth Press, 1999.

Blinderman, Barry, ed. *The UFO Show.* University Galleries, 2000.

Bowie, Angela, with Patrick Carr. *Backstage Passes—Life on the Wild Side with David Bowie.* G. P. Putnam's Sons, 1993.

Brown, Tony. *Jimi Hendrix "Talking."* Omnibus Press, 1994.

Buckley, David. *Strange Fascination—David Bowie: The Definitive Story.* Virgin Books, 1999.

Buhlman, William. *Adventures Beyond the Body—How to Experience Out-of-Body Travel.* Harper San Francisco, 1996.

Childs, Marti Smiley, and Jeff March. *Echoes of the Sixties.* Billboard Books, 1999.

Dalton, David. *The Rolling Stones—the First Twenty Years.* Alfred A. Knopf, 1981.

Dannemann, Monika. *The Inner World of Jimi Hendrix.* St. Martin's Press, 1995.

Doss, Erika. *Elvis Culture—Fans, Faith, & Image.* University Press of Kansas, 1990.

Flippo, Chet. *Graceland—the Living Legacy of Elvis Presley.* Collins Publishers San Francisco, 1993.

Giuliano, Geoffrey and Brenda. *The Lost Beatles Interviews.* Plume, 1996.

——. *The Lost Lennon Interviews.* Adams Media Corporation, 1996.

Giuliano, Geoffrey, and Vrnda Devi. *Glass Onion—the Beatles in Their Own Words.* Da Capo Press, 1999.

Goldman, Albert. *Elvis.* McGraw-Hill, 1981.

——. *The Lives of John Lennon.* A Capella Books, 2001.

Green, John. *Dakota Days.* St. Martin's Press, 1985.

Harry, Debbie, Chris Stein, and Victor Bockris. *Making Tracks—the Rise of Blondie.* Da Capo Press, 1998.

Hatay, Nona. *Jimi Hendrix: Reflections and Visions.* Pomegranate Artbooks, 1995.

Havens, Richie, with Steve Davidowitz. *They Can't Hide Us Anymore.* Spike/Avon Books, 1999.

Hayes, L. Christine, with contributions by Wanda June Hill. *Magii From the Blue Star—the Spiritual Drama and Mystic Heritage of Elvis Aaron Presley.* Johannine Grove, 1995.

Henke, James, and Parke Puterbaugh, eds. *Higher—the Psychedelic Era, 1965-1969.* The Rock and Roll Hall of Fame and Museum, 1997.

Heylin, Clinton. *Bob Dylan Behind the Shades—a Biography.* Summit Books, 1991.

Hinds, Mary Hancock. *Infinite Elvis—an Annotated Bibliography.* A Capella Books, 2001.

Holzer, Hans. *Elvis Speaks From the Beyond—and Other Celebrity Ghost Stories.* Gramercy Books, 1999.

Hough, Peter, and Jenny Randles. *Looking for the Aliens—a Psychological, Scientific and Imaginative Investigation.* Blanford, 1991.

Jackson, Michael. *Moon Walk.* Doubleday, 1988.

Jones, Cliff. *Another Brick in the Wall—the Stories Behind Every Pink Floyd Song.* Carlton Books, 1996.

Jordan, Joel T., Summer Forest Hoeckel, and Jason A. Jordan. *Searching for the Perfect Beat—Flyer Designs of the American Rave Scene.* Watson-Guptill Publications, 2000.

Knight, Curtis. *Jimi Hendrix: Starchild.* Abelard, 1992.

Leng, Simon. *Soul Sacrifice—the Santana Story.* Firefly Publishing, 2000.

Levin, Laura Victoria, and John O'Hara. *Elvis & You.* Perigee, 2000.

Mandelker, Scott, Ph.D. *From Elsewhere—Being E.T. in America.* Birch Lane Press, 1995.

Mannion, Michael. *Project Mindshift—the Re-education of the American Public Concerning Extraterrestrial Life, 1947–Present.* M. Evans & Co., 1998.

Marcus, Greil. *Dead Elvis—a Chronicle of a Cultural Obsession.* Doubleday, 1991.

Marsh, Dave, ed. *For the Record—George Clinton and P-Funk—an Oral History.* Avon Books, 1998.

McCall, Tara. *This Is Not a Rave—in the Shadow of a Subculture.* Thunder's Mouth Press, 2001.

McDermott, John, with Eddie Kramer. *Hendrix—Setting the Record Straight.* Warner Books, 1992.

Mist, Cherokee (compiled by Bill Nitopi). *Jimi Hendrix—the Lost Writings.* Harper Collins, 1993.

Moody, Raymond A. *Elvis After Life.* Peachtree Publishers, 1987.

Moyer, Susan M. *Elvis—the King Remembered.* SP, L.L.C., 2002.

Norman, Philip. *Elton—the Definitive Biography.* Arrow Books, 1991.

Noyer, Paul Du. *John Lennon—Whatever Gets You Through the Night—the Stories Behind Every John Lennon Song, 1970-1980.* Thunder's Mouth Press, 1999.

Obstfeld, Raymond, and Patricia Fitzgerald. *Jaberrock—the Ultimate Book of Rock 'n' Roll Quotations.* Owl Books, 1997.

Owen, Ted, and Denise Dickson. *High Art—a History of the Psychedelic Poster.* Sanctuary Publishing, Ltd., 1999.

Pang, May, and Henry Edwards. *Loving John.* Warner Books, 1983.

Parker, Ed. *Elvis: The Secret Files.* Anaya, 1993.

Paytress, Mark. *The Rise and Fall of Ziggy Stardust and the Spiders from Mars—David Bowie.* Schirmer Books, 1998.

Paytress, Mark, and Steve Pafford. *Bowie Style.* Omnibus Press, 2000.

Pegg, Nicholas. *The Complete David Bowie.* Reynolds & Hearn, 2000.

Presley, Reg. *Wild Things—They Don't Tell Us.* Metro Publishing, 2002.

Rodman, Gilbert B. *Elvis after Elvis—the Posthumous Career of a Living Legend.* Routledge, 1996.

Sagan, Carl. *Murmurs of Earth—the Voyager Interstellar Record.* Random House, 1978.

Sandford, Christopher. *Bowie—Loving the Alien.* Da Capo Press, 1998.

Schaffner, Nicholas. *Saucerful of Secrets—the Pink Floyd Odyssey.* Delta, 1991.

Sereda, David, forward by Dan Aykroyd. *Evidence—the Case for NASA UFOs.* Terra Entertainment, 2002.

Shadwick, Keith. *Jimi Hendrix: Musician.* Backbeat Books, 2003.

Shapiro, Marc. *Carlos Santana—Back on Top.* St. Martin's Press, 2000.

Sitchin, Zecharia. *The Earth Chronicles* series. 10 vols. Bear & Co., 1991-2004.

Solt, Andrew, and Sam Egan. *Imagine John Lennon*. Penguin Studio, 1998.

Stanley, David E., with Frank Coffey. *The Elvis Encyclopedia*. JG Press, 2002.

Stearn, Jess, with Larry Geller. *Elvis' Search for God*. Greenleaf Publications, 1998.

Steiger, Brad, and Sherry Hansen-Steiger. *Hollywood and the Supernatural*. St. Martin's Press, 1990.

Stern, Jane and Michael. *Elvis World*. Alfred A. Knopf, 1987.

Strassman, Rick, M.D. *DMT—the Spirit Molecule—a Doctor's Revolutionary Research into the Biology of Near-Death and Mystical Experiences*. Park Street Press, 2001.

Strausbaugh, John. *E—Reflections on the Birth of the Elvis Faith*. Blast Books, 1995.

Taraborrelli, J. Randy. *Michael Jackson—The Magic and the Madness*. Birch Lane Press, 1991.

Thompson, Dave. *David Bowie—Moonage Daydream*. Plexus, 1987.

Thompson, Elizabeth, and David Gutman, eds. *The Bowie Companion*. Da Capo Press, 1996.

Troy, Sandy. *Captain Trips—A Biography of Jerry Garcia*. Thunder's Mouth Press, 1994.

Weir, Wendy. *In the Spirit—Conversations with the Spirit of Jerry Garcia*. Harmony Books, 1999.

Welch, Chris. *David Bowie We Could Be Heroes—the Stories Behind Every David Bowie Song*. Thunder's Mouth Press, 1999.

West, Red and Sonny, and Dave Hebler, with Steve Dunleavy. *Elvis: What Happened?* Ballantine, 1977.

Woolbridge, Max. *Rock 'n' Roll London*. St. Martin's Griffin, 2002.

Yancey, Becky, and Cliff Linedecker. *My Life With Elvis*. St. Martin's Press, 1977.

# Articles

Black, Johnny. "We Have Lift Off!" (UFO Club). *Mojo* (London), February 2004.

"Bowie, T-Rex, Queen and the Glory Years of Glam Rock, 1970-75." *Uncut* 1, no. 15 (March 2004).

Brunell, Doug. "UFO Rock 'n' Rollers." *UFO* magazine 18, no. 3 (June/July 2003).

Clerk, Carol. "Dark Side of the Moon—Pink Floyd." *Uncut,* June 2003.

Du Noyer, Paul. "David Bowie Special." *Mojo* 104 (July 2003).

Fenwick, Lawrence J., Henry Tokarz, and Joseph Muskat. "Canadian Rock Band Abducted?" *Flying Saucer Review* (London) 29, no. 3 (March 1984).

Friedman, Andrew. "Contact! UFOs, Aliens & L.I." (Maria Cuccia). *Long Island Voice,* September 11-17, 1997.

"George Harrison Special Commemorative Section," *Daily News* (New York), December 1, 2001.

*The Guide* (London). Interview with Bill Wyman of the Rolling Stones. June 3-9, 2000.

Keller, Martin. "Space Is the Place—Rockers Look to the Skies in Search of UFOs." *Rolling Stone,* May 16, 1996.

*Mojo* Special Limited Edition, "Bowie—Loving the Alien." November 2003.

Rabinovitch, Simona. "Jamiroquai's Two Sides." *Remix* 3, no. 11 (November 2001).

Rayl, A. J. S. "UFO Update" (Phoebe Snow). *Omni,* August 1986.

*Relix.* Interview with Jerry Garcia. August 1995.

Roberts, Andy. "An Acid Test for ESP" (Grateful Dead). *Fortean Times* (London) 186 (February 2004).

*Rolling Stone.* Interview with Carlos Santana. Summer 1999.

Seaman, Fred. "Why John Lennon Believed in UFOs." *National Enquirer* (November 5, 1991).

*Sun Ra Research* 33 (April 2001) and 38 (1999). Millbrae, CA: Omni Press.

Sutton, David. "King of Kings—the Cult of Elvis." *Fortean Times* 166 (February 2003).

"Swinging London." *Uncut* 1, no. 11 (2003).

Willsher, Pete. "Moody Blues UFO Encounter in 1967." *Flying Saucer Review* (London) 36, no. 2 (Summer 1991).

# WEBSITES

The following Internet sites are just the tip of the iceberg of what is available on the subjects covered in this book:

GLOBE IN TRANSIT.
"Alien Life-Forms Influence Rock Music and Popular Culture."
www.xdream.freeserve.co.uk.

ELVIS
krystos@spiritheart.org
www.elvislightedcandle.org
www.spiritheart.org
Maia Nartoomid, Spirit Heart Sanctuary
P.O.Box 1357, Kapaa, HI 96746

DAVID BOWIE:
"Uncut Interviews Tony Visconti on Berlin."
www.bowiewonderworld.com.

"The Ziggy Stardust Companion."
www.5years.com.

FS ANCIENT MYSTERIES NEWS:

"'Wild (Reg) Thing' Presley's Book."
www.100megsfree4.com/farshores/amreg.htm.

THE RAVE SCENE:

"Techno Music and Raves FAQ."
www.hyperreal.org/~mike/pub/altraveFAQ.html#definition.

"The History of Rave Music."
www.planetpapers.com?Assets/2484.php.

"Rave New World."
www.hartfordadvocate.com/articles/raves.html.

THE GRATEFUL DEAD:

*The Bam Review.* "The Grateful Dead in Egypt."
www.users.senet.com.au/~tortoise/egyptbam1.htm.
Extraterrestrial Musical Forces: Many quotes in this section have been taken from *Playboy, Circus, Hit Parader, Reader's Digest, Rolling Stone,* and *Down Beat* magazines, as cited in this religious website:

# BIBLIOGRAPHY

Way of Life Literature. "Rock Musicians as Mediums."
www.wayoflifeorg/fbns/rock-musiciansmediums.html.

MUSIC IN SPACE:

www.hobbyspace.com.

www.space.com.

"SF-References in Music List."
www.faqs.org/faqs/music/sci-fi-refs/.

# PHOTO CREDITS

# INDEX

# ABOUT THE AUTHOR

MICHAEL C. LUCKMAN, author of *Alien Rock: The Rock 'n' Roll Extraterrestrial Connection,* is director of the New York Center for Extraterrestrial Research and founder of The Cosmic Majority, an organization that seeks to advance the views of the majority of people living on planet Earth who believe in UFOs, life on Mars and other planets throughout the universe, the paranormal, the New Age, and the sanctity of the environment.

Luckman taught the nation's first college-level course on rock music and the youth culture at New York's School for Social Research in 1971. Among his guests were producer Sid Bernstein, the man who brought the Beatles to America; singer-songwriter Johnny ("Secret Agent Man") Rivers; legendary program director Scott Muni of WNEW-FM and later Q104.3; and 1960s protest leader Abbie Hoffman, Chicago Seven defendant and founder of the Yippies. Hundreds of colleges and universities the world over have since added rock music to their curricula.

Luckman's freewheeling *Underground Tonight Show* live on cable television in New York City paved the way for television programs like *Saturday Night Live.* His guests included the Beatles' first manager, Allan Williams; and singers Tiny Tim, Phil Ochs, Patti Smith, and Screamin' Jay Hawkins.

Luckman produced several major UFO events in New York City featuring rock and folk musicians including Richie Havens, and is the visionary behind the Signal to Space Concert, a historic event that will beam live rock and pop music to Mars, the Moon, and other locations in this solar system and beyond.

In his role with New York Center for Extraterrestrial Research, Luckman recently announced the discovery of two new human-like faces on Mars photographed by NASA's *Global Surveyor,* was the first investigator to expose television's infamous "Alien Autopsy" as a hoax, and broke the story of a special initiative by billionaire philanthropist Laurance Rockefeller to open the government's secret X-files.

A frequent and outspoken guest on television news and talk shows, Luckman was asked by Bill O'Reilly, the controversial host of Fox News Channel's *The O'Reilly Factor*, to bring a live space alien onto the show so that O'Reilly could score an exclusive interview with an extraterrestrial. CNN's *Show Biz Today* program compared Luckman to Mel Gibson's character in the hit movie *Conspiracy Theory*. Fifteen cameras rolled when Luckman replied to the official U.S. air force report about the crash of a flying saucer with aliens aboard in Roswell, New Mexico, in 1947.